中译翻译文库·口译研究丛书

实战同传（英汉互译）

Field Simultaneous Interpretation

林超伦 著

中国出版集团
中 译 出 版 社

图书在版编目(CIP)数据

实战同传：英汉互译/林超伦著. —北京：中译出版社，2012.11（2023.2重印）
ISBN 978-7-5001-3377-3

I. ①实… II. ①林… III. ①英语-同声翻译-高等学校-教材 IV. ①H315.9

中国版本图书馆CIP数据核字（2012）第225997号

出版发行/中译出版社
地　　址/北京市西城区新街口外大街28号普天德胜大厦主楼4层
电　　话/(010) 68359827（发行部）；68359725（编辑部）
邮　　编/100088
传　　真/(010) 68357870
电子邮箱/book@ctph.com.cn
网　　址/http://www.ctph.com.cn

责任编辑/范祥镇

排　　版/北京竹页文化传媒有限公司
印　　刷/北京玺诚印务有限公司
经　　销/新华书店

规　　格/700毫米×960毫米　1/16
印　　张/20
字　　数/360千字
版　　次/2012年11月第一版
印　　次/2023年2月第五次

ISBN 978-7-5001-3377-3　定价：48.00元

中译翻译文库

编　委　会

门顺德（大连外国语大学）
牛云平（河北大学）
潘志高（解放军外国语大学）
彭发胜（合肥工业大学）
屈文生（华东政法大学）
邵　炜（AIIC 会员，北京外国语大学）
石　坚（四川大学）
宋亚菲（广西大学）
孙迎春（山东大学）
王　宏（苏州大学）
王　宁（清华大学）
王振华（河南大学）
文　旭（西南大学）
肖维青（上海外国语大学）
杨　柳（南京大学）
姚桂桂（江汉大学）
张德禄（山东大学、同济大学）
张其帆（AIIC 会员，香港理工大学）
章　艳（上海外国语大学）
郑海凌（北京师范大学）
朱振武（上海师范大学）
孟凡君（西南大学）
潘文国（华东师范大学）
彭　萍（北京外国语大学）
秦潞山（AIIC 会员，Chin Communications）
任　文（四川大学）
申　丹（北京大学）
石平萍（解放军外国语大学）
孙会军（上海外国语大学）
陶丽霞（四川外国语大学）
王建国（华东理工大学）
王克非（北京外国语大学）
文　军（北京航空航天大学）
温建平（上海对外经贸大学）
闫素伟（国际关系学院）
杨全红（四川外国语大学）
张春柏（华东师范大学）
张美芳（澳门大学）
张秀仿（河北工程大学）
赵　刚（华东师范大学）
朱纯深（香港城市大学）

特约编审（以姓氏拼音为序）

Andrew C. Dawrant（AIIC 会员，上海外国语大学）
戴惠萍（AIIC 会员，上海外国语大学）
高　伟（四川外国语大学）
黄国文（中山大学）
李长栓（北京外国语大学）
李亚舒（《中国科技翻译》）
罗新璋（中国社会科学院）
孟凡君（西南大学）
屠国元（中南大学）
王立弟（北京外国语大学）
谢天振（上海外国语大学）
杨　平（《中国翻译》）
杨士焯（厦门大学）
俞利军（对外经济贸易大学）
张　鹏（四川外国语大学）
祝朝伟（四川外国语大学）
柴明颎（上海外国语大学）
冯庆华（上海外国语大学）
胡安江（四川外国语大学）
黄忠廉（黑龙江大学）
李凌鸿（重庆法语联盟）
刘军平（武汉大学）
梅德明（上海外国语大学）
苗　菊（南开大学）
王东风（中山大学）
王明树（四川外国语大学）
徐　珺（对外经济贸易大学）
杨全红（四川外国语大学）
杨晓荣（《外语研究》）
张　健（上海外国语大学）
赵学文（吉林大学）

前　言

首先，无论是中国还是西欧，对于同传的理论研究都很少。现有的大多数出版物或者文章都是有关同传现状、实践、培训的看法和体会。英国过去20年里只出版了一本有关同传的英文专著*Conference Interpreting Explained*，也只是教材，内容都是作者对于自身实践经验的描述以及个人看法，没有实证研究，不是可以作为凭证的理论。

笔者也没有做过同传方面的实证研究，本书讲解的是在过去6年里通过努力思考、反复验证而发展起来的体系。这个体系从一些基本概念上与通常的看法完全不同，在有些关键问题上反其道而行之。这并不是笔者别出心裁，而是在反复实践中得出的必然的结论。

但是由于我们都极其缺少实证研究，即使是采用某个理念或者某种方法培养出合格的同传译员，也无法断言是何种结论或者方法以何种方式产生了作用。本书肯定有考虑不周或者描述不当之处。如果使用本书有所收获，则笔者无限宽慰。但是万万不可把本书中为了培训需要所做的描述或者所采用的手法当做教条或者标准来评判其他理念和方法。笔者的愿望只是提供一个对于同传认识的不同角度，提供培训同传译员的一个不同体系，希望能够促进对于同传的认识，为推进同传研究和实践做出一点微薄的贡献。

笔者希望强调说明的是，本书完全没有任何显示自己高明或者贬低别人的用意。在拟写中已经尽量小心措辞，以免造成误解。但是如果读者发现仍有言语冒犯之处，敬请指出，笔者将及时去函道歉。如果有错误和不当之处，承蒙来邮指出，笔者不胜感激。邮箱地址是：mail@linchaolun.com.。

其次，本书的培训目标是帮助具有一定双语基础的学员在一定条件下从零开始，在大约70-100个小时内达到可以在比较有经验的搭档译员的关照下做第一场一般难度同传会议的水平。这个定位是经过思考而拟写的，具有特定的含义。

所谓一定双语基础特指相当于英文雅思7分及其上，一定条件指每次集中上课或者练习至少为 4 小时。做第一场一般难度同传会议的水平不等于是个熟练的同传译员，而只是入门。同传的职业发展具有很明显的线性规律，即是从第一场会议起，每做一场都会有进步，做过几十场之后就基本熟练。所以，本书的目标不是训练出达到相当于做过几十场会议水平的译员，而是训练出具有能够做第一场会议水平的译员。

为了确保本书的实战价值，所有练习单元均采用未经编辑的讲话原稿，所有例句和参考译语均完全按照实战的环境和标准提供。凡是在实战里遇到的难题均坦白地承认，凡是在实战里很可能处理不好的译语均老老实实地展示，不做任何文字上的修饰。由于忠实于实战，难免从抽空了现实的学术角度来看会有不完美、不顺当甚至不够标准的情况。

最后，由于同传缺少理论研究基础，在认知和培训同传的过程中笔者不得不采用自己界定的概念来做说明，从而帮助理解。这就不可避免地产生一些概念有待商榷的情况。所以特此说明，这些概念仅仅是为了有助于培训，而非权威界定，欢迎大家参加讨论，共同提高对同传的认识。

另外，常言道：矫枉必须过正。本书里有些概念的使用正是出于这个目的，所以尽管听上去可能有些过头，但是如果说得方方面面都照顾到了就容易淡化要点，影响培训效果。因此，在使用中应该按照概念使用后可以产生的实际培训效果来理解，有关可以如何改进文字上的表述，欢迎来邮件赐教。

本书既可以作为高等教育正式教材，也可以用作自学或作为论文参考。大学高年级可以使用，研究生尤其合适，职业译员也可以把本书作为职业发展的参照。

由于英译汉和汉译英需要不同的方式、方法和技能，所以将在两课里分别讲解，而且两课讲解的技巧不完全对应。

同传是一种非常特殊的口译形式，无论是从语言转换，还是从思维方式上都为职业翻译开辟了崭新的天地，对翻译的理论及其研究带来全新的挑战。同传还是一种特殊的智慧体现，同传译员在双语之间转换的速度远远超出不会同传者，资深同传译员能够分脑使用的能力及其由此体验到的意境是其他形式的译员无法领略到的，更不要说其他职业的工作人员。这项特殊技能所带来的喜悦，以及在这种被旁人看来高不可攀、神秘不可解的工作上能够驾驭自如、稳操胜券的感觉是无数同传译员乐于此道的主要原因之一，也是激励后来者投身其中的动机之一。本教材便是为了帮助你在实现同传目标的道路上迈出举足轻重的这一步。

目　录

第一部分　理念阐述

第一课　基本概念

同声传译在本书中除非有特殊需要，否则将一律简称为同传。

本书中翻译这个词涵盖口译、笔译。口译涵盖交传、同传。所以，本书特指口译、笔译、交传、同传时将分别使用这些概念以示区分。口译时，译员听到的和看到的将统称“来源语”，译员说出的译入语将统称“译入语”。本书使用“英语”“汉语”这对概念以区别于“英文”和“中文”。“语”特指说的话，“文”特指写的文字。所以，本书称“英译汉”和“汉译英”。在谈及笔译时则采用“英翻中”和“中翻英”。

本书中“讲者”统称说话人，不区分性别与人数。“受众”指通过译员口译而听讲者讲话的受众。由于在这种场合，受众不光是听，有时也要看，比如电脑幻灯片的演示就是这样，所以用“受众”来统称听众和观众。

笔者对于同传的定义为：同传是在有组织的活动中，译员借助设备担任讲者和受众之间的跨语言传话筒；讲者具有双重动机，译员总是双角色。如此定义比较啰嗦，但是比较全面地概括了构成同传概念的几个特性。本课前半部将逐一讲解这些特性，讨论这些特性是如何共同定义同传的，使其不同于笔译以及其他形式的口译。本课后半部将讲解与同传相关的其他基本概念。

另外，为了明确区别口译和笔译，本书一概采用译入语或者译入语版本表达译员传译出来的语言，以此与笔译里的译文相区别。本书在其他词汇的使用上也都注意强调“语”和“文”的区别。

有组织的活动

同传主要用于在两个组织机构之间出于官方或者组织机构的目的而举行的有计划、有组织或者是双方商定的会谈或者活动。其主要特征是这种活动往往有双方商定的日程或者框架。这个特征决定了同传的其他一些重要特点。实践中，使用同传的场合主要有：

- 大会
- 会议
- 会谈
- 谈判
- 演讲
- 演示
- 培训
- 座谈会和研讨会
- 参观或者游览

由于正规同传需要设备，所以采用同传作为跨越语言障碍手段的活动就有了地点的限制，一般都在室内。只有在实地参观时，可以采用便携式导游设备在户外使用同传。

一般情况下，同传采用正规设备，译员坐在专用的同传箱（或者室）内，借助设备上完全分开的听、说频道做同传。译员所说的话由红外发射器传给受众佩戴的耳机收听。在这种情况下，译员听清讲者的话基本不受环境的影响。

但是如果是使用便携时导游设备，则译员不是通过耳机，而是必须直接听讲者的话做同传，所受到的环境影响就比使用正式设备时大得多。讲者声音不够大、受众里有人咳嗽或者翻动纸张，都会给译员的听力带来困难。另外，由于译员可以听见自己的话，容易导致听、说相互干扰。

还有一种形式的口译与同传有类似之处，即耳语口译。耳语口译指的是一名译员坐在或者站在一到两位受众身边或者身后，基本按照同传的要求轻声地把讲者的话传译给受众听。耳语口译无需设备，但是一次能够服务的受众难以超过两位，否则译员将不得不提高音量，会影响周围直接听来源语的受众或者直接影响到讲者。

讲者双动机

讲者作为口译的服务对象往往不仅是通过讲话提供信息，而且是在影响受众。最典型的例子恐怕就是带有宣传性质的演讲了。如果纯粹是为了提供信息，那么完全没有必要由讲者发表演讲，把讲稿发给受众看就行了。发表现场演讲为的就是获得文字稿起不到的效果。也就是说，讲者利用声音、语调、目光、肢体语言和个人的感情来产生远远超出文字表达能力的效果。

即使是一次日常会议上的一般发言，当场听讲者的话也和事先或者事后阅读其文字稿件感觉很不一样。绝大多数讲者讲话都会自觉、不自觉地带有希望影响受众的意图。所以，即使是同传，译员也在“一定程度上”担负了帮助讲者传达这种影响力的责任。

之所以说是在“一定程度上”是因为由于同传本身条件的限制，译员无法像交传那样与受众面对面交流，能够传达的效果有限。同传是流水运作，无法像交传那样听完了整段话再组织译入语。这就给传译某些内容带来困难，比如传达幽默就是这样。因为译员跟着讲者的话译，等到听到最后发现是幽默时可能已经来不及修改之前的用词。

尽管同传译员有交传译员没有的困难，但是仍然应该在同传的局限内尽力传达讲者意图达到的效果。同传再现幽默不容易，但是高水平的译员仍然能够做到。不过需要说明的是，传达讲者的意图有个先决条件，那就是讲者及其话语没有与译员的道义准则发生冲突。有关口译里道义准则的考虑，请参阅第三课以及笔者的《实战交传》。

译员双角色

不仅讲者有双重动机，而且译员也担任了双重角色。一重是宏观角色，另外一重是微观角色。从宏观层面看，译员是所参与的有组织活动的一员，其角色是为活动中听译入语的受众提供译入语。从微观层面看，译员口译时需要尽量准确，使受众能够尽可能地获得与来源语受众类似的信息和感受。

同传时，译员的宏观角色占主导地位，微观角色占次要地位。也就是说，译员的宏观任务，即：首要任务，是保证译入语的受众能够尽量像听来源语的受众一样参加活动，而不是口译的准确。所以，在特定条件下，译员可以、有时甚至必须牺牲准确性以达到完成宏观任务的目的。

比如，如果讲者没有使用话筒，译员听不见讲者，就需要向译入语的受众解释一下，以免他们不知道耳机里怎么突然没有声音了。如果讲者忘记打开话筒，则译员可以利用同传系统的方便请受众提醒讲者打开话筒。如果讲者语无伦次，译员可以用比较规范的译入语总结、归纳讲者的话，而不是跟着讲者语无伦次。

另外，越是正式的场合，越是有组织的活动就越是依照事先确定的程序进行。国际会议就是比较典型的例子。即使译员什么话都没说，活动也会依照程序继续下去。有时还会是必须按照程序继续下去。在这种情况下，即使译员一时听不见讲者，无论什么原因，也不能打断活动进程去要求排除听不见的障碍。即如果译员的宏观角色与微观角色之间发生冲突时，必须以让活动平稳、顺利进行为主，口译的准确程度为次。

但是如果没有其他因素的干扰，即：译员的宏观与微观角色重合的情况下，译员就应该争取利用口气、音色和抑扬顿挫这三大手法，在译入语里体现讲者的双重动机。比如，讲者发表演讲时往往说话抑扬顿挫，译员不会或者没有采用同样方式，译入语平平淡淡就不能算传达准确。遇到讲者使用幽默，译员可以在听到最后发现讲者是在使用幽默时，可以马上动用比较调侃的语调，帮助受众体会到幽默。

口气和音色还可以用来区别讲者。如果遇到数名讲者热烈交谈，互动程度很高，语速又比较快的时候，无法采用“他说”来区别讲者时，如果能熟练地运用较高、较低和中间这三个音调就能有助于受众区别出三个不同的讲者。当然，这是具有相当水平的译员才能做到的。

同传设备

同传所使用的设备有两大基本功能，一个是传输译员需要听到的内容，另外一个是传输译员口译的内容。两者必须完全分开。来源语和译入语都熟悉的受众可以选择直接听讲者，也可以选择通过无线耳机收听译员的口译。

同传所使用的设备基本有两大类，正式场合最常用的是同传室（固定式）或者同传箱（移动式）外带技术员。前者是会场建筑的组成部分，联合国、欧盟这样的国际组织都是根据三人一组的原则建筑同传室，即有三个座位。后者往往是双座式，可以根据需要向设备供应商租用，临时搭建在会场内或者近处，用后拆除、交还。

同传室（箱）内都配有一个台面，放置供译员使用的同传控制器。不同厂家设计、生产的控制器看上去可能很不一样，但是基本功能相差无几，都有译员所需的听和说两个功能区域。每个区域内都有一些按钮或者开关，提供选择，或者控制音量大小。所需的选择既有听的频道，也有说的频道。之所以需要选择听的频道是因为如果是多语种国际会议，有时需要做接力同传。比如，英语译员把法语译入英语，然后汉语译员再把英语译入汉语，如同田径运动里的接力跑一般。另外，译员还需要根据自己现在的译入语而选择译入语频道，以便受众准确选择所希望听到的语言。

非正式场合为了节省开支有时也采用便携式导游系统。这种系统也有很多不同厂家的不同设计、型号。基本构成分为两大部分：播放和接收。播放部分就是一个小型便携式发射器外加一个微型话筒，话筒可以戴在耳朵上或者头上。接收部分往往就是一个可以调节音量的耳机。由于便携式导游系统设备比较便宜，无需技术员监测，所以成本大大低于同传箱。

由于导游系统不是为同传所用而设计的，使用效果比较差。比如，由于发射器的功率有限，无法保证所有受众都能在任何时候听清译员的话。另外，这种设备对译员的要求比使用同传箱要高很多。比如：译员必须直接听讲者而不是通过耳机，不仅周围的干扰无法排除，而且增加了听不清讲者的风险。

跨语言

跨语言指的是讲者与受众使用不同的语言，通过同传译员进行交流。由于同传借助设备，所以可以同时有多种语言的受众参加同一个会议。比如，讲者说阿拉伯语，一名同传译员把阿拉伯语译成英语，然后再由其他译员把英语译成汉语、法语、德语等，即前述的接力同传。

如果光从语言角度考虑，接力同传的效果不理想，因为如果来源语是阿拉伯语，接力之后到英语就已经在讲者和译员之间产生了时间差，而英语再传译到其他语言的时间差还会延长。往往是讲者已经结束，有些受众尚未听到尾声，出现受众根据所听的语言不同而对讲者做出反应的先后有明显差别的局面。更不用说跨越两种语言之后很容易出现所表达的意思与原话不完全相符的情况。

传话筒

之所以说同传译员像传话筒是因为同传译员对于活动进程的影响由于存在以下限制而远不如交传。首先，如果活动在两种语言之间展开而且讲者正在发言过程中，则往往无论译员译好译坏，甚至说不出话来，讲者都会继续讲下去。唯一的例外是当活动本身互动性质很强，即如果讲者提出一个问题，等待受众答复时，译员译不出来或者是严重错译时才会导致活动停顿或者影响走向。

其次，坐在同传箱里的译员与讲者和受众完全隔离开来，所以无法与他们直接互动。比如，同传译员如果遇到没听见或者没听懂的地方，就无法像交传译员那样有向讲者提问的机会。在绝大多数情况下，同传译员只能是尽力而为，听见或者听懂多少传译多少。

上述两点与交传有天壤之别，交传时任何时候译员被卡住往往马上就会导致活动暂停（交传也有一个例外。比如举办仪式时，即使译员译不出来，仪式往往也会按照计划进行下去）。在很多情况下，交传译员都可以与讲者或者受众互动或者担当讲者的助手。比如：

- 可以向讲者或者某位受众提问
- 可以在需要的时候增加自己的解释而不仅仅是传译，
- 可以为受众用手指出应该看印刷材料的哪个部分
- 可以站起来用手指出刚才讲者谈到的是电脑幻灯页上的哪个数字

以上这些都是在传译的话语之外的行为，是同传里没有的现象。尽管这样，译员还是必须争取在有限条件下尽力实现讲者的双重动机。作为传话筒，译员必须争取传得有声有色，不仅仅是传达所说的词、句。

语言方向

同传里的语言方向挺有讲究。西欧业界普遍接受的一个原则是：为了保证受众听到的质量，译入语必须是母语。欧盟机构内的会议同传基本都遵循这个原则，在西欧占主导地位的行业组织国际会议口译协会就要求申请加入者明确说明自己的母语和外语，并且要求会员遵守仅限译入母语的原则。

欧盟国家里有很多人都熟练掌握了不止一种语言，所以可以坚持译入语必须是母语的原则。中国绝大多数人的母语都不是英语，所以形成了在担任同传译员时必须双向口译，即不分英译汉和汉译英的局面。其实，这种情况不仅限于中国。在所有缺少真正意义上的双语译员的国家里，同传译员都不可避免地要做双向口译，不分母语、外语。

语言方向的另外一个层面是所需的技能和技巧。人们往往会以为英译汉与汉译英只是方向不同，所需的技能、技巧、方式、方法基本相同。但实际上，汉译英从根本理念和具体技巧上都有不同于英译汉之处。所以，本书在讲解同传技巧时就区分了英译汉和汉译英的内容，以两课分别讲解。

外语水平

至于同传培训所需的最低外语水平，迄今尚无科学的论证。纵观中国大陆、英国、法国和美国的现状，虽然每所院校的要求以及商业市场培训课程的要求都不一样，但大体上有三种模式。

一种可以称之为精英式，即认为只有两种语言都掌握得非常流利，近乎双母语的水平才能学好同传。法国的 esit、上海外国语大学高翻学院和对外经济贸易大学的欧盟口译硕士项目就都属于这种类型，他们在招收学生的时候通过高难度的考试录取外语水平等同或者比较接近母语水平的学生。

第二种可以称之为择优录取式，即并没有明确要求外语水平接近母语，而是从申请的学生中择优录取。除了中国大陆，香港、台湾、英国、美国、澳大利亚的绝大多数院校都采取这种模式。这些课程对于申请者外语水平的要求往往与自我定位及其所在大学的总体声誉有很大联系。比如，总体来说，北京外国语大学高翻学院的学生入门外语平均水平会高于大部分省级大学。

第三种可以称之为大众式，基本上是只要达到最基本的外语水平而且愿意学，就能被录取。此类学生往往需要同时上不同形式的外语补习课，为同传培训提供支持。比如，英国有些大学同传招生的标准定在英语雅思 6.5 分，国内有些商业培训班里学生的英语水平还不到雅思 6.5，有些没有正式考过雅思。

这三种模式的培训目标不同，培训对象不同，培训成果不同，这是不可避免的客观存在。无论什么行业或者职业，都有多个水平的层次，形成橄榄形。两头尖，中间宽。一头是水平极高者，为少数。另外一头是水平极差者，也为少数。大多数人都在两个极端之间的某个位置上。同传也不例外，供应方如此，需求方也同样。需要高水平同传并且愿意为此支付市场最高价的客户总是少数，出于无知或者为了省钱而使用水平很差的译员的客户也是少数。大多数客户都处在高质高价与低质低价这两个极端之间的一个位置上。

主要特点

同传是两种语言之间转换的特殊形式。首先，同传时，讲者一般不考虑译员，完全根据自己的希望和速度讲话，而且完全根据自己的需要决定是否停顿。讲者的话就像一江春水向东流，不停顿、不回头。译员也只能跟着讲者不能停，无论是回顾还是改口都会导致此后的话无法顺利传译。在其他口译形式里，比如在交传时，译员就有一定的决定余地。由于交传译员是在讲者暂停时口译，所以在一定程度上可以回顾讲者的话，在译入语里重新组织句子，还可以根据自己的掌握采取比讲者稍快或者稍慢的速度口译。

另外，同传只能是边听边译，无法统筹兼顾整个句子，更不用说整段话了。

这也就是为什么同传很难把俏皮话或者笑话传译成功的主要原因之一。无论是英语还是汉语，笑话的基本结构都是先让听众形成某种预期，最后话锋一转，形成与听众预期的反差但又符合情理，由此引出会意的笑声。比如，讲者采用双意或者双关词，故意让听众产生其中一意的感觉，最后却点明另外一个意思。但由于同传是边听边译，无法统筹兼顾。势必把双意或者双关词根据目前为止的背景译成其中一个意思，等于无意中破坏了讲者的意图，结果是没啥好笑的。

第二，同传时，译员边听、边理解、边转换并且说出译入语，必须能够在脑子里同时完成多项性质完全不同的任务，边听、边理解刚刚听到的话、马上转换成译入语、说出来，与此同时还在听、理解、转换、说。所以，同传是多项任务既同步开展，又交错进行。

第三，由于同传是一江春水向东流式的，译员对于每个听到的内容仅仅有大约 1 秒左右的思考时间。由于同传是多项任务交错进行，除非是资深译员，大多数人都无法在说出译入语、注意听讲的同时思考新内容超过 1 秒。也就是说如果思考时间不超过 1 秒，基本能够保证不影响译、听。如果不是资深译员，超过了 1 秒钟就会明显地影响到译或听。

第四，由于同传时必须采用顺序口译的方式，即译入语的顺序很接近来源语，势必要求译员在英汉两种语言之间通过处理技巧做出调整。这种调整往往会改变原话的重心、修饰关系。再加上由于讲者口音、速度、话题难度等其他原因，同传译入语的质量无法达到交传可以达到的准确程度。但是同传的目的不同于交传，受众的需要也不同于交传，不能简单地用交传的准确程度来衡量同传。有关如何看待同传的准确程度这个问题将在下一课里进一步讨论。另外，有关口笔译里准确幅度的概念，请参阅笔者的《实战交传》（中国对外翻译出版有限公司，2012）。

最后，同传的受众很难当场评估译员的质量。难以评估的特点可以通过与交传比较来看。在交传里，由于讲者讲了一段话后需要停顿下来让译员口译，这就使得凡是知晓来源语和译入语的受众都可以根据刚才听到的来源语来比较、判断现在听到的译入语，决定质量高低。

而同传则非常不同。如果想比较、判断译员的质量，首先必须使用两套耳机，左右耳朵各自戴上其中一套的一个耳机。一个耳朵听讲者的话，另外一个耳朵听译员的同传。与此同时，还必须自己在脑子里也做同传，然后才能把自己的同传版本与译员相比较。由于做比较者自己必须能够熟练同传，而大部分受众即使双语熟练也往往不会同传。所以，除非出现明显的词汇错误，比如某个词汇、人名或者数字等等，绝大多数受众都无法比较准确地当场判断同传质量。

常见问题

初练同传时最常见的问题就是感到无法在听、译、说这几个行动之间同步、交错展开。造成这个问题的主要原因有三个：一，两种语言的掌握程度差距明显；二，在双语转换时遵循的是笔译的原则；三，沿用不符合同传本质的思维习惯。

同传里，讲者主动，想说什么说什么，凡是说出的话都是讲者知道怎么说的。译员被动，讲者说什么就必须跟着说什么，即使不熟悉、甚至不懂的用语也无法避免。除非译员传译的两种语言都是自己的母语，即所谓的双母语译员，否则对于外语的掌握总是不如母语，总有语言掌握不足的困难。

虽然外语不如母语的情况在交传里也是问题，但是由于交传里译员有比较大的思考空间与时间，而且是在讲者暂停后口译，可以自己掌控速度，这些都在一定程度上给交传译员以回旋余地。所以，译员外语水平明显不足是同传汉译英质量不高的主要原因之一。

中国学生外语水平往往不如学习欧洲主要语言的欧洲学生，其主要原因之一是英汉两种语言的差别很大，给英汉两语的译员带来很大挑战。首先是汉语里的外来语或者类似表达法远远少于主要欧洲语言之间的量。比如，汉语里的外来语数量比主要欧洲语言相互之间的外来语要少很多。

由于缺少外来语，绝大多数的英文单词的发音都与其汉语译入语没有任何联系。而很多欧洲语言里的单词都相近，经常顺着来源语发音就进入了译入语，而对于英汉口译却此路不通。

其次，在一词多义的情况下，欧洲主要语言之间对应程度比英汉之间的对应程度高。这就大大增加了英汉同传时译员的难度，更多地需要仰赖译员的熟练记忆，无法借助语音、拼写或是词义这样的因素。比如，无论是法语的 tableau，还是英语的 table，都既可以是桌子，也可以是表格。而中文则不然，桌子和表格完全是两码事。

第二，几乎所有英语学生在学习英语的过程当中都已经被培养出一些与同传的要求恰恰相反的思维习惯。这些思维习惯都是把英语作为外语使用，或者是笔译所需要的，但却是同传中常见问题的症结。这些习惯就是：根据上下文判断词义以决定翻译成什么。

同传不能仰赖上下文的原因有两条。第一，笔译可以通读全篇，然后再动手翻译，所以可以看完上下文，然后决定其中某个词如何翻译。同传是边听、边说，永远是只有上文，没有下文。这就经常导致讲者目前为止所说的话无助于理解下面即将说的话。请看例句：

Thank you for inviting me to this conference on energy efficiency. In our department, I'm known as a back seat driver. But I've come to listen and learn.

在上述例句里，讲者是在一个有关能源效率的大会上讲话。能源效率与 back seat driver 没有任何关系。只有当听到后面的 But I've come to listen and learn 才能猜出 back seat driver 大概是指教训人的意思。同传里这种上文根本无助于理解的情况司空见惯，习惯于根据上下文判断处理方法的思维定式会导致同传做不下去。

第三，不懂的词需要想想。这不仅限于英语，绝大多数人从小到大，无论是家长还是学校老师都教：想好了再说。而同传需要的是瞬间说出，说了就过。第三课有关同传技能的部分将有详细讲解。

这里需要说明的是同传由于其特性决定了译员必须以特殊方式运用语言、进行思维。这些方式不同于日常外语学习，但这不是说日常外语学习的方式本身有什么过错，只是说同传特殊而已。

本课小结

同传是一种特殊的口译形式，虽然在一些原则上与交传类似，但是和交传有本质上的不同。对于同传的认识缺少研究，即使是在人们经常作为参照的西欧，也缺少像笔译理论那样的研究和认识水平，有很多误解和人云亦云的说法。

同传与交传类似之处可以从译员的角色上看出，但不同之处在于同传译员几乎与讲者同步说话，所以需要使用特殊设备，采用特别的语言转换技巧和特有的思维方式。如果对于这些特殊之处有比较科学的认识就能有助于学会同传，如果缺少比较科学的认识就容易事倍功半。

工作坊

全班分成小组，根据本课有关同传的理解和理念，讨论除了“同声传译”之外，还可以用什么词汇为这种口译形式命名？这个练习既可以在课上做，也可以作为课下作业完成，然后在课上讨论不同版本之间的长短。

第二课　议题探讨

大凡不了解之事，认识往往容易走极端。不是将其顶礼膜拜，就是将其贬得一钱不值。在有了一定了解之后，就会认识到事情的复杂性，比较能够一分为二地做分析，获得比较全面，有一定深度的认识。

同传在学术界里的研究无论从质还是量上看，都与对笔译的研究无法相比。从笔者过去十多年里在英国接触到的正式出版的英文书籍中，有关同传的教材只有 *Conference Interpreting Explained* 这一本，而且是欧洲人的教材。国内出版有关同传的书也基本属于教材性质，即重点在于解决诸如顺序译这样的语言处理。对于同传本身的理论研究往往只有介绍，或者提出一些个人的看法。其中既有真知灼见，也存在误导、误解。本课将于后半部就一些常见的说法开展讨论，以期达到更加全面地认识同传的目的。

不过需要说明的是：笔者对同传的认识也是首先基本仰赖于自己的实践和思考，再在参考他人以及其他学科的思路基础上总结出来的，难免会有局限性而且也是个在发展中的过程。所表达的观点旨在开阔思路，不能作为金科玉律学习。

参照西欧?

欧洲二次大战结束后审判战俘首次采用同传作为口译的方式。自那以来，同传便逐渐发展成为国际会议跨越语言障碍的主要手段。无论从理论研究还是实践上看，西欧似乎都是同传的鼻祖并且领先全球。口译学术界的领军人物和重头论文、著作几乎全来自于西欧。同传界最有权威的业内协会，即国际会议口译员协会设在日内瓦，绝大多数成员都在西欧。在这种情况下，很容易形成以西欧为标准，向西欧看齐的情况。其实，中国的情况与西欧有本质的不同，必须发展符合中国需要的体系、标准、行业组织。

比如，中国大陆的同传基本上是从同传培训——即当年联合国设在北京外国语大学的译训班开始的，而不像欧洲是从大规模使用同传开始。也就是说，中国的同传史与西欧很不相同。西欧是先使用，后发展正规的培训。中国是先有正规的培训，后来才出现大规模的使用。中欧的差别不限于此，在译员的身份、双语水平、语言环境和培训条件诸多方面都很不相同。

西欧同传译员里除了日内瓦的联合国和布鲁塞尔的欧盟系统以外，其他政府部门、商业公司、学术研究机构几乎都没有全职的同传译员，绝大多数译员都是根据需要临时聘用的自由职业者。这是由于西欧的历史发展形成的局面。而中国政府和机构一向都有外事办公室专职翻译人员的传统，自由职业译员是十几年前刚刚发展起来的。所以，部门政府机构和商业公司一直有自己的同传译员。随着同传需求的不断增长，今后完全有可能在更多的政府部门、机构以及大型商业公司里出现拥有自己的全职同传队伍的情况，使同传的供应呈现全职译员和自由职业译员共同存在的局面。这种局面在欧洲几乎是不可能出现的。

西欧的译员基本来源于两大渠道：一个渠道是通过正规培训拿到学位或者培训证书，另外一个是自学成才，边做边提高。但是无论上述哪种，西欧译员中有很多是双母语者，即两个工作语言都是母语或者外语水平很接近于母语。而中国的绝大多数译员外语水平都明显低于母语，双母语译员寥若晨星。目前活跃在同传市场上的少数几位接近双母语的译员基本都是汉语熟练的其他国家人，不是中国本土产生的译员。

西欧译员经常是生活、工作在自己工作语言的环境里，绝大多数中国译员往往仅仅生活、工作在汉语里，往往只是在做口译的时候才用外语。由于上述原因，在中国培训同传译员不能照搬西欧的做法，需要根据中国译员的特点设计、安排培训。

比如，西欧的同传培训都以培训生外语水平很高为先决条件，培训课没有提高外语水平的内容。在中国，即使是一流大学的同传课里，学生的外语水平和国际知识也只是相对高于没有考上的学生，远远没有达到接近母语的水平。继续提高外语水平，大大增加国际知识是中国同传培训不可缺少的内容。

吃青春饭?

从媒体渲染中曾经看到“同传时大脑细胞大量死亡”、“同传用脑过量，职业生涯不过三十岁”之类的说法。这些说法没有任何科学根据，大多是想象而来，人云亦云，添油加醋。同传是有特性，与未经训练者现有的知识、技能和能力有很大差距，需要相当大的努力才能掌握。但是这并不等于做同传时需要超人的本领。凡事刚学时总是比较费劲，刚学骑自行车，刚学开汽车，刚学很多手艺时都会动不动出一身汗。学会之后，驾轻就熟，无需那么费劲。

由于同传的特性很像学手艺，只有操业十年、八年之后才会有胸有成竹的感觉。所以，优秀的同传译员都有一定年纪。20 世纪 90 年代传说的所谓同传职业生涯不出三十现在已经不大有人说了，其中部分原因也在于 90 年代毕业的同传学员，如今是口译职场里的强手，个个都在三十岁以上。

再看欧洲口译市场，活跃其中的译员 40–50 岁的比比皆是，60 多岁的也不乏其人。道理之一是手艺越精、功底越厚、用力越少。年龄 40–50 岁的译员，做了十几、二十年，积累了相当的知识、经验和能力。虽然体力、脑力不如年轻人，但是他们在做同传时所需的体力、脑力大大减少。生理因素的重要性大大下降，知识、经验和能力起到主导作用。

同传准确吗?

本课以及本书所讨论的同传质量，除了特别说明以外，一般都指同传译入语的质量。

同传译员和交传译员一样，也是担负着双重任务。首先是保证活动能够按照计划进行；其次是以力所能及的最高水平完成口译任务。从这点上看，同传尤其如此。除非是互动性质很强的活动，否则无论同传质量如何，讲者都会持续发言，活动都会进行下去。比如，无论是联合国还是欧盟的全体大会都有固定的时间、日程和会议进程的惯例。除非出了很大的问题，会议进程一般不会因为个别译员一段时间内同传质量不好而中断。

从这个角度看，同传本身的质量与会议的进行并没有直接的关系，只是会影响到部分听众对于活动内容的理解。这部分听众的人数越少，同传质量对于活动质量的影响就越小。相反也成立。

这就提出了一个具有原则性质的问题——既然译员在一段时间里的译语质量与会议或者活动的进程没有直接的关系，那么译员的首要任务仍然是保证译语的准确吗？如果不是的话又是什么呢？有否可能是紧跟讲者，不停地传译呢？这点听上去好像说话过了头，不过仔细想想似乎也有一定道理。

如果译员听到的都是很熟悉的内容，都能很顺利地传译，自然不成问题。而一旦遇到不熟悉甚至不懂的内容，译员就只有两个选择，一个是没有想出解决方案之前不开口，即所谓被卡住；另外一个是放弃暂时不会译的内容继续往下译。如果被卡住，不仅之前的话没有译，由于卡住时在思考前话而没听清后话，连后话也会漏译、错译。所以，与其被卡住，不如扔掉不会的内容把之后会的内容传译过去。除了上述两个方案之外恐怕没有第三个方案。

假设同传时准确性仍然很重要，那么同传的准确尺度与交传和笔译一样吗？由于同传时必须采用顺序口译的方式，即译入语的顺序很接近来源语，势必要求译员在英汉两种语言之间通过处理技巧做出调整。这种调整往往会改变原话的重心、修饰关系。再加上由于讲者口音、速度、话题难度等其他原因，同传译入语的质量无法达到交传可以达到的准确程度。

但是同传的目的不同于交传，受众的需要也不同于交传，不能简单地用交传的准确程度来衡量同传。有关如何看待口笔译里准确幅度的概念，请参阅笔者的《实战交传》（中国对外翻译出版有限公司，2012）。以下举例展示同传里的准确幅度，每个例子右栏里的三个不同版本听上去都属于准确或者可以接受。

英语原话	同传版本
Vice President, distinguished guests, my lords, ladies and gentle-men	• 副主席阁下、贵宾们、女士们、先生们 • 副主席、各位来宾、勋爵们、女士们、先生们 • 尊敬的副主席阁下、各位女士们、先生们、各位来宾们
We’re well positioned to supply to such projects.	• 我们条件优越，可以供应此类项目所需 • 我们完全能够胜任此类项目的供应 • （接之前的话）完全可以保证供应
There is total commitment from the senior management to drive the strategy forward	• 决心是由高层经理人员下定了的，要驱动战略实施 • 决心很大，高管层决意推进战略实施 • 高管层决心驱动战略的贯彻执行

一般来说，正式的文章往往用词比较讲究，句子结构比较严谨，句子比较长。这种文章阅读起来还比较容易，但是听人家念便会不容易理解。这里基本有两个原因：一个是句子本身难度较大，阅读时如果不明白可以回头再看一下，并且没有时间的压力；二是听别人朗读时不仅没有回顾的机会，而且理解的速度必须与朗读者同步。由此可见，如果是听，反而在句子结构比较零碎，并不工整，用词比较接近于口语时比较容易理解。

由于上述原因，同传的准确幅度比交传时大。即：与交传相比，受众在听同传时对于什么是准确有更大的宽容程度。交传里很可能被认为不准确的地方在同传里有可能被认为很准确，这也是为什么在上述例子里不同的表述听上去都挺准确的原因。但是在同传里听上去质量很高的话语同样用在交传里，就有可能被认为不够准确。

由此看来，衡量同传的准确程度不能像是采用一根准绳，偏离了准绳就不准确，而是允许准绳上下各有一定的余地。只要是在这个余地幅度之内，就都会被认为是准确的或者没有错误。如果同传的准确幅度不同于交传、笔译，那么是否必须在同传培训时避免用交传甚至笔译的准确概念来衡量译语呢？如果是的话，那么无论是教、还是学，恐怕都必须经常提醒自己在看到同传文稿时，不要自然而然地就把注意力放在了文字的准确程度上，导致用笔译的概念评判同传。

在本教材后半部分的练习材料里，所有的参考译入语都完全是按照实战同传的要求提供的，在使用中一定要按照听人说话的标准来听，一定不要按照阅读文章那样来阅读，否则会觉得很不准确。只有按照听的标准，才能体会到同传里译入语需要达到的水平，从而达到以实战标准学习同传的目的。

有关同传的准确程度还有另外一个值得讨论的层面，这就是有关同传译员是应该按照讲者所说的话传译呢？还是可以对讲者的话做个总结概要，也就是说只要传达一个大意就可以了，不必讲究讲者说什么译什么？无论是教学界、还是同传业内都有人持后一种看法，而且有些同传译员也经常按照传译总结概要的标准去承接同传任务。

总之，有关同传中的准确、准确程度、听众的评判、会议的质量和效果这几方面之间的关系缺少科学的论证，所以是个很值得开展实证研究的话题。

道义标准

译员和其他职业人员一样，也面临行为准则的问题。英文里的相关概念是 ethics 及其形容词 ethical，两者都没有十分合适的中文对应词汇。中国常见的概念是道德，但是道德是全体社会的，道德标准是在社会发展过程里形成的。同传译员在业界遇到的问题有时并不是道德性质，而是译员个人自己给自己的行为准则确定什么标准，即什么事情应该做、可以做，什么事情不应该做，不可以做。

“比如，如果邻居想送小孩上个好学校但是经费不够，你没有慷慨解囊，这不能说你是缺少道德，但是根据本课的定义可以说缺少道义。即，从社会角度来看，没有慷慨解囊不是过错；但是从个人角度来看，可帮人而没有帮缺少道义。”（《实战交传》，中国对外翻译出版有限公司，2012）

由于口译中的 ethics 问题是个比较新的概念，为了能够展开讨论，不得不在没有更加合适的词汇之前，暂且先用道义一词。笔者在《实战交传》里对于口译的道义问题有更多的讨论，可以参阅。以下从三个方面探讨自由职业同传译员的道义考虑：搭档合作、评论他人、发展业务。

由于同传译员绝大多数情况下是至少两人合作，但两人又往往不是日常的同事，有时甚至是素昧平生，这就产生了如果是在一个只能容纳两人的同传箱里工作时的行为标准问题。即使是在同传比较发达的欧盟国家，在这方面也没有权威的规定，更不用说问责体制。译员的行为标准完全是个人决定。是谦让还是霸道？是以我为中心还是相互关照？是体谅搭档还是给对方穿小鞋？是照顾总体同传效果还是让搭档出丑？是做无名英雄还是抢出风头？这些都是同传译员搭档合作时不可避免的考虑，也是每个译员通过自己的行为肯定会反应出来的问题。

自由职业同传译员经常应客户的要求推荐其他搭档译员或者发表对曾经合作过的译员的看法，这个看似简单的问题涉及到很多方方面面，很容易产生道义问题。是向客户推荐最佳译员还是自己最熟悉的朋友？如果自知有位译员的水平超过自己还愿意推荐这位译员吗？在发表对于其他译员的看法时是尽量从客户需要的角度评论译员的业务能力，还是从自己的角度由于不喜欢某人的穿戴打扮、生活习惯、曾经上过哪个大学、接受过哪个教师的培训而贬低这位译员？

笔者在《实战口译》（外研社，2005）里就曾以单独一课的篇幅讲解自由职业口译的商业性质，自由职业同传译员从法律实体的角度看其实就是提供同传服务的个体户。这就决定了每个自由职业译员都必须通过自己的努力发展业务，增加客户数量和客户聘用自己的次数。个体户译员的业务发展途径相当有限，主要是靠现有客户或者是其他译员的推荐。如何保持和发展与客户以及其他译员的关系就成了自由职业同传事业发展的关键。那么采用什么做法保持和发展这种关系是应该的、可以接受的，什么做法是不应该的，不可接受的，这些问题都完全由译员本人根据自己的行为准则决定。

比如，根据你个人的道义标准，你会采用以下方法吗？如果其他译员采用以下方法你会反感吗？

1. 印制精美的名片附上自己由专业人士摄制的照片
2. 使用电子设备保证自己无论在哪里都能在一小时之内回复客户
3. 每次收到客户信息都热情致谢
4. 定期招待客户方的联系人（请吃饭、游玩）
5. 节庆必定给客户发贺卡
6. 给新客户打折

7. 给回头客打折
8. 与常客商定全年优惠价格（而不是每次报价）
9. 以报价略微低于相识译员的方法把同传机会争取到自己手里
10. 奖励为自己介绍机会的人或者译员
11. 被其他译员邀请搭档做同传时顺便把自己推荐给客户
12. 被其他译员邀请搭档做同传时趁机把客户拉过来
13. 以学习的名义出席客户会议但主要是去发放自己的名片
14. 应客户要求推荐译员时只推荐水平不如自己的人
15. 聘用专业人士设计精致的简历
16. 为所有经常使用的与客户往来邮件精心设计内容与格式
17. 在被客户问及对某位译员的看法时尽量多说些负面的话以免客户对那位译员产生兴趣
18. 在被客户要求发表对某译员的看法时谢绝做具体评论
19. 争取加入设在日内瓦的国际会议口译员协会
20. 考上并且宣传自己拥有国内的所有口译证书
21. 乐于和同传新手搭档、帮助他们走上同传的职业道路
22. 遇到搭档是新手而且遇到困难时谢绝提供帮助
23. 对想学同传的人强调同传很难、学不会
24. 对想学同传的人说鼓励他们的话，帮助他们学好同传

从理论上讲，自由职业同传译员相互之间除了在同一个任务里是合作关系之外也都存在不同程度的竞争关系。如何既能够发展自己的业务，又保持比较高的道义标准是所有译员都面临的挑战。从总体上看，保持较高的道义标准往往会有业务损失的风险。说白了，这就是一个为了赚钱什么事情能做，什么事情即使能多赚钱也不能做的问题。不过如此尖锐的价值观上的抉择不局限于中国的自由职业同传译员，在欧洲的同传业界同样存在。在其他职业、行业也有类似情况。

用新闻练同传?

在中国，新闻同传往往是指电视节目的同传。如果发生了两国战争这样的重大国际事件而又无法派中国的记者前往时，采用同传方式转播其他国家的电视报道确实是一种好办法。在每日电视新闻中使用同传向另外一个语种的受众广播始于 1992 年英国广播公司为香港卫视提供的服务，节目时间从每天半小时逐渐增

加到最多时每天 2.5 小时。最初只有英语，后来又增加了日语。

新闻同传与会议同传有四大不同。首先，新闻同传的信息密集程度和速度都远远超过一般会议的发言和演讲。英国广播公司的新闻速度是每秒 3 个单词，15–20 秒的一条新闻需要包含所有最新、最重要的信息。编写人反复推敲，尽量在极其有限的字数内传达更多的信息。而同传时如果想把所含信息全部传译就会时间不够，导致信息遗漏或者由于难以组织译入语的句子而产生误译。这个道理如同被紧紧地压缩在一个小盒子里的东西，一旦打开盒子拿出来就会出现体积超过盒子大小的情况一样。另外由于新闻朗读速度快，译员缺少思考的余地，很容易出现口误。

第二，新闻顾名思义是新信息。突发新闻更是有可能包含完全超出译员现有知识的信息，导致漏译或者错译。另外，按照常规，电视新闻正点开播 10 分钟，往往有 10 来条内容完全不同的新闻，对译员知识面的要求经常超过一般会议口译。

第三，新闻同传有很多技术处理上的挑战。比如：电视新闻的惯用手法是主持人说一段引语，然后记者报道的声音紧跟而入。而同传译员本来就至少滞后讲者 1 秒，稍微一犹豫就滞后 2 秒，会导致画面已经是记者了，但是听众听到的还是主持人的话正在被传译的情况。或者画面已经是主持人了，译入语还在说刚才记者报道的话。另外，电视新闻里被采访者的身份总是用字幕打出。如果同传译员不马上增加对被采访者的介绍，就会导致节目主持人或者报道记者的话与被采访者的话连在一起，造成混乱。但是如果译员介绍被采访者就会明显增加在极其有限的时间里所需要说的话，导致落后太多而无法跟上原话，乃至漏译其后的内容。

新闻同传是同传的一种特殊用途，有明显的特殊性质，需要特别的训练，不是会议同传译员自然就能胜任的工作。另外，使用同传转播电视新闻需要一组技术和运作体系上的支持，不能提供一套会议同传所需的设备而了之。

由此可见，电视新闻节目不适合于同传的初级培训。不仅如此，新闻稿件也不适合于同传的初级培训。以英国广播公司的英文新闻稿为例：结构非常特殊，以最新内容开始，以相关背景结束；大量使用无主句、被动语态以及 there is/are 之类的结构。（有关英文新闻稿件的结构特征在外研社出版的《实战笔译》里有详细介绍）。这些语言上的特征都是同传里最难处理的现象，集中出现就大大增加了同传的难度。由于只有新闻文体里才常见这种情况，所以初学者不应该采用英语新闻作为培训材料。如果不是特地为了攻下新闻同传的难关也没有必要涉及。

口译的巅峰?

同传时常被人描绘成口译的巅峰，这点很值得商榷。同传有其独特之处，为了强调这些特点说同传是口译的巅峰有一定道理。但是其他口译形式恐怕也有各自的特点。比如，交传里笔记的使用就是一个需要培训才能掌握的技能，是同传里没有的。没有经过笔记培训的同传译员难以胜任高难度的交传任务。欧洲很多同传译员做不了高端的交传口译。

目前为止，在同传和交传各自的难点在哪里、困难程度如何比较方面，缺少令人信服的科学根据，缺少实证研究。交传在中国的历史与中国对外交往的历史一样长。尤其是改革开放开始之后，所有政府部门的涉外活动都大大增加，担任交传任务的人也相对较多，各个单位外事办公室的员工都有可能临时担任交传译员。相比之下，大规模使用同传在中国只有十几年的历史，再加上需要专门培训，同传译员相对交传来说少得多，这也有助于形成对同传的特殊印象。

不可否认，同传入门的门槛比交传高很多。交传可以从很低的层次开始，比如在国内一个办公室里，领导在迎接国外来访者并且与之寒暄几句。这种要求的交传无需特殊训练，只要能用外语会话就基本能完成任务。所以，交传往往被看做是只要会外语就会做的事情。而同传需要一组与笔译和交传完全不同的技能，其中最难掌握的是一组不同于交传以及其他语言形式的思维技能，没有经过有效的培训无法掌握，而是会戴上耳机听着讲者说话，自己张不开口。也就是说，同传没有一个交传那种很低层次的起点，如果没有经过培训达到相当的水平就根本做不了。

但是如果由此得出同传比交传难的结论就有失全面。交传起码在以下三个方面比同传难。

首先，虽然交传的入门门槛比同传低很多，但是交传可以达到的质量高度是同传由于形式本身的局限而达不到的。比如，从语言转换的角度看，由于同传时必须采用顺序口译的方式，译员往往不得不在英汉两种语言之间通过处理技巧做出语序和词义表达的调整。这种调整往往会改变原话的重心、修饰关系，而且这种调整基本上无法考虑原话的风格。

换个角度看，人们从概念上都接受了同传的特性，所以不会超出同传本身的局限去要求译入语里的语言质量和严谨程度。也就是说，受众对同传译入语质量的预期不高，再加上绝大多数同传受众都不具备评判同传质量的能力（具体说明请看上一课的有关讲解）。所以，只要译员持续口译，没有明显的大错误，受众都会觉得质量不错。

但交传却十分不同，译员需要达到而且可以达到的译入语质量明显超过同传。比如：同传里遇到幽默时是一闪而过，译员很难处理好，受众也不计较。但是交传里听来源语的受众已经笑过了，听译入语的受众会等待听明白为什么他们笑了。如果听完译入语仍然莫名其妙，受众马上就会产生译员没有译好的印象。再如：当讲者采用比较工整、优美的语言时，同传译员只能采用同一组顺序传译的技巧，没有运用于工整、优美语言的专门技巧。但是如果交传译员没有在译入语里反映出原话的优美风格，就很容易让受众产生译员水平不够高的印象。

换个角度看，同传是跟着讲者的话走，听到哪里、跟到哪里。靠的主要是熟练运用顺序译的技能和技巧，基本没有在紧跟讲者之外而需要自己思考之处。但是，交传译员必须在讲者暂停之后马上综合笔记、短期记忆和自己的知识，迅速回忆起原话，然后与此同时迅速在瞬间决定采用结构完整、词汇恰当的汉语在译入语里做表述。由于交传笔记无法齐全，译员短期记忆会力不从心，瞬间之内组织好汉语结构和修辞需要有出口成章的水平，所以，要让交传的受众感到译入语质量高是非常难做到的。再加上双语受众和译员一样，也是刚刚听完讲者的话，可以一边听译员的版本，一边与自己的理解比较，很容易听出译员处理不当之处，更不用说遗漏或者误译了。

但是尽管交传里有上述挑战，高水平的译员仍然能够以超出同传可能的质量传译幽默、笑话，可以在译入语里做到句子工整、句法正确、用词恰当、再现讲者原话的效果。这些都是同传受到形式本身的局限而很难做到的。

其次，交传译员所必须承受的心理压力大大超过同传。这里有两个主要原因。第一，同传译员与听众隔离，而且每次任务至少两人承担，有时还是三人轮换。译员心里知道听众一般不清楚在某个具体时间段是哪位译员在传译。而交传译员必须单枪匹马面对听众，所有听众全部都听着、看着每一位译员，无处藏身。场面越大，在场听众的层次越高，译员的心理压力就越大。

再次，交传译员对于译入语的质量所承担的后果远远超出同传译员。在典型的同传环境下，受众与译员完全隔离，受众无法直接挑战译员的质量。即使个别受众对译入语质量很有意见，也不愿意因此去打断讲者。也就是说，除非是高度互动式的对话，同传译员极少需要对于译入语的质量当场承担责任。

交传则恰恰相反，译员往往是必须当场为译入语的质量承担责任。这主要有两个原因，一个是译员遇到难点，一时不知如何处理，整个活动的进程马上就戛然而止，所有受众包括讲者都知道译员遇到麻烦了。另外一个是在典型的交传环境下，受众与译员面对面，可以直接挑战译员的质量。由于交传时需要打断的是译员而不是讲者，这就大大减少了受众的顾虑，对质量有不满意之处就会打断译员，导致译员不得不当场承担质量后果的责任。

最后，交传对于译员的体力和耐力要求时常会超过同传。凡是做过正规交传的译员都知道，一个人担任一整天交传比两个人搭档完成同等长度、同等难度的同传要辛苦得多。同传搭档轮换休息的道理就在于要让大脑在感到疲劳之前得到休息，回复到之前的状况。但是交传译员的脑力活动是完全不间断的：讲者说话时，译员需要做笔记，而做笔记就是在处理信息；讲者暂停说话时，译员马上开始传译。周而复始，循环不断，译员没有喘气之机。连续三天做交传和连续三天做同传的感觉是很不一样的。

总之，同传和交传是两种口译形式，两者之间有着本质的差别，不能简单地做比较。在没有实证研究的科学根据之前断言哪种形式比哪种形式更难或者更高级容易得出谬误的结论。

本课小结

同传是一种特殊的口译形式，由于对同传缺少研究和了解，不少流行的说法其实是误解。同传既不是青春饭，也不能简单地称作是口译的巅峰。以比较客观、科学的眼光看待同传有利于比较准确地认识到同传的难处以及达到同传水平所需的技能，有利于学会同传。

由于同传一般需要两位译员合作，这就给同传这种口译形式带来了其他形式没有的挑战，其中包括两位译员之间的关系如何对待。自由职业译员在一定程度上是业务的竞争对手，但是在担任同一个任务期间又必须妥善合作，这就对同传译员在职业道义标准上提出了其他形式的译员无需考虑的问题。

工作坊

分组讨论本课有关同传译员如何开展业务时列举的二十多个选项，说明哪些做法你认为符合你个人的道义准则，哪些不符合以及为什么你认为可以或者不可以接受。

第三课　同传技能

同传是一种特殊的口译形式，需要三大组能力，即：核心能力、知识能力、辅助能力。核心能力是指同传特需，即定义同传的一组技能。而知识能力和辅助能力属于同传所需但并不是同传特需，在其他形式的口译里也同样需要的能力。以下是笔者理念中同传所需能力及其构成技能的示意图：

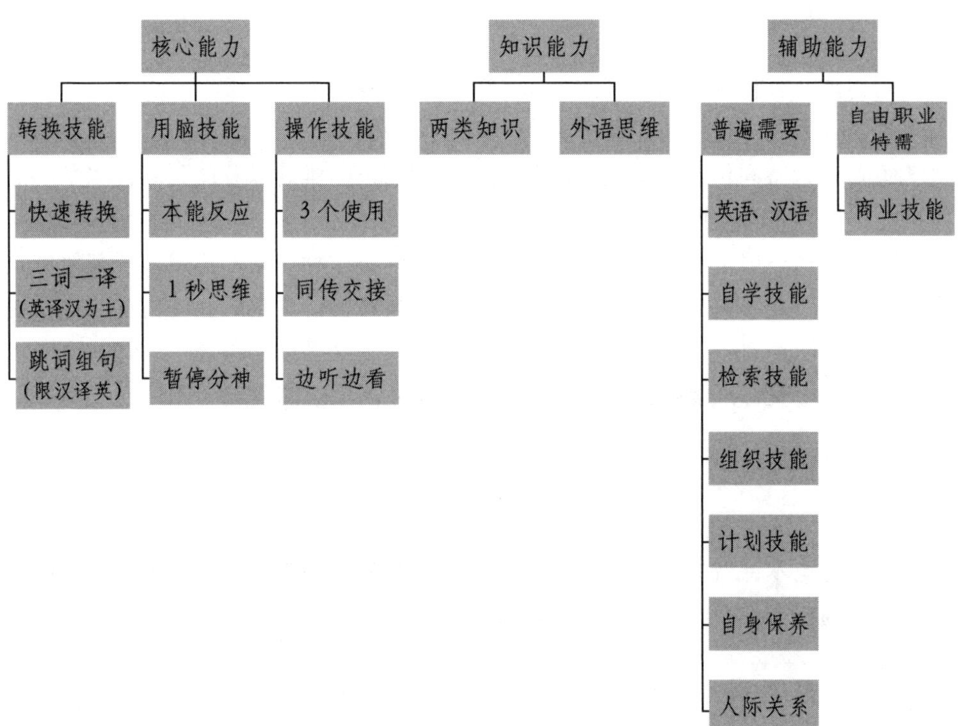

本课将分别讲解核心能力和辅助能力，下一课讲解知识能力。

核心能力

同传所需的核心能力具有多层次结构的特性，而且根据语言方向的不同而有差别。所谓多层次结构指的是三大能力都由一系列技能构成，而每个技能又由具体分技能构成，形成一个多层次结构。比如：英译汉需要以下三大组核心能力：

1. 转换技能：指译员在把来源语转换成译入语时对于译入语所作的处理。
2. 用脑技能：指译员通过培训，能够在一定程度上驾驭思维，按照同传的需要运作，即：能够同步交错地完成边听、边译的任务。
3. 操作技能：指译员在同传操作过程中需要使用的技能。

而汉译英还需要增加诸如跳词组句这样具有明显译入语方向的技能，以下逐一讲解。

快速转换

转换技能由三大具体分技能组成，首当其冲的就是快速转换。这指的是译员以所需的速度把听到的来源语迅速转换成译入语。在练习同传之前，绝大多数学英语的人都从来没有被要求过按照限定的速度说英语，也就是说没有经过速度的训练。绝大多数学翻译的人都从来没有被要求过在一眨眼间把来源语转换成译入语，即使是自己熟悉的单词，也无法按照同传所需的速度转换成译入语。

我们来做个小实验：请按照你自己平生最快的速度把下述英语词组口译成汉语：

Good morning
Good afternoon
Good evening
Nuclear non-proliferation

请问刚才口译最后一个单词的时候是否反应速度比前面三个单词明显慢了很多？这是自然现象。前三个单词对于大多数学习英语的人来说，都已经从英语口译到汉语无数次，属于熟练转换。而除了熟练 Nuclear non-proliferation 这个话题的译员，恐怕绝大多数人都极少转换过，甚至可能这是有生以来第一次。如果不熟悉，甚至是有生以来第一次，反应速度肯定比较慢。

同传要求的是所有听到的单词都必须属于可以熟练转换的范围，即如同此生已经无数次转换过。如果遇到一个不能马上转换的词汇或者概念，就会迟疑、甚至停顿下来思考，影响随后继续听。

快速转换是同传能力里的第一个也是最关键的一个，同传里常见的绝大多数问题都是由于转换速度不够快而导致，这些问题也都可以随着转换速度足够快而迎刃而解。比如，速度足够快时，分脑的负担就能下降到一般人都可以胜任的水平。请看以下用脑技能的讲解。

三词一译

转换技能里的第二个具体技能是三词一译，即英译汉时遵循每个意群处理一次的原则。每个意群指由三个具有实际意义的单词组成的单位。译员边听、边处理、边说出译语。

所谓“三词”是一个笼统的概念，在英语里指除去了语法所需的比如定冠词、介词和其他语法所需之词（如：has been）之后的名词、动词、副词或者形容词这些实义词。之所以说处理是因为有些意群听到之后可能需要暂时不译，甚至完全不译。

汉译英时，由于绝大多数汉语表达法都是由两个汉字组成的词，所以相当于英语里的“三词”大约为5–6个汉字。三词一译在汉译英里就是5–6个汉字一处理，既可能把这5–6个汉字所代表的内容传译到译入语里，也可能暂时不译，甚至完全不译。

之所以把目标定在“三词”有几个原因。首先，英语演讲的平均速度大约是每秒三个单词。英国广播公司BBC就是按照这个速度计算每条新闻的单词数量，据说这是因为一般人大脑处理信息的速度是每秒三个英语单词，超过了就容易处理不及而听不懂，低于这个速度又没有必要。当然，在口译的实战中，讲者的速度既可能因为过度兴奋或者时间不够用而超过每秒三个单词，也可能因为个人习惯而不到每秒三个单词。

其次，根据笔者多年的实践、观察，发现经过一定同传训练之后，普通人大脑同时处理不同信息的能量大约为2秒。也就是说，边听边说时，如果是落后于讲者1秒则相当轻松。可以长时间一边处理刚才听到的三个单词，一边同时听下面三个单词而不感到疲劳。如果是落后于讲者2秒，通过训练也能够对付，但是不能持久。而如果落后于讲者 3 秒，这时边听边说对于脑力的使用就会明显增加，往往只有训练有素或者经验丰富的译员才能做到，否则就会开始遗漏。而且即使能够做到滞后于讲者 3 秒或者以上，也往往很容易因为大脑压力过大而过早疲劳。

边听边译的能力经常被称作分脑，这种描述很形象。分脑是同传不可或缺的能力，但是分脑并不是同传特有的能力。同时完成多项任务也是交传不可缺少的技能，译员必须能够边听、边理解、边记笔记甚至快速决定如何记录某个内容。大脑同时做几件事情的能力绝大多数人都有，只要是在认真听别人讲话，就势必同时在理解所听到的话，有时还同时稍作思考，形成看法。歌手边唱边给自己伴奏是分脑，在家一边炒菜一边聊天也是分脑。不过，同传译员需要同时完成的任务更多，更系统，难度更大，持续时间更长。所以，如果没有经过专门训练，光靠大脑的自然能力无法胜任。

由于分脑很不容易，所以初学者需要尽量减少大脑同时处理的信息量。三词一译就是减少分脑量的一个有效技能。在三词一译的状态下，大脑在听新内容的时候需要处理的上一个内容一般都在三个英语单词之内。这就能大大减轻由于不必在大脑里保留 5–6 个英语单词，甚至把句子结构像笔译那样倒装所带来的负担。

再次，三词一译为如何决定修辞顺序是否可以或者应该颠倒提供了量化的依据。根据三词一译的概念，只要是在英语 3–4 个单词的范围之内，为了符合汉语语法或者习惯而颠倒词汇的顺序不成问题。即这样小范围之内的颠倒，一般人的大脑都能胜任，无需大量的特殊训练。以下是一些在三个英语单词之内颠倒译语词序的例子：

英语原话	汉语译语
the book of the library	图书馆的书
The role of a leader	领导人的角色
Gathered here this evening	今晚在此相聚

刚才讲解的是英译汉，汉译英时由于正常字数比例是 2:1，所以，同传的所需速度大约为每秒 5–6 个汉字。为了便于记忆，笔者仍然称其为三词一译，指在相当于英语里的三词一译。汉译英如何三词一译将于第六课详细讲解。

这里需要说明的是三词一译的实现会受到其他因素的影响，比如，讲者的口音、译员对于所听到内容的熟悉程度、译员的双语水平等等。克服这些其他因素的影响需要其他知识和技能。不过，同传的任何技能和技巧都会受到同样其他因素的影响。

要想做到三词一译，就需要熟练地掌握一系列技巧，帮助译员跨越英汉两种语言之间的鸿沟，无论是在做英译汉还是汉译英，都做到听上去好像每三个单词就有一个对应一样，不等待，不改变顺序，听到哪里，译到哪里。要做到三词一译除了需要双语转换技巧之外，还需要培训用脑技能，使大脑服从同传的需要而流水思维。有关运用大脑的技能将于稍后详细讲解。

跳词组句

汉译英的转换除了上述技能之外，还需要善于“跳词组句”。这指的是汉译英同传时不能象英译汉那样每听到三个单词都反映到译入语里，而必须有选择，即边听边扔汉字。有关哪些汉字必须扔、哪些应该扔、哪些可以扔，笔者在即将出版的《实战笔译—中翻英》里将有详尽的讲解。另外，在中国对外翻译出版有限公司出版的《实战交传》第六课辅助能力里也有涉及，可以参阅。以下根据同传的需要概要讲述。

汉语至少有两个特点直接影响到同传的处理。首先是汉语词汇大多数为两个汉字组成一个意思。必须把这两个汉字当做一个英语单词处理，而不宜分别译入英语。请看以下例子：

汉语词汇	建议译作	不宜译作
成功	success	realise the effort
学习	study	Study and review
大学	university	Large institute of learning

其次，汉语里有很多重复表达的用法，有时是为了强调，有时是因为指称关系所需，有时是为了修辞。但是由于英汉语言文化不同的原因，这些重复表达法不能全部译入英语，而需要删去。否则，在英语里不仅完全失去汉语里的作用，而且会听上去啰哩啰唆。请看以下例子：

汉语表达	建议译作	不宜译作
出口增长的局面	Export growth	The situation of export growth
受剥削的悲惨命运	Being exploited	The sad life of being exploited
无数仁人志士苦苦探索救国救民的道路	Many struggled in their search for a way to save the nation.	Numerous people of good character struggled bitterly to experiment with a way to save the country and its people.

同传里跳词组句时还需要摆脱句子结构的束缚。首先，同传完全靠听而且是边听边译，往往是译完一句之后，有时甚至是第二句开始译了才知道上一句话结束了。其次，如果达到三词一译的水平时，译语经常是自然而然地跨原话句子的。把减字和跨句这两个技巧结合起来能够在保证准确的前提下大大提高同传的速度。

比如，如果单独看"微不足道"，不译成 too minute to mention 就有不准确的感觉。但是如果听到这句话："世界市场很大，我们的份额微不足道"，同传就可以处理成：The world market is very big. But our share is insignificant。

再如，如果单独看"强国建设"，不译成 development to strengthen the nation 就有不准确的感觉。但是听到这句话"我们行业已经进入了强国建设的关键时期"，同传就可以处理成：Our industry is helping to build a strong nation. We're at a critical juncture。不能按照笔译那样统观全句，重新组织为：Our industry has entered the critical period of the development to strengthen the nation.

有关跳词组句的具体技巧将于第六课里详细讲解。

本能反应

接下来讲解同传的第二组技能，即如何培训自己的大脑使其按照同传的需要运转，即：用脑技能。这听上去可能有点玄乎其玄，大脑怎么能够培训呢？其实，同传给人留下很难学的一个主要原因就是需要大脑以非同寻常的方式运作，所以练同传有独特的难度。同传培训效果不尽人意也经常是因为缺少对于同传时大脑需要如何运作的正确理解，导致不是缺少对译员进行大脑思维运作方式的训练，就是对培训生提出短期内无法达到的要求。

同传是边听边译，不像交传那样可以听完一段话之后再重新组织句子。这就好像一江春水向东流，只能往前，不能回头。而人们大脑习惯的思维、运作方式是既可以停顿，也经常回头，反思刚才听到的或者自己说过的话。无论是停顿下来思考，还是回头反思，在同传时的结果都一样，译员会被卡在前一个内容的思考上，听不见接下来的话。练同传的一个关键内容就是练成流水思维，即：能够控制住大脑的思维方向，使其如同讲者的话，一江春水向东流。不停顿、不回头，一直译下去。

要实现这个目标就需要集中练两个技能：本能反应和1秒思维。前者指听到一个意群（三个单词）或者一个需要马上译出的单词的时候就能够像本能的反应一样说出来，不假思索。打个比方，这就像伸手去拿玻璃茶杯，忘了刚刚加过滚烫的水，杯壁很烫，手指刚一接触马上就缩回来。缩回的速度比眨眼还快，完全是本能驱使，不是经过思考："我的手指感到杯子的温度很高。如果不马上收回手指，就会被烫伤"之后的行动。

以本能反应的速度传译往往会产生"话音未落"就已经译出的印象。以下对比"听完再说"和"话音未落"式本能反应在同传时的效果。左栏展示的是"先听后说"，即栏内的话是先英语，后汉语。右栏展示的是"话音未落"，栏内的话是英语未完，汉语已经开始。

先听后说	话音未落
Library 图书馆	Libra**ry** 图书馆
Contribution 贡献	Contribu**tion** 贡献
Political 政治	Politi**cal** 政治
Climate change 气候变化	Climate change 气候变化
Global economic downturn 全球经济衰退	Global economic downturn 全球经济衰退

在同传培训的初期，根据转换时的速度可以把译员拥有的词汇量分成三种情况：已知很熟、已知不熟、尚且不知。同传培训初期的一个内容就是需要尽快地把现有的双语词汇越来越多地变成能够以本能反应的速度转换成译入语的知识。请看示意图（如下图）：

一秒思维

同传里的1秒思维指两种能力：首先是译员经过培训能够控制大脑对于一个单词或者词组如何转换成译入语的思考时间一般不超过1秒钟，即一边听接下来的内容，另一边还在思考上一个内容这种分脑使用的持续时间不超过1秒钟。1秒钟内想不出解决方案马上就抛弃上一个内容，集中脑力听下面的话。这叫做“有疑便扔”，即凡是1秒之内没有解决方案者马上就扔掉不管，继续听、译接下来的话。如果不能果断地扔掉有疑之处而继续思考，则势必影响接下来几个单词的听，导致大脑负荷过重而漏听以至于漏译后来本来会译的内容，得不偿失。对于上个内容的思考时间过长，乃至于听下一个内容的脑力不够导致听不懂，甚至没听见是同传时遗漏内容的最主要的原因之一。

1秒思维是一种特殊的技能，没有经过培训的大脑是没有如此严格的自律能力的，很难在想某件事情时仅仅想1秒钟，然后马上不想上个语言点而想下个语言点。

其次是同传译员必须习惯于在1秒钟之内想出解决方案。绝大多数人都具有1秒思维的潜能，所以才有“急中生智”的说法。但是由于同传要求顺序传译，在英汉双语之间不停地采用各种技巧保证三词一译，所以需要经常、大量地“急中生智”。这就需要经过培训，逐渐地把急中生智变成在同传时大脑运转的习惯。

同传译员必须能够完全、自如地控制自己的大脑运作方式，在开口同传前还是普通人的思维，可以花几秒钟想一个想说的词或者内容。但是一旦开口同传就即刻进入1秒思维状态，并且在做同传的整个时间段里保持这种状态。

培训起1秒思维的能力就能保证译员紧紧跟着讲者，即使偶尔遇到比较难处理的内容滞后于讲者超过2秒，也能采用其他相关技巧尽快重新跟上。总之，1

秒思维既是大脑的自律能力，又是大脑的创作能力，是个需要经过训练才能掌握的技能。

暂停分神

同传时必须绝对集中精力，不能分神。这个道理很简单，但是做起来不容易。同传时分神有两个层次，表面层次的分神比较容易避免。只要没有一边同传、一边想比如中午饭吃什么就行了。但是分神还有一个更深层次的表现，很少有人注意到，即使是经过训练能够做同传的人也常常没有意识到有这个问题。这就是一边在做同传，一边时不时怀疑自己刚才是否听错了、说错了，或者为刚才的某个语言点的处理感到满意。这就如同分身了一般，译员把自己变成了两个人，一个仍然在做同传，另外一个担任评估员，评估刚才的同传表现。请看示意图：

这种深层次的分神是人们从小长大期间养成的习惯，日常生活里对于自己的言行都会不由自主地自我评估，判定刚才的言行是否合适，这是在社会中生活的人保证自己言行合适的重要措施。由于绝大多数人十几、二十年来都已经习惯于此，极少有人注意到自己有这个习惯，更不会想到这是同传的一大障碍。

每当分神自我评估时，除非译员水平很高，已经达到能够持续分脑的境界，否则无法听清讲者于此同时说的话。如果经常分神做自我评估，势必导致不断地漏译、错译，使同传质量明显下降。如何通过培训养成在做同传时能够暂停分神的技能将于第九课里讲解。

3个使用

同传核心能力的第三个组成部分就是实际操作的能力，由三个主要技能构成。第一个是“3 个使用”，指的是：使用声音、使用麦克、使用设备。首先，同传译员是通过麦克传译，所以可以使用远远低于演讲的音量就可以顺利完成任务。不过，初练同传时往往容易非常紧张，而且不习惯于边听边说，自己的音量会越来越大。不仅没有必要地增加了自己的劳动强度，而且容易在有其他语种时干扰隔壁译员的工作。即使只有英汉互译，由于便携式同传箱往往隔音效果不尽人意，音量大了有可能给受众带来干扰。

麦克的使用也有讲究，业内称 microphone manners，汉语可以称之为麦克礼貌。这指的是译员通过培训，养成良好习惯，除了译语以外，没有其他声音输入麦克，保证受众只听到译语，而不受噪音之苦。麦克礼貌欠缺的主要表现有受众从耳机里听到了与译入语无关的声音：译员的咳嗽声、谈话声（忘了关闭话筒）、翻动面前讲稿的纸声、用手触摸麦克的噪声、梳理头发的噪声等等。译员必须时刻牢记麦克没有大脑，不会选择，凡是在一定距离之内的声音全部都会进入麦克被受众听到。要想达到麦克礼貌的要求就必须从思想上养成对于麦克状态的敏感，麦克一开，一切小心。一旦口译结束，甚至暂停时也及时关闭麦克，以免其他声音进入麦克。

使用同传设备说起来简单，但是也需要经过一段时间的练习才能掌握。虽然说同传设备大同小异，但是遇到从来没有使用过的设备而且自己又是同传新手，常常出现手忙脚乱、由于设备使用错误而影响同传质量的情况。不过，使用同传设备最复杂的情况当属双向口译多位不同语言讲者的快速互动。这是因为译员使用同传设备时有两个操作步骤，一个是选择听的频道，另外一个是选择说的频道。

比如，假设译员的工作语言是英语和汉语，而发言人说英语，译员就可以选择听原语频道。如果下一位发言人说法语，译员就必须马上选择英语频道，听英语箱的译员把法语译成英语，然后把所听到的英语译成汉语。如果接下来的发言人说汉语，译员就必须马上选择原语频道听汉语，同时马上把输出频道改选成英语。即：需要快速做两个选择。如果三个讲话人分别说英语、法语、汉语而且在讲话中激烈交锋的话，译员就必须在每次开始口译之前快速地做出两个选择，选定合适的听以及合适的说频道。而且这些动作都必须在传译持续不断的过程中完成，没有一定的培训，译员很容易顾此失彼。

同传交接

联合国系统的规定是同传团队由三名译员组成，其他国际机构以及私营市场上经常是两人一个团队。业内的惯例是如果三人一个团队，则每人 20 分钟，这相当于每位译员每个小时里只负责 1/3 的同传量。

这 20 分钟可以是毛的，也可以是净的。前者指完全按照钟点排班，不论是否做了同传。比如，如果安排给你的时间段是每个小时正点开始，而本来上午 9 点开始的会议拖到 9 点 20 才开始，则你已经完成了你的时间段，应该由负责 20-40 分的同事开始传译。如果按净时算，则安排的是顺序，无论几点开始，你都做 20 分钟，然后由搭档的同事接。

如果是两人一个团队，一般由两人商定每次的时间长短。即可以参照联合国的标准做法，每人每个时间段译 20 分钟，也可以长一些或者短一些。谁先谁后可以商定，也可以抽签而定。

同传的交接指的是一个团队里后一位译员根据事先约定的安排，在同传不断的前提下从前一位译员那里接过话头，打开话筒，继续往下译，并且在同传一段时间之后意识到后一位译员的提示时，恰到好处的停止传译，关闭话筒。

虽然同传交接时由下一位译员为主导，但是前一位译员需要配合，才能保证交接平稳，听上去只是换了声音，丝毫不影响译语的完整。

由于同传过程如同流水作业，译员常常需要在没有明显间歇的时候交接，所以需要通过培训初步掌握这个技能。达到得心应手的水平还需要经过一段时间的工作，与不同习惯的众多其他译员合作之后才能达到。

交接有三个关键：第一，选择恰当的交接点；第二，提示搭档译员；第三，手势与口译协调一致，果断地切入。交接点应该选在话语的自然结束或者停顿点。为了保持交接时不打断流水般的译语，下一位译员必须在前一位译员仍然在口译的同时脑子里也开始做同传，然后在听到自然结束或者停顿时切入。所谓切入即示意前一位译员停止说话、打开自己的麦克、正式开始口译。

在交接之前必须示意前一位译员，以便对方做好戛然而止、关掉自己麦克的精神准备。用什么方式示意没有硬性规定，理想的方式应为明显、清楚、适度。只有“明显”对方才能感觉到；只有“清楚”对方才知道这是交接的示意而不是出于其他原因或者与己无关；只有“适度”才能避免干扰前一位译员仍在进行中的同传。

交接示意并没有业界的硬性规定，译员往往都有自己习惯的方式。有些人打手势，有些人轻触对方。不过，需要注意的是，有些译员不喜欢被对方触碰。所以，打手势是比较保险的办法。

这里还需要说明一下使用同传箱的礼貌。虽然这不属于技能性质，而是行为性质，但是能反映出译员的职业标准，不可忽视。有些需要常规使用同传的机构拥有专业设计的高标准同传间，但是在商业市场上的同传经常需要使用移动式同传箱，而且最常见的是双位座，即为两人合用而设计。这种同传箱总体来说空间很有限，放两把椅子以后就很挤了。另外，桌面空间也十分有限。如果是三名译员合用，就不得不轮流，这就尤其需要注意相互之间的礼貌。

同传箱内需要遵守的首先是桌面礼貌，每次起身都应该争取把自己的东西全部带走，把空间腾出给下一位译员。其次是地面礼貌：译员往往都带有自己的物品，电脑包、手提包之类。同传箱里的有限空间是所有使用译员的共享空间，相互尊重就能避免产生没有必要的紧张关系。

边听边看

边听边看指的是译员一边听讲者的话，一边看面前的文稿或者电脑投影的屏幕。

前者一般有两种情况，有时是讲者提及某段文件内容，然后开始念这段。这在国际机构的会议讨论文件时经常出现，译员必须有相关文件，然后快速找到相关段落，然后视译，否则会跟不上讲者的速度。有时是译员持有讲者的讲话稿，而讲者基本按照稿子念，译员便可以边听着把握讲者的速度并且注意讲者是否脱稿，一边视译面前的讲稿。

后者指的是译员利用电脑屏幕上可以看到的内容协助同传。善于边听讲者、边看屏幕至少在两种情况下对译员很有帮助。一种是讲者提及很多复杂的数字，而这些数字都列在打在屏幕上的表格里，译员可以看着屏幕念，减轻完全仰赖大脑转换的压力。另外一种情况是当讲者描绘屏幕上的内容时使用了译员感到生疏的个别词汇，如果光靠听懂就会被卡住。但是由于屏幕上的内容很形象，译员知道讲者在描述其内容就可以用自己的话描述，避开生疏的词汇而完成同传的任务。

边听边看需要译员在正常的边听、边译上增加一层脑力活动，所以是一项需要通过培训才能掌握的技能。如果培训不够，或者不当，会导致看和听相互冲突，丢三落四，无益于同传质量。

辅助能力

同传的辅助能力有两种，一种属于译员作为一名职业人员所必须拥有的，具有普遍性质。这些并不是同传所特有的技能，而是译员在其他工作里或者改行之后可以携带到其他工作领域里的技能。另外一种技能属于同传特有或者在同传里的使用特别突出。

同传的主要辅助能力如下：

1. 自学技能：设定并且实现目标，分析、监测、评估自己的能力和表现，以及相关的组织和计划技能的运用
2. 检索技能：通过在线、电话、电邮、阅读或者其他手段弥补知识上的缺陷
3. 组织技能：善于安排时间、工作量以及自己的活动，善于区分轻重缓急
4. 计划技能：能够策划好行程、时间、交通工具，计划好前往外地担任口译任务所需的物品、行装
5. 自身保养：妥善安排饮食起居，保证总是处于最佳生理和精神状态
6. 人际关系：善于应对各种人和要求，其中包括其他译员、翻译公司、公关公司等
7. 商业运作：（仅适用于自由职业译员）设计口译服务项目、定价、宣传、报价、确认预定、收款、做账、税务管理等

有关人际关系和商业技能在笔者的《实战口译》一书里有比较全面的阐述，欢迎参阅。至于同传译员相互之间的关系，除了本课内容之外，还可以参阅第二课里有关道义标准的讨论。

同传译员按照从业性质可以分成两大类：全职雇员、自由职业。如果译员是全职雇员而且是与同事搭档完成一个同传任务，则两人的关系比较简单、透明。两人本来就是同事，所以，无论在所负责口译的讲话人的分工上，还是在所分担的时间段方面都可以比较灵活。同事之间往往也不大计较谁多译或者少译一、两分钟。

如果搭档的两位译员都是自由职业，两人关系就比较复杂。由于自由职业属于商业性质，所以从理论上看，所有自由职业译员相互之间都在一定程度上是竞争对手。当然在实际中，这种竞争关系可能由于两人的主要工作地点或者客户群体不同而几乎不存在。另外，大多数自由职业译员在职业发展初期都会经常遇到

第一次与某位译员搭档的情况。同传职业的一个特点就是完全可能之前与某人没有任何联系，之后可能也没有任何联系，仅仅在搭档完成某天的同传任务时与其人共事。

本课要点

同传译员需要拥有三大方面的能力，其中的核心能力特指同传特需、特有能力，其他两大方面的能力属于同传非常需要，但是不是同传特有，而是其他口译形式也非常需要的能力。每个能力都有一系列具体技能组成，以下结构图总结了同传所需的技能：

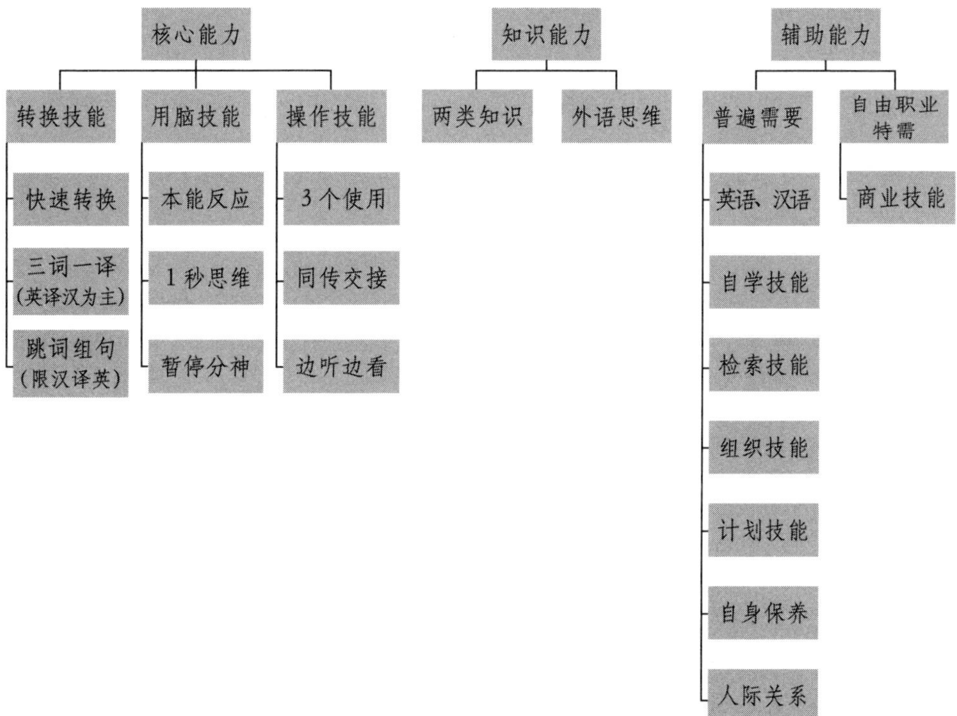

工作坊

分组讨论上述技能图中哪些是交传也非常需要的技能以及为什么这样认为。

第四课　知识能力

本书采用的“知识能力”这个概念有三个组成部分，一是知识，这属于大脑长期记忆性质；二是在有限时间内快速获得知识的能力；三是口译现场认知、理解的能力。

人们的一般看法是同传译员需要有广泛的知识才能胜任，没有广泛的知识就做不了同传的说法听上去也挺有道理。笔者在《实战交传》（中国对外翻译出版有限公司，2012）里已经提出必须区分某次任务所需的知识量和整个同传事业发展累积起来的知识量，认为广泛的知识往往是同传事业发展的结果，对于大部分同传译员来说，广泛的知识不是而且也不大可能是事业初期能够实现的目标。译员的知识量总是从初期的不广泛逐渐发展，口译越做越多，知识量越来越大，经过多年的实践和学习直至进入知识广泛的境界。

有关知识量的概念还需要做另外一个区分，那就是译员目前为止的知识量和每次任务时可能需要的所有知识量。前者总是相对的定量，即在某天、某个时刻，译员的知识是个定量。但是与此同时，译员为了胜任当天的口译任务可能所需的知识量却是不定量，甚至有可能是无限的。

比如，一位到访中国的欧洲国家元首发表有关两国友好关系的公开演讲。这种有关两国友好关系的讲话按理说是同传里难度比较低的类型，只要有一定的同传水平，对两国的情况有一定的了解就能胜任。但是这位国家元首在谈到大学生应该尽早接触社会的重要性时这样说：...whether it’s taking a summer job or pull a pint...。

只有熟悉英语文化的人才知道 pull a pint 说的是在啤酒吧里给顾客上啤酒时需要拉把手，而 pint 原意是一品脱，即一大杯啤酒。讲者是以在酒吧打工举例说大学生接触社会可以有多种形式。

同传里经常遇到讲者顺口提及家乡或者在他们国家里司空见惯的事情。由于中国的同传译员与这些事情根本没有接触，所以往往一头雾水，甚至一闪而过都没听见，更不要说传译了。

这种类型的知识就属于译员可能所需而且是无限的知识，因为译员基本上无法预料当天的讲者都知道什么而且会在什么时候谈及他们生活中的哪个具体细节。由于大多数中国译员都长期生活、工作在国内，与欧美国家的生活相隔甚远，光靠平常抽出点滴时间阅读一些材料是根本不可能获得与欧美国家人士基本重合的知识量。

综上所述，既要区分某次任务所需的知识量和事业发展积累起来的知识量（可以简称为阶段性不足），也要区分译员担任某次任务时已经拥有的知识量和胜任此次任务可能所需的知识量（可以简称为当天不足）。以下第一个示意图描绘的是前一个区分，每个圆圈代表一定的知识量，而且外圈包括内圈。第二个示意图采用同样的圆圈方式描绘后一个区分。

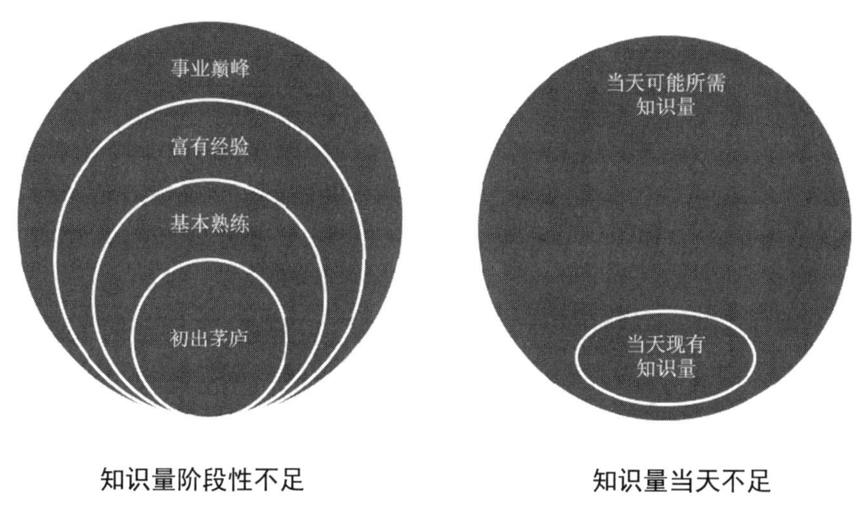

知识量阶段性不足　　知识量当天不足

由此推理，同传译员在事业初期几乎肯定是需要在知识不够广泛的情况下完成口译任务，即使是有了多年经验的译员也时常会遇到不懂的内容。此外，既定同传译员在每次任务中所面临的局面都很可能是自己所拥有的知识无法覆盖所有讲者的知识总和。由此进一步推理，同传译员不可缺少的不是广泛的知识，而是能够以有限的知识完成同传任务的能力。只有这样，才能随着不断实践，不断扩大知识量，越来越好地完成任务。也就是说，译员的知识能力才是真正的关键。

那么如何建立、发展知识能力呢？首先看属于记忆部分的知识，这部分知识可以从两个角度来看：任务知识和个人知识。前者按照同传任务的时间线界定，后者特指译员作为个人所拥有的知识，与所担任的口译任务没有直接的联系。

任务知识

任务知识有以下四种：

1. 预有知识：译员在接受同传任务之前已经拥有的与该任务直接相关的知识
2. 准备知识：译员通过同传任务之前的准备而得到的与该任务直接相关的知识
3. 现学知识：译员在同传时根据讲者的话马上掌握之前不懂的知识。这是知识能力的第三个组成部分，即在口译时当场学会的知识
4. 后续知识：译员通过同传任务以及之后的继续学习而掌握的知识

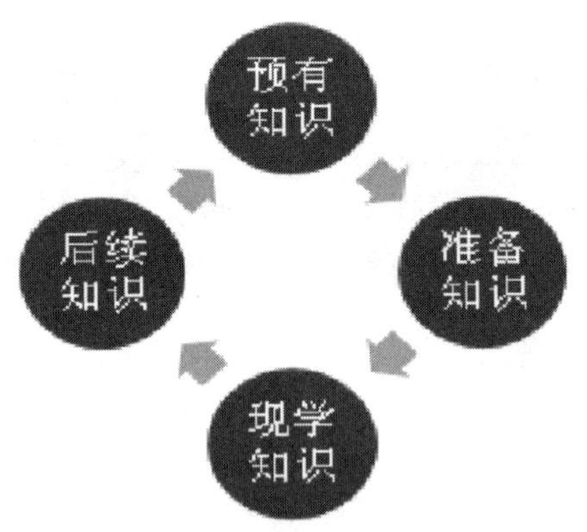

预有知识非常必要，但在译员职业发展的初期总是不够，总是需要准备知识的补充才能胜任同传任务；在任务期间以及其后继续学习所获得的知识又成为下一次同传任务的预有知识。在这个反复不止的过程中，译员在特定话题或者活动方面的知识量不断扩大。请看示意图（不同知识量的区分仅为示意，不是准确的描绘）。

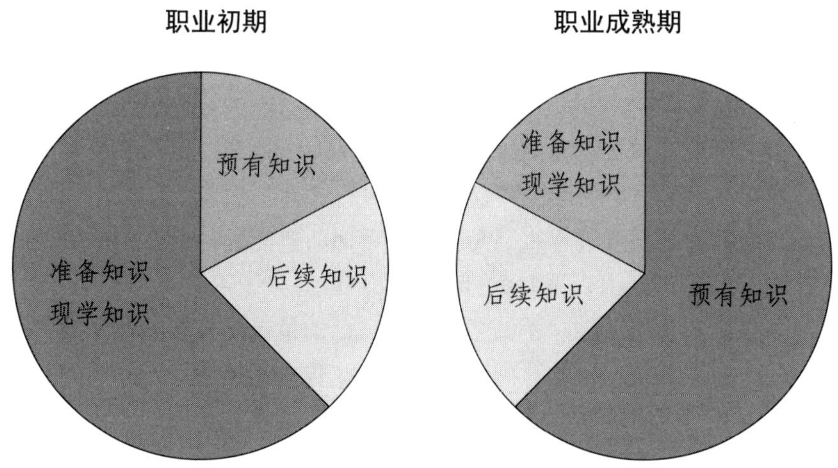

预有知识有两种：主题知识和非主题知识。前者是有关当天同传任务的话题的知识，后者是有关当天活动的知识，比如在哪里开会、有哪些人出席、会议的进行方式、之前发生过的情况等等。国际组织的定期会议、公司与组织机构的年会、年度活动都有各自的习惯做法。熟悉这些情况的译员比较胸有成竹，不仅知其然而且知其所以然。当讲者采用暗喻、暗指、间接提及的说话方式时，做过多次同一会议的译员往往从容不迫，而第一次做的译员，即使是资深译员，有时也会猛一下不知所云。

预有知识需要靠准备知识来补充，而准备知识所需的恰恰是知识能力里的第二个组成部分，即在有限的时间内快速获得知识的能力。其中包括快速地确定所需准备的知识范围、快速检索以收集好需要学习的材料和信息、快速学习（包括阅读、建立词汇表、背诵词汇）。具体内容将于第七课同传任务周期里详细讲解。

预有知识加准备知识仍然不够，这就是前述的知识量的当天不足，译员需要依靠知识能力的第三个组成部分，即通过自己的认知和理解能力，边听讲者的，边增加知识量。

由于焦点比较清楚，任务知识范围相对有限，所以是比较容易建立起来的，而且可以在短期内建立起来。同传乃至所有口译里最难的是建立个人知识体系。

个人知识

个人知识特指与当前的同传任务没有直接关系，而是讲者作为个人所拥有的超出当前话题的知识。这种知识无法准确界定，所需要的量防不胜防，经常给同传译员，甚至是做过多年同传的译员带来麻烦。之前所举的一位欧洲国家元首的演讲就是一个很好的例子。即使是在英国留学多年的中国译员恐怕也不一定马上能想到 pull a pint 是什么。

个人知识体系由哪些内容构成是口译研究的一大难题，以下介绍这个体系的一种描绘方式。由于这是仍然在探索、发展中的体系，不能作为教条，仅供参考，希望能借此推进对于同传所需的个人知识体系如何建立的讨论。

个人知识体系可以由以下几大部分构成：世界、国家、社会、工作、生活，每个部分都有很多细分层次。译员需要根据自己的情况确定知识体系的具体构成内容。不过，总体来看，一般都需要掌握近 100 多个具体话题，阅读几百万字的材料，背诵成千的双向词汇，掌握众多的热点议题（了解议题的背景和在每个具体议题上的至少两种完全不同的看法）。

这听上去很吓人，但又恰恰说明中国学生现有的个人知识远远不够同传所需，所以只有尽快地把个人知识体系的建立作为同传培训不可分割的组成部分，才能掌握同传所需的基本个人知识。

本课最后一页以在英国担任同传译员为例，以标题方式概括描述个人知识体系里有关英国部分的基本构成。英汉双语译员还必须参照这个体系列出所需的有关中国的个人知识，然后必须知道所有英国知识体系里的所有语言的汉语对应说法以及所有中国知识体系里的所有语言的英语对应说法。

系统地建立起个人知识体系很重要，但个人知识体系无法定量，不能单独作为同传的衡量尺度。既要认识到个人知识的重要性，又必须清楚地认识到个人知识在整个知识能力中的所处地位及其与其他组成部分的关系。以下从两个具体方面讲解认知、理解能力的作用，首先从思路开始。

英语思路

做同传光有知识还不够，还需要熟练掌握来源语和译入语的思路。绝大多数中国的译员母语都是汉语，所以比较熟悉汉语的思路，但不熟悉英语的思路。他们经常遇到单词都懂，但是不知道讲者在说什么或者为什么这样说的情况，并且因此导致漏译、错译。

中国的同传译员非常需要学习、掌握英语的思路。以下举一系列同传里英语思路的常见表现，把这些表现与相对应的汉语思路做个比较。由于本课不是对于两种方式的专题研究，所以只是列举实战里观察到的部分例子，既不是全面阐述，也不一定完全正确，只是说明问题的存在而已。

常见不同点	典型的英语方式	典型的汉语方式
会议发言结构	经常是开场白以幽默揭幕，中间是论证阐述，要点以不超过三个为好，如果较长则中间需要用幽默调节气氛，最后以妙语或者再次使用幽默结束。	几乎肯定是以客气或者赞扬的话开场，中间以论点阐述或者信息提供为主，连续说十大点为好，有时大点里还有小点，最后以豪言壮语结束。
对事物和讨论的看法	认为没有真理，只有不同看法，所以讨论时除了表达自己的看法之外也是为了更多地了解不同看法，以修正或者丰富自己的看法。	认为有真理；看法可以不同，但是有对有错；必须坚持正确的，反对错误的。讨论的目的是表达自己的正确看法，说服他人，达成共识。
细节分析	讲究在概念上做精确的定义，不追求宏观上的全面。	注重宏观上的全面，不注重具体概念是否有精确的定义。
世界观	从小到大，从里到外，最重要的最先说。	从大到小，从外到里，最重要的最后说。
表达看法的手段	用西方三段式论证，修辞多采用比喻，明暗喻兼用。	从中国历史上引经据典，修辞多采用成语和排比。
遣词造句的特征	以极其简练的语言来加重语气。	以多重表达，连续使用成语的方式来加重语气。
指代方式	避免重复，采用不同描述指同一人物或事情。	同一人物或事情常常以完全或者部分重复表达。

掌握英语思路能明显减轻同传时听和理解上的负担。比如，国际研讨会开始时，如果是英美人士担任主席，那么开场白就很有可能以幽默开始，即：讲者很可能故意说反话。请看这个例子：

I really didn't want to be here. But the Secretary General threatened me with a vote of no confidence. So, here I am.

如果译员知道英美人士的这个特点，就可以做好思想准备，听到不符合情理的反话大胆照原话译，同时用比较调侃口气处理一下，达到传译幽默的目的。如果译员不知道这个特点，从汉语的思路去理解就很有可能怀疑自己听错了或者误解了讲者，导致不敢开口译或者自己去纠正反话而曲解讲者的话。

在以下例子中，讲者谈到做研究时统计数字的使用：

"The way you display statistical data can have a significant impact on the impression you give. What seems like a significant trend when looking at a small scope, may be an insignificant trend if you look at the wider picture."

如果熟悉统计学里的基本概念就不难顺利地同传这段话，那属于靠知识同传。但是如果不熟悉统计学，而是熟悉讲者的思路，也能够理解讲者是在比较局部和全面之间的关系，而且做这种比较是因为在讲者的思维里统计数字并不一定代表事实，以不同方式取统计数字或者以不同方式展示统计数字都会产生不同的结果，得出不同的结论。如果对于讲者的思路心中有数译员就能充满信心地把原话传译到汉语里。也就是说，熟悉英语的思路能够帮助译员弥补当天知识不足的缺陷。

在汉译英时也是这样。如果熟悉汉语思路，就能在同传时有似曾相识的感觉，从而增强自信心，不仅有助于紧跟讲者，减少在听讲者的话时的疑惑，而且有助于跳词组句，提高预测先说时的准确率，降低预测先说时的过失率。

但是熟悉了思路还不够，还需要有相应的思维能力。对于中国译员来说，具有汉语的思维能力不成问题，需要训练的是英语的思维能力，尤其是在英语里进行抽象思维的能力。

抽象思维

同传译员经常要在三种情况下仰赖抽象思维度过口译难关。第一种情况是讲者的话本身就很抽象，有些专家、学者的讲话经常带有抽象内容。第二种情况是虽然讲者的话本身并不抽象，但是译员听不出讲者现在说的话与之前的话有什么关联。第三种是译员听不出讲者的话与自己所知的哪件或者哪类事情有关联。

上述三种情况下，译员都会遇到知讲者所言，但是不知讲者所指，或者说莫名其妙的局面，即：译员遇到的不是语言问题，而是需要在不知道直接关系在哪里的情况下继续口译的能力。以下两个例子属于上述的第二和第三种情况，在同传里时不时都会遇到：

The sheer waste of time in a typical corporate establishment defies belief. From ill-conceived initiatives and CEO's projects that lead nowhere to endless and endlessly dull workshops, staff buried themselves in work that has no real benefit and even less significance.

Nor is he particularly happy with the current state of rock music—recycling itself, he feels, into irrelevance—or the Internet-driven madness that says absolutely anyone can be a rock star.

在上述这两句话里，似乎所有单词都不难，但是很容易让译员感到不知所云，即无法把听到的话与译员的现有知识联系起来。在这种听不出关联的情况下，译员很容易失去自信，开始怀疑自己的听力或者理解。译着译着大脑就不知不觉地开始放慢速度，失去边听、边译的焦点，开始思考讲者所言的关联（所指）在哪而无法同传下去。

本课要点

知识能力由知识和能力两部分组成。与每次具体任务直接相关的是任务知识，与每次具体任务没有直接关系但仍然可能起到成败关键作用的是个人知识。任务知识通过事前准备获得，个人知识仰赖有结构、有系统的建立和发展。光有知识还不够，还必须熟悉英语思路，掌握在英语里抽象思维的能力。同传译员需要以知识和思维能力以及辅助能力来支持自己的核心能力，完成同传任务。第三课里，有关这三大能力的构成图就是一个很好的总结，请复习一下。

工作坊

以下是在英国英汉同传译员的个人知识体系里必须包含的部分内容。请参照这些内容，以类似清单的形式列出在中国担任同传译员所必须掌握的有关中国的知识内容。

英国英汉同传译员的个人知识部分内容

1. 世界
    1.1. 地缘政治
        1.1.1. 英国与中国
        1.1.2. 英国与美国

1.1.3. 英国与欧盟
1.1.4. 英国与阿拉伯
1.1.5. 英国与非洲
1.2. 重大议题
1.2.1. 气候变化
1.2.2. 国际反恐
1.2.3. 其他热点
2. 国家
2.1. 历史事件
2.1.1. 布莱尔 12 年
2.1.2. 撒切尔 11 年
2.1.3. 二战与丘吉尔
2.1.4. 一战
2.1.5. 工业革命
2.1.6. 英格兰内战
2.2. 君主制宪
2.2.1. 著名君主：亨利八世、伊丽莎白一世、维多利亚
2.2.2. 当今王室及其家人
2.3. 议会两院
2.3.1. 下议院
2.3.2. 上议院
2.3.3. 立法程序
2.3.4. 大选、地方选、补选
2.4. 三级政府
2.4.1. 中央政府（与中国相关的主要部门）
2.4.2. 区域自治政府（苏格兰、威尔士、北爱尔兰）
2.4.3. 地方政府
3. 经济
3.1. 宏观架构
3.1.1. 财政部
3.1.2. 中央银行
3.2. 主要行业
3.3. 各大市场

3.3.1. 伦敦股市
3.3.2. 保险、再保险
3.3.3. 金属交易所
3.3.4. 商品交易所
3.4. 公司财务
4. 社会
4.1. 法律治安
4.1.1. 法庭体系
4.1.2. 警察体系
4.1.3. 监狱体系
4.2. 婚姻家庭
4.2.1. 恋爱
4.2.2. 同居
4.2.3. 结婚
4.2.4. 离异
4.2.5. 生儿育女
4.2.6. 子女教养
4.2.7. 两代关系
4.3. 民族构成
4.3.1. 血统
4.3.2. 移民
4.4. 宗教状况
4.5. 终身教育
4.5.1. 幼儿
4.5.2. 小学
4.5.3. 中学
4.5.4. 大学
4.5.5. 职业培训
4.5.6. 继续学习
5. 医疗卫生
5.1. NHS
5.2. 初级医疗
5.2.1. 保健诊所、医生

5.2.2. 保健护士
5.2.3. 家庭服务
5.3. 医院信托、医院
6. 工作
6.1. 寻招应聘
6.2. 上下班
6.3. 自由职业、个体户
7. 生活
7.1. 夜晚周末
7.2. 度假旅行
7.3. 锻炼身体
7.4. 购物饮食
7.5. 节庆活动

第五课　三词一译：英译汉

本课讲解英译汉里三词一译的技巧，其中包括汉译英和英译汉共用的技巧，而汉译英特有的技巧在第六课里讲解。

由于英汉语言结构很不相同，而且常常是完全相反。只有熟练地采用一系列语言转换技巧，才能在同传时保证能够基本按照讲者说话的顺序传译。如果按照笔译的习惯，听完整句或者大半句之后才开始传译，势必导致大脑无法承受同时听、译、说所需的信息处理量而遗漏或者误译。

同传所需的这组技巧早年经常被称作“断句”，英语里有人称之为 trunking，如今国内常称之为“顺序驱动”。笔者采用的概念是三词一译，这个概念没有经过理论上的论证。但好处是直接点明笔者认为在英汉双语之间同传时所需要达到的目标。

第三课里已经讲解过，三词一译指每听到三个具有实际意义的单词就处理一次，边听边译。在英语里指除去了语法所需的比如定冠词、介词和其他语法所需之词（如：has been）之后的名词、动词、副词或者形容词这些实义词。在汉语里，由于绝大多数汉语表达法都是由两个汉字组成的词，所以“三词”大约为 5–6 个汉字。

三词一译所需的技巧细分起来很多，以下按照笔者的理念讲解一组最有用、最常用的技巧，可以解决初学同传时的绝大部分问题。这些技巧在不同作者的书或者教材里有不同名称，笔者采用四字词组的方式，为的是有利于形象记忆：

1. 缺省传译
2. 原话直译
3. 重复谓语
4. 介词转动
5. 先存后译

6. 反话正说
7. 被动变的
8. 点到为止
9. 预测先说
10. 弃卒保车

指导原则

有关如何培训同传技巧将于第九课讲解。不过，三词一译技巧与如何练习的关系非常密切。练习方式正确，事半功倍；练习方式有误，事倍功半。所以，本课首先讲解三词一译技巧培训时的指导原则。这些原则可以归纳为：顺藤摸瓜、左右逢源、弃前补后、宁少勿多。

顺藤摸瓜指的是以边听边译而且是三词一译为目标，在绝大多数情况下都可以通过对于原话的处理而无需等待，无需在听到更多内容之后颠倒顺序。也就是说，只要遇到无法顺序译的话，基本可以肯定是尚未找到合适的处理方式，而不要轻易认为是同传无法处理的障碍。如此边听边译就如同顺藤摸瓜一般，不知瓜在哪，只是顺藤摸下去而已。

左右逢源指的是无论在原话的哪个点上，只要是需要动用三词一译技巧之处，就必须拥有至少两种不同的处理方案。之所以必须这样是因为第三课里讲过，同传的思考余地每次只有大约 1 秒钟。如果三词一译练的只是一种处理方法，就容易增加在实战里出现一时想不起来的发生几率。相反，如果平常练习时就养成了两种方案的习惯，实战里就能大大增加想起其中一个方案的几率，加快反应时间，避免被卡住。

弃前补后指的是三词一译时如果 1 秒之内没有反应过来，不知如何处理为好，就马上译接下来的话，在之后合适之处把句子补齐。也就是说练习三词一译时必须符合同传为流水思维的原则，不停顿、不回头、一直往下译。有关弃前补后在实战中能够帮助译员渡过难关的例子，在本书的练习单元里有很多。

宁少勿多指的是从练习同传的一开始就培养自己能够用词精炼的习惯，能少用一个汉字就少用一个，削减所有的多余字。在同传里，每少说 5 个汉字左右就省下了 1 秒钟时间。如果持续用词精炼，就能每隔几句话省出 1–2 秒。同传里往往就这 1–2 秒的空间之内决定是成功地做到三词一译，还是漏译、误译，其重要性不可低估。

宁少勿多应该作为一种技能培训，而不是作为教条遵守。即：掌握这个技能之后同传时一旦感到有滞后讲者超过 2 秒的危险时便自动以简练的译入语抢时间。如果讲者速度缓慢，译员就可以采用比较长的译入语，填补时间。

以下是几个宁少勿多的例子：

英语原话	常见习惯	宁少勿多
Vice Minister of the National Commission for Reform and Development	国家发展与改革委员会副主任	发改委副主任
We're pleased to be able to gather here this evening.	我们感到很高兴，能够今天晚上聚集在这里	很高兴今晚相聚
I would like to begin by reflecting recent events	我想开始时先反思一下最近的一些事件	首先反思最近的一些事件

以下分别举例讲解上述 10 大技巧。所有技巧都必须通过大量的练习熟练掌握之后才能实现三词一译的目标。具体有关如何培训、练习的详细讲解，请看第九课。

缺省传译

由于同传译员的思维空间只有 1 秒左右，最多不过 2 秒钟。为了达到这种思维的速度就必须善于缺省传译。这是个从电脑语言借用过来的概念，指的是在没有足够的上文（同传只有上文，没有下文），甚至根本没有任何上文的情况下快速地把单词或者词组转换成译入语。

翻译里有一个具有根本性质的理念，这就是根据上下文判断如何把来源语翻译成译入语。这个根据上下文做判断的理念从学习英语一开始就不断地被老师教诲，不断地被巩固。对于几乎所有学习外语的人来说，这个概念都已经根深蒂固，成为大脑的思维习惯。这种根深蒂固的思维习惯是练习同传时被卡在一个单词或者词组上的一个重大原因。

培养缺省传译能力的第一步就是为所有单词确定缺省译法，这不是说为每个单词确定一个最常见的译法，而是为每个单词都决定一个如果没有上文译什么的版本。一旦为所有单词都确定了缺省译法并且熟练掌握，就不会因为上文不明而不知道译成什么，而是会让缺省译法脱口而出。当然，在实战中，如果之后发现应该用另外一种译法更合适，那么届时再修正。

缺省传译版本的决定可以参照单词最常用的译法，但是一定不能停留在自己知道用哪个为缺省版本上，而是必须反复练习几次，在大脑留下深刻印象。一旦听到，只要没有上文作为判断依据，马上就能脱口而出。

以下举几对意思相近的词汇为例子，显示采用缺省版本的好处。这些词汇由于是近义词，按照传统的理念每次出现时都需要考虑上下文再做译作什么的决定。但是如果按照下面的缺省传译的版本就不需要任何上下文，看到或者听到就能够马上译出。

Cooperation — 合作
Partnership — 伙伴

Help — 帮助
Assist — 协助

Principle — 原则
Code — 准则

Rules — 规则
Regulations — 规定（尤指监管）

当然，如果在同传时听到这些词应该传译成其他汉语词汇更加合适，就按照更加合适的版本传译。缺省版本是在上文不足、下文不知情况下的译法。

原话直译

这个技巧指的是在英译汉时，除非很清楚应该如何处理，凡是暂时还不清楚的一律按照原话直译，不考虑是否符合汉语习惯用法。

原话直译有三大作用。第一，有助于紧跟讲者，滞后不超过 2 秒钟，而且绝不停顿下来。第二，这是应对抽象概念、自己没听懂的话、幽默、笑话以及其他修辞手法的重要手段。只要讲者所使用的单词、词组、分句和整句话的语言本身没有障碍，就按照话面的语言直译，不管自己是否真正理解话意。

要做到这点需要克服两大障碍。第一个障碍是人们从小长大期间养成的习惯，即：只愿意，而且只能够重复听懂了的话。小孩刚开始学讲话的时候往往毫不在意重复自己根本不懂的话，但是逐渐长大之后就失去了这种能力，直至不懂意思的话就难以重复。这就相当于在同传时，不懂意思的话就马上译不下去。

第二个障碍是绝大多数中国学生在学习外语过程当中都接受一个理念，即看懂了再翻，听懂了再译。经过多年的外语学习、培训，这个理念根深蒂固，从潜意识里左右了大脑的反应。但是同传译员必须具有一种特殊的技能，那就是暂时不懂仍然继续传译，边译边懂。有时甚至译完之后听众都懂了，译员自己还是不懂。

当然，人脑的能力是有限的。在不懂的情况下完全仰赖原话直译的持续时间也有限。初学同传者往往几个词没听懂就卡壳。再资深的译员也难以在不懂的情况下持续传译并且保持准确。但是，资深译员能够不懂而译的持续时间能够大大长于初学者，经常能够连续几分钟不懂仍然准确传译，或者在相当长的时间里多次不懂仍然保持传译。这也说明了为什么资深译员能够做到在专业研讨会或者专业培训课上，即使是听众自己都不懂的内容，译员仍然可能传译到位。

原话直译的第三大作用是避免回头错。笔者在《实战交传》（中国对外翻译出版有限公司，2012）里对回头错有详细的讲解，指的是译员根据之前讲者的话所传译的版本，在听了讲者后来的话之后那样处理不合适，甚至是谬误的。

以下是件很多人都听说过的事情。中国政府的一位部长宴请外宾，席间交谈时说："这个问题很简单，如同小葱拌豆腐一清二白。"译员记得学习翻译时老师讲过要用外宾听得懂的方式，要用地道的英语表达中国文化，于是传译为："The matter is crystal clear"。谁知部长又接着说："你们国家有豆腐吗？"至此，译员已经无法改口，只好硬着头皮说："Do you have crystal in your country?"

由于同传是边听、边译，出现回头错的几率超过交传，听到讲者在英语里明显采用修辞手法时尤其需要按照原话直译。这样就能在之后万一讲者延伸其修辞用语时，照样按照原话的用词继续同传。比如，在上述例子里，如果译员按照原话直译，就很可能避免出现麻烦。

为了比较直观地展示同传译入语和原话之间的关系，以下例子里表示译入语部分的文字按照同传时的说出顺序列出，而不是按照文章那样逐字排列，空当代表停顿。另外，原话和译入语在一行不够时交错展示，保持上行为原话，下行为译入语的格式。

汉语原话	这个问题很简单，如同小葱拌豆腐一清二白。你们国家有豆腐吗？
英语译入语	It's simple like spring onion blended with Tofu. Do you have Tofu in your country?

在同传里，按照原话直译并不是个语言处理问题，原话直译的先决条件就是原话里基本没有语言问题。原话直译的难处在于改变过去十几年来的大脑思维习惯，所以需要在指导下经过一段时间的培训才能掌握。

重复谓语

英语句子结构的特征是谓语 + 状语，而汉语恰恰相反，是状语 + 谓语。英译汉同传时不能在听到谓语、知道之后还有状语时就不译谓语，等听到状语之后才按照笔译的方法颠倒两者之间的顺序。如果那样处理，势必造成大脑在颠倒顺序时无法认真听讲者还在说的话，导致漏译或者错译之后部分。

同传必须根据三词一译的原则，必须先译出谓语，不能等待状语，然后以简化方式重复谓语并带出状语。采用这样技巧的关键有两个：一个是重复谓语，另外一个是以最少的字数来重复谓语。初学同传常见的一个问题就是没有重复谓语："我们开了个短会。5 月 1 日"，导致译入语残缺的结果。以下举三个例子，用表格方式来说明如何采用重复谓语的技巧来保证三词一译：

例 1

英语原话	We held a short meeting on 1st May
重复谓语	我们开了个短会，5 月 1 日开的

例 2

英语原话	Welcome to New York in this beautiful autumn season.
重复谓语	欢迎来到纽约，在美丽的秋季来纽约

例 3

英语原话	The G20 is fast becoming the centrepiece of today's international economic, social 20 国集团快速成为中心，是当今国际经济、
重复谓语	and environmental governance architecture. 社会和环境治理架构的中心。

介词转动

这个技巧指的是把引出状语的介词转换成动词以达到三词一译的目的。以下表格里用黑体标出同传时被处理成动词的介词。

例 1

英语原话	It is now focusing on the very important issue of exit strategies.
介词转动	它现在聚焦于非常重要的议题，**考虑**退出战略。

例 2

英语原话	My desire to be here reflects just how important China has become 我希望来这里，这就反应出中国已变得
介词转动	for the global economy. 何等重要，**如何影响**到全球经济。

例 3

英语原话	During Asian Financial Crisis, China demonstrated its leadership in the region 在亚洲金融危机期间，中国显示出领导作用，**引领**该地区
介词转动	and the rest of the world. 以及整个世界。

介词转动靠两条，一条是经过训练之后比较熟悉的一小组介词。这些介词转变为什么动词都已经比较熟悉，可以听到就自动转。另外一条是在 1 秒之内通过创意思维想出应该转变成什么动词合适。这后一条的能力需要从一开始练同传就注意培养。在练习中需要掌握的是善于根据讲者的话找到顺应话题走向的动词。

比如在上述第一个例子中，在说了“……聚集于……议题”之后听到“of exit strategies”，就说“考虑推出战略”。在第二个例子中，在说了“……何等重要……”之后听到“for the global economy”，就说“如何影响到全球经济”。在第三个例子中，在说了“……领导作用”之后听到“in the region”，就说“引领该地区”。关键就在于顺着讲者的话译一个相关的动词。

先存后译

这个技巧指的是把听到的名词暂时储存在短期记忆里，在此后的第一时机补上。这个技巧与前述必须避免的等待、颠倒顺序有两个根本性质上的区别。首先，先存后译是以公式的方法，仅限于特定表达法的使用。这些表达法的结构完全一样，在英语句子里的所处地位基本一样，所以经过短期练习就可以掌握。其次，先存后译是在三词一译范围之内的技巧，没有违反三词一译的原则。

需要采取先存后译技巧最常见的表达法有：

- The role of . . .
- The responsibility of . . .
- The importance of . . .
- The opportunity of . . .

以下将以表格方式展示这个同传技巧的使用。第一行为原话，第二行为译员采用相关技巧之后的译入语，译入语里词汇所列之处基本反应与原话的时间顺序关系。另外，空格表示译入语的持续时间或者译员的停顿：

例 1

英语原话	The role of the central government is to . . .
先存后译	中央政府的角色是……

例 2

英语原话	The responsibility of the executive board as described in . . .
先存后译	执行委员会的责任已经写在……

例 3

英语原话	The importance of this conference and the urgency of the matter . . .
先存后译	本次大会的重要性以及此事的急迫性

例 4

英语原话	The opportunity of joining the company appeared non-existent.
先存后译	加入公司的机会看上去不存在。

使用先存后译技巧时需要注意三点。首先，由于是先存后译，不得不短期内超过三词一译的界线，但是必须尽快开口。在练习时从不超过 6 个单词入手，养成习惯。第二，由于等待时间超过 1 秒，所以必须尽快把这 1 秒再抢回来。最简单的方法就是加快语速。第三，必须在第一时机把之前存在脑里的词传译过去。否则会忘记，或者因为占用脑力太多而影响之后的听或者译。

最后需要说明的是，根据左右逢源的原则，凡是采用了先存后译技巧之处都必须练习如何用简单重复的方法作为另外一个方案。切记不要仅仅练习了先存后译便满足，如果只练一个方案，就容易在实战中卡壳。比如，除非是资深译员，实战里大脑往往不一定每次都能做出最准确的判断而采用最合适的技巧。如果刚听到 the role of 就脱口说出"角色"，就必须能够采用简单重复的技巧说"角色，中央政府的角色是……"，以避免在译入语里出现残句。

反话正说

这个技巧指的是听到英语以否定句式开始的话就在汉语里采用肯定句式开始，把否定的意思放到之后的合适之处表达，既可以是直接采用否定词（不，没有，不行等等），也可以是采用反义词。如果遇到以否定句式开始的话不会反话正说的技巧就会出现张不开口，说不出话，听到后来可以张口说时已经太晚了，不是遗漏、误译，就是下面的话没听见。

反话正说是这种技巧的名称，也包含了正话反说的技巧。原理一样，只是方向相反。以下例子中，反话正说或者正话反说部分以黑体标出。

例 1

英语原话	It was not until last year that we had a library
反话正说	**直到**去年我们才有了图书馆

例 2

英语原话	I never cease to be amazed by the speed of change
反话正说	**我总是**感到惊讶变化的速度很快

例 3

英语原话	It's not in our interest to continue this negotiation
反话正说	**符合**我们利益的做法就是**停止**谈判

采用反话正说技巧时，一定不要忘了否定词或者肯定词是推迟出现了，一定要在之后补出，否则就会把意思完全译错。

被动变的

这个技巧指的是听到英语里的被动语态就顺口把谓语动词转换成"谓语 + 的"的句式，绝大多数由于被动语态带来的问题都能凭借这个技巧迎刃而解，保证三词一译。在以下例子中，译入语"谓语 + 的"的句式以黑体标出。

例 1

英语原话	Initial investment was boosted by a fresh round of cash injection
被动变的	最初投资**的增加**来自于新的一轮现金注入

例 2

英语原话	We are all affected by each other's policy actions.
被动变的	我们所受到**的影响**来自各自的政策行动

例 3

英语原话	We, the peoples of the United Nations, are bound by certain sacred duties.
被动变的	我们，联合国的人们**的联系**来自于一些神圣的职责。

点到为止

这个技巧指的是在边听边译过程中，如果感觉到译入语里意思已经到位了，即使听到更多的英语单词也果断地决定省略不译，接着译之后的内容。由于英语句法、表达习惯与汉语有很大差别，时常会出现根据之前的话，译入语已经在汉语里表达出英语直到句尾才阐明的意思，没有必要再译这部分英语。

掌握好点到为止的技巧有两大好处。首先是译员能够借此赶上讲者。由于种种原因，译员时常无法保证与讲者的滞后距离保持在 2 秒之内。所以，每次点到为止的机会都能帮助译员抢回时间，缩小滞后的距离。其次，即使译员滞后时间保持在 2 秒之内，如果善用点到为止，则能够时不时与讲者同时结束一句话，听上去同传感很强，效果很好。在以下例子中，采用点到为止技巧后不译的部分用黑体标出。

例 1

英语原话	Importantly, these policies have resulted in actual cost savings **for businesses**.
点到为止	重要的是，这些政策 带来了 实际成本 的节省。

例 2

英语原话	I've been to Shanghai many times. I never cease to be amazed at the speed of change **that's taking place here.**
点到为止	我去过上海多次，总是惊讶这里变化的速度。

例 3

英语原话	We're investing to cut energy waste, helping American families save money on energy bills **in the process**.
点到为止	我们投资减少能源浪费，帮助美国家庭节省能源开支。

预测先说

这个技巧指的是译员预测讲者尚未说的话并且提前于讲者译出。预测的根据往往有以下几种，一是在前述话语的背景下把语言里固定搭配的后半部分提前译出；二是具有相对固定格式的套话；三是译员把在事前准备时已经了解到的内容或者说法在尚未听到讲者说到时就预先译出。

在以下例子中，译员根据词汇搭配预先说出讲者尚未说出的话以保证译入语流畅（预测先说的词用黑体标出）：

例 1

英语原话	One must take account of all factors involved. For example, one must take the duration 必须考虑到所有相关因素。比如，必须考虑到
预测先说	the event **into account**. 事件的持续时间。

在以下例子中：译员知道讲者是在说赠送礼品时常用的套话，所以提前说出讲者尚未说的话：

例 2

英语原话	May I present this locally produced crystal vase **to you**.
预测先说	请允许我向您赠送这个本地生产的水晶花瓶。

在以下例子中：译员在事先准备中了解到了主旨发言人的背景，所以提前说出讲者尚未说的话：

例 3

英语原话	He is a researcher at **the Economic Research Centre**.
预测先说	他是经济研究中心的研究员。

弃卒保车

这个技巧指的是由于两种语言之间的句法差别导致难于转换时，就果断地扔掉部分细节内容以保证译入语总体上的完整。比如：连续多个时间、地点状语就很难对付。如果每次都重复谓语就会使译入语琐碎而且来不及说完，但此时无法采用介词转换成动词的技巧，因为状语太短而且接二连三，来不及转动词。在这种情况下，译员就必须果断地扔掉一个甚至两个状语。这样处理虽然细节不够，但是总体流畅，不会影响之后内容的传译，故称弃卒保车。

在以下三个例子中，都是由于状语里的细节太密集，无法既保证信息完全，又保证译入语流畅而且速度不能落后于讲者太多，译员必须采用弃卒保车的技巧，舍去部分细节不译：

例 1

英语原话	We met at a small hotel in the centre of Paris on 3rd Oct 2005.
弃卒保车	我们的会见是在巴黎，2005 年 10 月 3 日。

例 2

英语原话	Prices increased 20% ahead of the new policy announcement in September this year.
弃卒保车	价格上升了 20% 赶在新政策 9 月宣布之前

例 3

英语原话	It requires simple majority in a vote within two weeks under Clause 3 of the Charter
弃卒保车	这需要简单多数两周之内投票这是 of our society. 我们学会的规定。

本课要点

同传时需要基本按照讲者说话的顺序传译，所需的句子处理技巧可以概括为三词一译，培训时的四大指导原则为：顺藤摸瓜、左右逢源、弃前补后、宁少勿多。三词一译所需的十大句子处理技巧如下：

1. 缺省传译
2. 原话直译
3. 重复谓语
4. 介词转动
5. 先存后译
6. 反话正说
7. 被动变的
8. 点到为止
9. 预测先说
10. 弃卒保车

十大技巧说起来容易，做起来难。难就难在必须把这些技巧练成译员的本能反应，即听到了马上就如此处理，就像手指碰到了烫手的茶杯会马上抽回一样，而不能是经过思考之后的决定。

工作坊

分成两人一组，找一篇英文讲话稿，按照三词一译的原则翻译成中文，借此尝试把本课的十大技巧运用于讲稿，探讨在多大程度上可以解决英汉两种语言结构不同的问题。这个练习的目的不是同传，而是体会三词一译给语言处理带来的崭新天地。所以，不必强调译入语完善，重点是能够遇到结构顺序上的难点时能够找到相应的解决办法。

这个练习既可以在课上采用培训教师统一提供的讲稿来做，也可以作为作业由培训生课下做了之后在课上讨论。

第六课　三词一译：汉译英

第五课讲解的是英译汉里如何做到三词一译，本课讲解汉译英里如何做到三词一译。由于绝大多数汉语表达法都是由两个汉字组成的词，所以“三词”大约为5–6个汉字。即：同传汉译英必须以每5–6个汉字为一个单位来处理。

汉译英所需的技巧中类似于英译汉的有：

- 先存后译
- 反话正说
- 预测先说
- 弃卒保车

而汉译英特有的技巧为：跳词组句和译所指也。前者用于句子的处理，后者用于词汇和词组的转换。跳词组句包含了四个分技巧：

- 减字近半
- 增加时态
- 实词开句
- 增补主语
- 译所指也

培训汉译英时同样需要遵循培训英译汉时的指导原则，即：

- 顺藤摸瓜
- 左右逢源
- 弃前补后
- 宁少勿多

另外，汉译英在思维方式上也需要掌握英译汉所需的技能，即：本能反应、1 秒思维、暂停分神。也就是说，练习汉译英时也需要训练凡是会译的内容都能够做到像手指头被烫迅速抽回那种反应速度；训练凡是需要思考之处，思考时间绝不超出 1 秒钟。一旦瞬间思考没有所需结果就马上扔掉不会之处继续往下听、往下译。与此同时，还必须训练绝不自我评判刚才译入语的自律本领。由于汉译英时的大脑使用技能与英译汉相同，以下将集中精力举例说明语言处理技巧，先讲解汉译英里与英译汉类似的技巧，然后讲解汉译英特有的技巧。

为了尽量从视觉上反映同传时的同步程度，以下例子里采用缩进方式体现译入语比来源语稍晚开始的特点。

先存后译

这个技巧指的是把先听到的话暂时存在短期记忆里待到后来再译出。在以下例子里，先存后译的部分用黑体标出。

例 1

汉语原话	**我**代表中国政府向英国人民表示感谢！
先存后译	On behalf of the Chinese government, **I would like to** thank the British people.

例 2

汉语原话	他是**中国社会科学院**的研究员
先存后译	he is a researcher at **Chinese Academy of Social Sciences**

例 3

汉语原话	**人民法院**在开庭三日以前公布开庭时间和地点
先存后译	Three days before the trial, **the People's Court** will publish the time and location.

反话正说

这个技巧指的是把汉语里的肯定表达法处理成英语里的否定表达法，反之也成立。

例 1

汉语原话	我国改革开放的基本面不会改变。
反话正说	Our Reform will continue.

例 2

汉语原话	我们不能无所作为。
反话正说	We must act.

例 3

汉语原话	没有大家的支持，我们就无法开始这个项目。
反话正说	It was with your support that we managed to start the project.

预测先说

这个技巧指的是译员预测讲者尚未说的话并且提前于讲者译出。第五课里讲解了预测先说在英译汉里的使用，不过这个技巧在汉译英时尤其重要。这主要是因为英语里主语和谓语动词往往很接近，听到主语之后很快就会听到谓语。比如：I thank you for your meticulous planning and relentless execution。但是汉语则很不相同，可以在主语之后跟上很长一段状语，然后才是谓语动词。比如：我对你们在过去几个月里的不懈努力表示感谢！在上述情况下，如果译员采用主语马上加谓语动词的译法就必须预测讲者的话，把“表示感谢”赶在讲者之前说出：I thank you for your efforts in the past few months。也可以动用弃前补后的原则加预测处理成：You have worked hard in the past few months. I thank you for that。

在以下例子中，译员知道中国领导人在国际会议开幕时的讲话里常常首先表示祝贺，所以预先译出祝贺这个词：

例 1

汉语原话	首先，我代表中国政府对中国经济改革国际论坛的举行表示祝贺！
预测先说	First of all, on behalf of the Chinese government, I congratulate you on this International Forum on the Economic Reform of China.

在以下例子中，译员在事先准备中了解到主旨发言人的背景，所以预先说出：

例 2

汉语原话	他是国际关系研究中心的研究员。
预测先说	He is a researcher at the Centre for International Relations.

在以下例子中，译员是根据对于当前时事的了解预先说出“方向”：

例 3

汉语原话	宏观审慎政策框架已成为危机后国际金融改革的主要方向。
预测先说	Macro prudential policy framework has become the direction for post-crisis international financial reform.

汉译英采用预测先说的技巧，尤其是在提前说出谓语动词的时候难免会冒一点风险，即：有可能预测错误或者讲者改变说话方向或者没有遵循惯例。所以在采用预测先说技巧时还需要掌握弃前补后的原则，如果预测失误而不符合讲者的话，则必须在此后第一机会以正确的话弥补之前的过失。比如，上述第一个例子里，如果领导人的话是表示感谢而不是祝贺，译员需要马上补过：

汉语原话	首先，我代表中国政府对中国经济改革国际论坛的联合主办方表示感谢！
预测先说	First of all, on behalf of the Chinese government, I congratulate you on this International Forum on the Economic Reform of China and express our thanks to the joint host!

在上述第三个例子里，如果后来发现讲者用的是“主要解决方案”，也需要采用‘补后’的方式修正：

汉语原话	宏观审慎政策框架已成为危机后国际金融改革的主要解决方案。
预测先说	Macro prudential policy framework has become the direction for post-crisis international financial reform. It's become the main solution.

这种先预测，如果不准确再随后纠正的手法是同传里弃前补后原则的一种运用。

弃卒保车

这指的是由于汉英两种语言的不同，在特定情况下会出现如果追求前面的话信息完整就肯定会由于来不及传译而导致后面的话丢三落四。在这种情况下，就必须主动省略部分细节，以保证总体信息完整。以下是三种常见情况的例子，首先是一连串数字外加百分比。请看例子：

汉语原话	我们的营业额上升到 5.63 亿，同比增长 14.3%；税前利润达到 56 万 4000，同比增长 12.6%；客户增加到 634 万 2000 人，同比增长 18%；而集团资本回报率达 11.2%。
弃卒保车	Our sales increased to 563 million, an increase of above 14%, pre-tax profit increased by 12.6%, our customers increased to more than 6 million, groupcapital return was 11.2%。

其次是由于汉英两种语言的结构不同，修辞顺序不同，如果再加上信息密集，为了保证译出的英语结构完整，往往不得不舍去汉语原话里的部分细节。请看例子：

汉语原话	近年来我国发生了南方严重雨雪冰冻灾害、北方和西南地区严重干旱、“5•12”汶川地震、“4•14”玉树地震，以及甘肃舟曲特大山洪泥石流。
弃卒保车	In recent years, China has gone through disasters in the South, North and South-west. There was earthquake in Wenchun, Yushu. Gansu had a big mudslide.

最后是一些组织机构、文件条约、计划或者活动的名称，也是由于汉英两种语言的结构不同而词汇顺序相反。除非是译员通过事先准备熟练掌握了这些名称的译法，否则，如果当时听到必须马上传译的话，就不得不舍去细节以保证总体信息完整。请看例子：

汉语原话	根据《核事故或辐射紧急情况援助公约》中的义务，中国政府在第一时间即向日本政府表达了愿意提供援助的愿望。
弃卒保车	Based on nuclear accident convention, the Chinese government promptly contacted the Japanese government to offer assistance.

再举一例：

汉语原话	先后实施了国土资源大调查、青藏高原地质矿产调查、 We've conducted national land resources survey, Qinghai plateau survey, 新疆"358"地质矿产调查、油气资源战略调查、危机矿山接替资源勘查等等 Xinjiang 358 survery, oil and gas survey, mine replacement survey and so on
弃卒保车	

跳词组句

这个理念泛指在汉译英时边听边挑选词组译入英语。这是同传汉译英的一个具有根本意义的概念，由一组具体的技巧组成。这些技巧主要有：

- 减字近半
- 增加时态
- 实词开句
- 增补主语

减字近半的根据是汉译英时必须减少所需译出的汉字。即如果原话由 100 个汉字组成，译入英语时大约只译其中的 50 个汉字左右。以下分别讲解跳词组句时具体技巧的运用。

减字近半

汉译英必须减字有数个原因。首先，相对英语而言，汉语里重叠、重复表达的现象很多，往往是为了强调或者表达清楚。由于英语里不用这些方式，所以，如果按照汉语全部译入英语，在英语里听上去就会显得多余、累赘。

汉语原话	建议译作	一般不译作
重点强调	Stress	emphatically stress
不断深入	Deepen	continuously deepen
再次重申	Repeat (doing it twice)	Reiterate once again (doing it three times)
不断扩大	Expand	continuously expand

其次，如果中心动词已经意思到位，就不必译汉语里起到加强语气作用的其他修饰词。

汉语原话	建议译作	一般不译作
奠定了经济增长持续发展的有力基础	lay the foundation for robust economic growth	lay the solid foundation for continued development of economic growth
富有远见卓识、高瞻远瞩的决策	A visionary decision	A decision with vision and foresight
欢庆春季的热烈气氛	The atmosphere of Spring Festival	The happy atmosphere of happily celebrating the Spring Festival

再次，不必译“总结词”。这指的是用一个词总结前面已经详细说过的内容。在译入英语时，只要把前面的具体内容译出来就足够了。

汉语原话	建议译作	不必译作：
从而形成了经济持续增长的喜人局面	Economy continues to grow	The situation of the continued growth of economy
产量连续上升的趋势	Production continued to increase	The trend of production increasing continuously
新系统产生了改善业绩的效果	The new system resulted in improved performance	The new system has resulted in the effect of performance being improved

由于汉译英需要减字近半，所以和英译汉的概念有根本上的区别。英译汉时讲究每个词组和分句都要争取译出才算保证质量，但是汉译英必须善于跳词组句。这就意味着探讨汉译英时不能抽出一个词组或者表达法来思考如何译成英语，因为在跳词组句时有些词组很可能是可以甚至是必须跳过不译。

比如，如果在笔译时遇到“微不足道”，不翻成 too minute to mention 就有不准确的感觉。但如果是同传里听到这个成语就很可能需要做更加简单的处理。

汉语原话	世界市场很大，我们的份额微不足道。
弃前补后	The world market is very big. Our share is insignificant.

再如，如果在笔译时遇到“强国建设”，不翻成 development to strengthen the nation 就有不准确的感觉。但如果是同传也需要简化处理。

汉语原话	我们行业已经进入了强国建设的关键时期
弃前补后	Our industry is helping to build a strong nation at a critical juncture

有关为什么汉译英必须减字以及为什么减字的比例是 2 : 1 的详细论述，请参阅笔者经由外语教学与研究出版社出版的《实战笔译》汉译英分册。

增加时态

这指的是虽然汉语原话里没有时态，但是译入英语之后必须加入时态。增加时态是汉译英的一大难点，难就难在判断采用哪个时态。汉语里的时间概念主要通过两大方式表达，第一是通过句子的逻辑顺序，先发生的事情先说，后发生的事情后说，其先后顺序本身表达了时间的先后概念。比如：“我们明天去吃饭、看电影”，“绿灯亮了按这个按钮”。

但是这种先后顺序的时间表达法只是表达两件都是过去发生或者都是将来发生的事情之间的关系，汉语句法里不注重区分过去发生的事情与现在的时间关系，从话面上往往不容易区分哪个是过去，哪个是现在。尤其是中文里有夹叙夹议的文体，其特点就是在当前的评论与过去发生事件的描述之间平稳过渡，形成一种不分现在和过去的状况，导致译员汉译英时态不容易把握，很容易出错，为汉译英带来巨大的挑战。

比如这句话：“我们很喜欢这种椅子，就买了几个。”刚听到“我们很喜欢这种椅子”时，很容易说出：we like this chair。接着听到“就买了几个”，很容易说出：and bought a few。在英语里，听上去很别扭。现在喜欢怎么会是过去买呢？由于这个句子很短，即使时态不对，也可能听懂，知道译员时态使用错了。但如果是话比较长，而且时间顺序直接影响到对句子的理解时就很可能导致听众误解。

比如这句话：“我们不赞成重新谈判价格，你们也不赞成重新谈判价格。但是却又通过谈判小组找我们，要求重新谈判。这让人觉得不好理解。”

We're not in favour of a renegotiation of prices. Neither are you. But you asked the negotiation team to contact us asking for a renegotiation. That's difficult to understand.

译入语逻辑混乱之处在于：如果对方过去要求重新谈判，现在不赞成重新谈判，岂不就是与己方立场相同了吗？那又怎么会不好理解呢？但是，如果时态使用准确的话就不会出现这样的逻辑混乱：

We were not in favour of a renegotiation of prices. Neither were you. But you asked the negotiation team to contact us asking for a renegotiation. That's difficult to understand.

汉译英增加时态的第一个难点就是在英语口语里能够准确使用时态对于大多数中国学生来说都很难做到，这往往是因为受到母语的影响，还没有在脑子里明确建立起时态的概念，对于时态不敏感，尤其是对过去时和虚拟语态不敏感。所以，过去时和虚拟语态是中国译员汉译英时最经常出错的两个领域。

由于过去时是英语几大常用时态之一，要想达到口译准确的目的必须尽早开始提高过去时的总体水平。本书由于焦点和篇幅所限，只能集中谈同传里现在时和过去时之间转换所需要把握的要点。

提高同传里现在时和过去时的使用水平需要注意三大要点。首先必须明确：时态的使用也和同传其他方面水平的提高一样，需要相当时间的练习、实践，无法一蹴而就。所以，在事业初期以及其后相当一段时间里都经常会错用时态。这是发展的一个不可避免的阶段，如果是译员，则不必灰心。如果是教员，则一定注意避免在同传练习初期强调这点，那样容易导致学员由于考虑时态而违反 1 秒思维的原则，顾此失彼，无助于总体质量。

其次，开始养成英语时态的思维习惯。这会是一个比较艰难的过程，需要毅力才能持之以恒，达到在说汉语时也对时态有感觉的境地。但是万里长征，始于足下。

再次，需要判断时态。在逐渐开始对于时态有感觉之后，就可以把这种感觉运用在同传之中。之所以说判断是因为由于前述原因，汉语原话里经常没有关于时态、时间的明确表述。译员需要根据对讲话人、讲话内容的了解以及到目前为止所说的话来判断。

比如，在之前有关价格谈判的例子中，虽然从这段话的开头无法准确判断是过去时，但是这段对话肯定不是从“我们不赞成……”开始的。假如之前有这样的话“我们当时就说过我们不赞成重新谈判……”这里的“当时”就足以判断是过去时，而且只需要用过去时，而不必用：at the time。即处理成：we said we were not in favour of renegotiation。

以下就简单过去时、过去完成时、过去进行时、过去将来时、过去将来完成时（即：虚拟语气）各举一个例子。在此需要说明一下，在以下例子里，英语译入语比起实战里的版本要长。这是由于为了集中篇幅讲解时态的使用而没有采用减字的原则。在实际同传里，完全可以根据之前的话而减少本句话里需要同传的汉字数量。另外，例子中的处理也不是标准答案，只是诸多可能方案之一。

简单过去时

汉语原话	你刚才说首席执行官需要亲自抓人才的培养，那你是怎么做到这点的呢？
英语同传	You said CEO needed to take charge of talents. How do you do that?

过去完成时

汉语原话	去了之后才发现，虽然本来有一些了解，但是亲眼看到感觉就是不一样。
英语同传	After arriving, I realised although I'd had some idea, seeing it was still different.

过去进行时

汉语原话	开会时我们没有看到文件，还没打印好，所以我们要求推迟讨论。
英语同传	At the meeting, we didn't see the document. It was being printed. We asked to postpone the discussion.

过去将来时

汉语原话	他们被告知，再不增加资源的投入，就要丢失生意了。
英语同传	They were told without increased resources, they'd be losing business.

过去将来完成时（虚拟语态）

汉语原话	他倒是想开始就把合同给签了。
英语同传	He'd have liked to sign the contract early on.

实词开句

指的是在同传时，如果句首遇到介词、虚词以及其他没有明显意思的词时就跳过去，从之后的第一个实词或者有明显意思的词开始译。

实词开句是跳词组句的一个具体手法，特别有助于解决汉译英时的两大问题。一大问题是听到介词就从介词开始译起，结果由于以介词开始的是状语，而这个状语本身又是由一个句子组成的，因此导致译入语成为病句。另外一大问题是由于听到介词后感觉需要多听一些再决定如何译而导致不敢马上开口，结果越听越无法开口，终于不得不整句扔掉。请看以下的几个例子及其讲解。

例 1

汉语原话	以中国出版集团为代表的 29 家出版集团，已经成为出版产业主力军。
弃前补后	China Publishing Group represents 29 publishers. It has become a major force.

在以上例子里，听到“以”不译，从“中国出版集团”开始译，问题迎刃而解。如果受到笔译影响而考虑如何处理“以中国出版集团……”就不得不继续往下听，等听到“……29 家出版集团”就会忘记之前的话，或者因为集中精力把原话译出而听不见接下来的话。

例 2

汉语原话	这对国土资源的合理运用提出了更高的要求。
实词开句	National resources need to be used more appropriately.

在听到“这对”时不译，而是把之后的“国土资源”作为主语开始，跳过虚词“的”而译动词“运用”。本来是准备译 need to be used appropriately，此时已经听到“提出了更高的要求”，正好加上“more”而处理成 more appropriately，完成全句。以 More appropriately 表达“合理……提出了更高要求”是采用点到

为止的手法达到了减字的目的。

例 3

汉语原话	我们决定，在核安全规划批准前暂停审批新的核电项目。
实词开句	We've decided nuclear safety planning approval is required before any new projects can be approved.

在听到“在”时不译，而是把之后的“核安全规划批准”作为主语。听到“……前暂停”，处理为 is required before。此时已经听到“审批新的核电……”，译 any new projects。此时已经听完这句，于是译 can be approved 补齐句子。当然，也可以按照原话顺序处理为 . . . is required before approval of any new projects。

例 4

汉语原话	对于刚刚登上世界经济舞台，
实词开句	They have just stepped up to the world stage, 并被西方看作渐成主导者的中国决策者们 The West is gradually seeing them as leaders. China's decision makers 应该反思中国的发展模式。 should reconsider their development model.

上述例 4 是汉译英里常见的难关，如果不会实词开句的技巧就会无法开口，等听到“中国决策者们”时只能继续往下译，前面一大段内容都会被遗漏掉。另外在这个句子里还采用了汉译英的另外一个技巧，那就是增补主语。

增补主语

增补主语有两大用途，一个是处理汉语里的无主句。另外一个是处理定语太长的句子。这两种情况在笔译时都可以等看完了全句再处理，但是同传无法听完全句，必须尽快增补主语开句。以下例 1 和例 2 都是无主句的处理方法，所增补的主语都用黑体字标出。

例 1

汉语原话	核安全无国界。吸取日本核事故的经验教训是一项紧迫的任务。
增补主语	Nuclear safety has no national boundaries. **We** need to learn from the Japanese accident. This is an urgent task.

例 2

汉语原话	国家“十二五”规划纲要提出，要推动文化产业成为国民经济支柱性产业。
增补主语	The 12th Five Year Plan says **we** want to promote the culture industry and make it a pillar of our economy.

以下的例 3 与上节的例 4 都是采用增补主语的技巧来应对主语暂时不明确的句子。不同的是上节例子讲解的是如何跳过介词、虚词而从实词开始，以便尽快译出英语，而本节讲解的是如何通过增补主语而尽快译出英语。

例 3

汉语原话	促进社会和谐和经济发展的主要力量来自于协调一致的行动
增补主语	The promotion of social harmony and economic growth is mainly driven by coordinated actions

译所指也

这个技巧是专门针对汉译英里词汇的处理手法，指的是词汇汉译英往往不能按照汉语的话面传译，而必须根据汉语词汇所指的含义传译。在以下例子中，由于为了说明问题不得不抽取了一些词汇和短句，没有上文，所以建议译作的版本有可能是多个版本之一。实战中的版本需要根据之前的话或者上文做决定。

汉语原话	可以考虑	避免译作
散步	take a walk	scatter steps
取笑（某人）	taking a mickey out of . . .	acquire a laughter from . . .
给力	fantastic	give power
裸婚	no frills wedding	naked wedding

（续表）

商品房	residential property	commercial property
民营企业	Privately owned companies	people operated enterprises
民主生活	democracy	democratic life
吸引眼球	eye-catching (or attractive)	catching eye-balls
闲人免进	Authorised personnel only	No entry to leisurely persons
不动声色	Composed (or without a sign)	Not using sound or appearance
坚持市场经济道路	stick to market economy	insist on market economy road
有意见请向我们反映	Please tell us what you think.	Please reflect to us if you have an opinion.

不可否认，汉语和英语里直接对应的词汇也有，尤其是像气候变化、市场经济、国际社会这样的词汇。他们是从 climate change、market economy、international community 翻译到汉语里的，所以汉译英也就可以再从字面上直接译回英语。但是汉译英必须译所指而非所言的情况更多，而且往往越是具有中华文化特色、越是汉语原有的词汇，就越需要译所指。这当然给译员的英语水平提出了很高的要求，即译员必须知道汉语某个词汇所指在英语里是怎么表达的。

本课小结

汉译英的首要关键是减少所译的汉字，即在同传时必须边听、边扔，跳词组句。熟练掌握减字近半、增加时态、实词开句、增补主语、译所指也这五大技巧就能够明显提高汉译英的质量。总体指导原则仍然是顺藤摸瓜（边听边译）、左右逢源（总有至少两种解决办法）、弃前补后（一秒思维无法解决者就果断扔掉，仰赖往下译为补救）、宁少勿多（养成译入语简练的习惯）。

工作坊

分组讨论如何运用宁少勿多的原则简化以下译入语：

1. 呃，在我自己看起来呢，呃，可以吧。

2. 今天早上的天气真正是令人感到很好。
3. 要不然你看一看是不是可以这样考虑一下这个方面的问题?
4. 所以说，也就是呢，没有办法更早一些时间离开家里。
5. 电影院里面有没有可以买到喝的饮料的这种地方?
6. 改革开放30多年以来到了今天这个阶段，国民的收入得到了十分明显的数量上的增加。
7. 我们从最初一开始就有感到很喜欢、很欣赏这样一种很好形式的表达、表示方法。
8. 他们上班的路上刚刚好是撞上了交通流量的高峰期，所以我们花费了很长的旅行上用的时间才最后赶到了办公室来上班。
9. 除了全组人员已经收到了通知的人以外，大家剩余的人都应该在规定的时间以内自己查看电子邮箱里面的邮件。
10. 工厂里的大多数车间都在继续持续以每一天大约五次左右的实际监测工作次数来保证产品质量不出现问题。

第七课　任务周期

本课讲解同传任务及其周期，旨在帮助学员建立起完成同传任务的流程和系统，帮助学员从一开始就以职业标准对待每次同传练习，以便增加担任第一次同传任务时便成功的机率。由于同传的任务周期与交传有很多相同之处，所以本课里的很多内容与笔者之前由中国对外翻译出版有限公司出版的《实战交传》(2012)很类似，学习过《实战交传》者需要注意本课里有关同传的特别内容。

同传周期

同传是实践性质很强的职业，学员毕业后需要通过每次同传任务来不断学习、进步，所以必须尽早建立起同传周期的概念。也就是说，不能孤立地看待每次同传任务，而是必须把每次任务都看做是一个周期里的一个阶段，还需要做好同一周期里的其他工作，才能保证周而复始，不断进步。

同传任务的周期基本上是从接受任务开始，然后是为任务做准备、完成任务、最后以任务后的学习结束（请看示意图）。

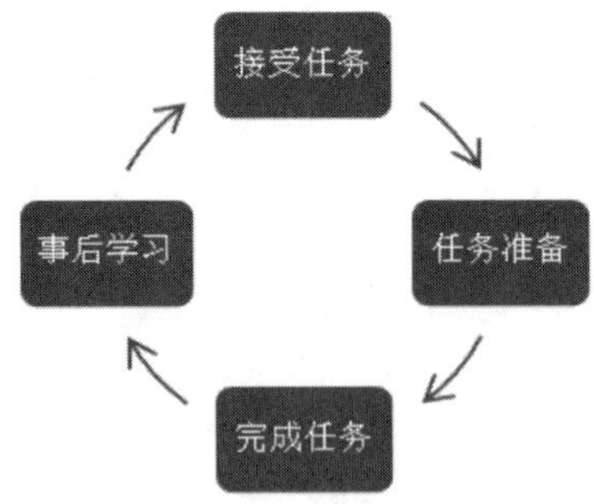

以下逐一讲解每个阶段的具体内容。

接受任务

接受口译任务是一个相当复杂的工作，牵涉到很多方面，需要建立起一个常用体系，否则容易顾此失彼，直接影响到同传质量以及给客户提供的服务。本课介绍的体系仅作为参考，必须根据个人的具体情况调整使用。

接受任务大致可以分成三个阶段：

1. 查询：客户询问译员是否有空并且愿意承担某项同传任务，收费多少。
2. 确认：客户向译员确认任务，形成合约关系。
3. 细节：客户向译员提供与任务相关的细节。

查询阶段没有合约关系，客户可能是货比三家，同时向多名译员查询，然后确定选择由谁承担任务。译员也不受约束，可以在几天后客户确认时说无法承接任务。但是一旦双方确认之后就已经形成合约关系，很多客户往往要求译员签署接受任务的合约。译员出于保护自身利益的考虑也愿意签署合约。

在查询阶段。客户与译员之间必须交换的信息不多，译员只需要知道是什么形式的口译和日期为几号到几号就可以了。到确认阶段，就必须掌握更多的信息。如果客户在确认阶段无法提供所有信息，则必须尽量在任务日期到达之前向译员提供。有些信息可能直到译员临出发甚至任务开始时都还没有。所以，译员必须非常清楚什么是客户必须提前提供的必需信息，什么信息可以稍后提供。

必须掌握的信息可以根据译员的经验多少而不同，新手应该争取多获得信息，以便有备无患；老手则可以凭借经验而到时随机应变。以下清单一列出的是需要在查询阶段掌握的信息，清单二是在确认时及其后需要掌握的信息，其中很多可以从客户提供的任务日程安排里获得，但是有些需要直接向客户询问。

清单一：

- 日　　期：几号到几号。
- 地　　点：在哪个城市。
- 口译形式：经常出现客户忘了提、译员忘了问，当发现双方各自的预期不一样时已经出现了麻烦。比如，客户要的是交传，译员以为是同传。
- 确　　认：客户大概什么时候可以确认对译员提供服务的预定。

清单二：

- 地　　点：任务地址以及具体到哪座建筑，哪个房间或者大厅。如果任务是在外地，是否需要提前一天到达。
- 活动形式：是大会还是小型会谈，是正式活动还是非正式交谈，是会议还是演示。
- 口译搭档：是否需要由译员请搭档？如果不要，那么为译员安排的搭档是谁？
- 口译语言：是否仅限英、汉语？还是有其他语言？如果有其他语言则需要做好接力的准备，而且尤其需要注重汉译英的准备，因为其他语种的译员有可能需要听你的汉译英，然后译入其他语言。
- 工作时间：几点开始，几点休息，几点午餐，几点结束，这些信息都有助于译员决定如何准备，准备多少，当天如何把握，是否需要自备午餐等等。
- 大概场合：是大会还是小会，是正式的同传设备还是便携式？
- 主　　题：是单一主题还是多个话题，什么话题，哪些方面？
- 材　　料：是否可以提供准备材料，比如讲话稿或者电脑幻灯文件（PPT）？什么时候可以提供？如何提供？
- 是否有着装要求？一般为商务装，但有些活动会要求穿商务休闲装。
- 食　　宿：如果是外地或者不止一天的任务，需要了解每天的中饭和晚餐是否自己解决？如果是外地则住在哪里？由谁定房？由谁付费？
- 旅　　行：是客户购买飞机或者火车票还是译员购买之后向客户报销？

催要信息或者材料的时候也有讲究。客户对于事先提供材料的重要性往往认识不同，有的很重视，积极配合译员；有的不重视，必须反复催要；有的虽然知道重要性，但是与译员联系的是客户机构里的低级人员，因为不敢向上司说明为什么讨要讲稿而没有这样做。译员需要根据对具体情况的判断决定采取什么行动，总体原则是：礼貌地说明提供材料是保证客户活动顺利进行的关键环节，而非译员为图个人方便。

任务准备

任务准备对于同传质量不是很重要，而是非常关键，对于新手来说尤其如此。

需要准备的内容大致可以分成五个方面：

- 任务性质与形式
- 发言人及其组织机构
- 话题与内容
- 限时视译
- 旅行、食宿和会务

每次同传任务都有其特别之处，就连同一公司的年会也常常是每年都有新内容、新形式、新活动。所以，应该把每次任务都当做是第一次来准备，才能立于不败之地。另外，上述五大方面也会由于任务不同而各有不同。

任务性质与形式。有些任务很简单，就是双边会谈，一天，一个房间，一个话题。但是有些任务就很复杂，可能是持续多天，换几个地点，讨论多个话题。最复杂的同传任务之一就是诸如“领导力培训”或者“全球化培训”这样的高管培训课程，或者是行业年会里的专业内容，往往是每天 4-5 个不同话题，各有不同的发言人。了解任务的性质与形式有利于译员当天比较有信心地完成任务。

发言人。如果是大会，则日程安排里很可能提供了所有发言人的名单（包括他们的职称）。如果是代表团会谈，则译员需要向客户索取代表团成员名单。这里有两大原因，首先，中国译员往往不善于听懂、记录、复述非中文的名字，在任务前熟悉可能需要多次口述的非中文名字就可以避免临场说不清楚甚至说不出来。其次，职称里的信息密集，几乎每个字都不可缺少，如果全靠当场同传就会跟不上速度。最好是手头有名单，一旦知道说谁，马上就照名单念。

知道主要发言人是谁还有一个重要作用，那就是如果客户没有或者无法提供讲稿，译员可以用发言人姓名和发言题目作为关键词上网检索，有时能够找到发言人之前发表的类似文章或者讲话稿，有时还能找到这位发言人的视频。

组织机构。组织机构的名称也是同传时很难当场译好的内容之一，最好是预先列成清单，笔译之后打印出来带入同传箱，放在面前，需要时就照着读。

组织机构除了需要知道其名称的翻译之外，还需要对其性质、工作内容或者业务有个概要的认识。这是因为对发言人所作的介绍往往提及组织机构的性质、工作内容或者业务。由于这种介绍往往说话速度很快，完全依靠当场译难免出错、遗漏。但是如果预先有了准备，就能减少当场口译的难度。

话题与内容。这里需要准备的内容基本上可以分为两大组成部分：

- 阅读材料
- 词汇表

最理想的局面是客户提供了所有讲稿和电脑演示文件，这种情况下熟悉所有已经提供的材料基本上就可以了。但是最常见的情况倒是客户提供的材料不全，甚至没有提供。以下讲解如何准备客户没有提供材料的部分。

自我准备时的最大问题是收集什么材料，收集多少？本课介绍两种做法，译员可以根据个人的现有知识和具体口译任务参考使用。一种做法可以称之为全面开花，另外一种可以称为单点深化。顾名思义，前者适用于知之甚少的话题，需要比较全面地阅读某个话题而形成话题的知识基础；后者适用于已经拥有相当的话题知识，只是需要在特定题目或者内容上深化知识，补充不足之处。

现在举一个来自实际的例子。假设同传任务是在国际建筑用塔式起吊机（tower crane）协会的年会上担任分会场的同传任务，而且译员过去没有接触过这个话题，这就需要形成有关塔式起吊机的基础知识。由于是业界年会，所以发言人往往从宏观上谈问题，不会在技术细节上太深入，如果时间有限就先覆盖行业的总体信息和最常见的词汇。具体做法是分别用中英文的关键词上网搜索，很快就会发现专业公司的网站和行业的门户网站，网站上的信息可以帮助译员了解该行业（行业现状、走势、主要议题）、主要塔式起吊机的类型与名称及其英中文的词汇对照。

如果任务是行业的技术研讨会，那就需要根据每位发言人的话题深入了解信息，词汇表也必须更加详尽。比如，为年会做准备可能只需要知道塔式吊机的基本原理和主要类型，为技术研讨会做准备就必须掌握塔式吊机的所有主要部件、功能、常见问题、解决方案和市场的最新动态。获得这些信息的渠道往往是行业协会的网站、领先公司的网站、学术论文。

词汇表。词汇表有三大考虑：内容、格式、运用。

内容指的是词汇表必须包括的条目，这里的关键是如果词汇表里的条目不符合要求，则会误导译员，以为准备就绪，其实没有覆盖口译所需。再举上述塔式吊机为例，词汇表必须包括以下三方面内容。

首先是中外与塔式吊机相关的组织机构的名称及其缩写；其次是专业词汇，即各种塔式吊机的类型及其主要部件的名称，塔式吊机使用中的常用词汇；最后是词汇表的运用，即词汇表必须是英汉对照，最好用 Excel 建立文件，以便增减、编辑、排序、查询。

决定词汇表长短主要有两大因素，首先是话题的复杂程度；其次是译员现有掌握程度。作为参照，1-2 天的行业大会需要上百个词汇是正常情况。

准备好了词汇表才只是准备工作的一半，另外一半是背词汇，译员的一个重要技能就是能在短期内记忆大批词汇。在同传任务的前一天，可以把上百个词条的词汇表浓缩到最常用，或者译员最担心会反应不过来的 20-30 个，用大字体、大行距打印在一张纸上，便于当天复习或者放在同传箱内的桌面上，扫一眼就能说出。

限时视译。很多人都知道在学练同传阶段，视译是个重要手段，但是很少有人想到视译，尤其是限时视译在已经可以担任同传任务的阶段也还很重要，是帮助译员做好同传任务准备的重要手段。限时视译指的是边看来源文，边用目标文口译并且在限定时间内完成。限时视译有两大作用，首先是帮助译员熟悉即将要做同传的内容及其英汉语之间的转换，其次是为译员增强成功完成任务的信心。

任务前的限时视译练习必须严格按照同传的实际情况，三词一译，采用一秒思维。主要内容一定要在练习中达到熟练的程度，否则即使是知道词汇也很有可能在同传时一时急切想不起来或者来不及说。

限时视译必须是双向练习，既要练英译汉，也要练汉译英，除非客户明确指示口译任务只是单方向，比如只是英译汉。

旅行、食宿和会务。这些是很容易被遗忘的事项，但是必须从接受任务开始就应该尽早了解清楚的内容。如果同传任务是在译员所在城市，旅行就比较简单。如果是在另外一个城市，甚至另外一个国家，旅行就会复杂很多。如果需要译员自己购买飞机票或者预定饭店，越早动手，就越能减少买不到满意的机票或者预定不到理想饭店的风险。

有时同传任务的地点就是客户安排的下榻酒店，有时是两个不同地点，需要有交通工具。有时客户安排接送，有时译员必须自己解决。有时客户安排译员和与会人员共进午餐和晚餐，有时客户要求译员自己解决。

酒店是否有互联网，多少钱？是否有健身房或者游泳池也是根据译员情况值得了解的内容。这些事情听上去琐碎，但是对于职业译员来说都是不可或缺的。有免费互联网有利于到达后继续准备，有健身设施可以忙里偷闲地锻炼身体。

有关会务事项的最主要内容有三个。首先是客户联系人，有些情况下，这就是一直与译员联系的人，有些情况下，当天译员需要向之报道的联系人是另外一位。所以，必须事先了解清楚，旅行时随身携带联系人的电话。如果出现万一而无法提前到达任务地点，就必须在第一时间通知联系人。如果译员顺利到达任务地点，可能需要有联系人带领才可以进入场地。无论如何，译员都必须事先约定报到的大约时间和方式（面对面还是手机电话或者短信息），在到达地点之后向联系人报到，等候任务开始。

其次是工作时间表，再次是餐饮安排。掌握工作时间表才好安排自己不可避免的活动，比如有时上午 9 点开始同传，11 点休息，然后下午 3 点再开始。这其中会有相当长的空当，译员需要知道去哪？如何渡过这段时间？

总之，客户往往各不相同，要求往往五花八门。译员必须尽量事先了解清楚，以避免误解或者当天无所适从的局面。

这里需要特别说明的是旅行安排，在做计划时必须遵循门到门的原则。即：计划必须涵盖从出家门开始，直到返回家门为止的整个旅程。如果是上午旅行，下午口译，晚上回家，第二天还有其他任务，这点就更加重要了。比如，家住北京的译员，如果去上海完成同传任务，不能光计划北京 - 上海之间的飞行时间，还必须计划从家到机场，从机场到市内具体地点的时间。此外，如果是当天旅行，当天口译，还必须留出足够的预防万一的时间，防止临时堵车。

完成任务

所有的准备工作都是为了当天顺利完成任务，当天需要注意的事项有：提前报到、熟悉环境、安排顺序、申请结束。

提前报到：如果客户有具体要求，则按照客户要求的时间到达地点并且向客户联系人报到。如果客户没有要求，则应该以提前半小时到达地点为目标，到达之后马上报到。如果客户联系人尚未到达，则以短消息方式通知对方，然后在约定地点耐心等待。

熟悉环境：一定要争取提前到达任务现场，熟悉设备。即使是有相当经验的译员也不能大意，同传设备大同小异，但是总有一天会碰上你没有用过的型号，总会有个按钮不同于其他型号。提前到达一旦发现设备特殊时能够事先尝试使用，以免届时太生疏。

安排顺序：由于同传几乎总是要与搭档合作，所以需要事先确定同传时谁先谁后的顺序。如何确定，请看第三课里有关同传操作技能部分的说明。

申请结束：任务完成之后，译员应该争取向客户联系人申请离去：“我们的任务结束了吗？可以走了吗？谢谢，再见！”当然需要根据具体情况调整申请结束的话，原则是礼貌到位便可，既不要啰嗦，也不要显得唐突。有时场面比较大时也有可能客户联系人忙其他事情了，对译员顾不上。这种情况下也可以自己离去，不过这样做时一定要慎重，以免留下过分着急下班的印象。

后续学习

顾名思义，这指的是完成任务之后的学习，是一个被很多译员忽视的环节。他们完成任务之后就不想了，马上把焦点转到下一个任务或者其他事情上去。后续学习之所以很关键是因为这个时候才知道：

- 自己在准备工作中哪些地方判断准确、用力适当而保证顺利完成了任务；
- 在准备工作中有哪些判断误差或者注意不够而导致执行任务期间力不从心；
- 在任务期间哪些地方口译恰当，哪些地方口译不当，本来应该怎样处理更加恰当；
- 在任务期间哪些事情处理恰当，哪些事情处理不当，本来应该怎样处理更加恰当。

即：既要回顾语言的处理又要回顾事情的处理，把每次任务都作为一次绝佳的学习机会，尽量扩大每次任务的学习量，举一反三，确保每次成功都重复再现，每次错误都永不再犯。

后续学习是同传周期的第四个，也是最后一个阶段。学习之后接受下一个任务，周而复始，不断进步。

同传装备

同传时一般都是由主办方安排设备的租用和安装，译员只需要到场便可。当然，同传译员需要面前有纸、笔，听到数字时经常需要先快速写下来，然后再传译，这在先听到数字后听到单位的情况下尤其重要。除此之外一般认为同传不需要其他装备，但是随着技术的发展进步，越来越多的译员开始为自己配备技术装备，提高口译质量、运作自己的口译业务。

常见的装备有电脑文件阅读装置，既可以是手提电脑，也可以是 iPad 以及今后可能出现的其他合适设备。另外，现在很多会场都有免费的无线互联网，可以在同传休息时间上网检索词汇、信息，或者处理自由职业的业务往来邮件。有些译员自己购置个人使用的耳机并且携带不同插孔的转换器，可以插在不同型号的同传器上使用。这样可以避免有时设备供应商提供的耳机太陈旧或者担心不卫生的问题。当然，如果自己携带设备就必须把设备的准备包括在任务准备的清单上。

本课小结

每个同传任务都应该是由四个阶段组成的周期，不局限于口译本身。译员需要在每个阶段上都把工作做好，就能够每次都有明显进步。这四个阶段是：接受任务、任务准备、完成任务、后续学习。

工作坊

假设下个月将前往伦敦为国际会议担任同传译员（会议日程请看下页）。两人一组讨论准备工作需要包括哪些内容，共同起草一份涵盖所有需要准备内容的清单。另外，假设将下榻于假日酒店（地址：Express by Holiday Inn, 106-110 Belgrave Road, London, SW1V 2BJ, UK），制定当天前往会场的旅行方案：何时从何地出发，乘坐什么交通工具，于何时到达何地。如果没有互联网，可以采用自己所在城市的一个会场或者饭店来替代做这个练习。

Mayors and Sustainable Cities in the 21st Century The Queen Elizabeth II Conference Centre Broad Sanctuary, Westminster, London SW1P 3EE	
08.30—09.00	Registration
09.00—09.10	Plenary/Opening remarks—The Mayor of Greater London
09.10—10.30	Plenary/New challenges facing mayors
10.30—11.00	Coffee break
11.30—13.00	Breakout Session 1—Key challenges to municipal governments Breakout Session 2—Funding changes
13.00—14.00	Lunch and networking
14.00—15.30	Breakout Session 3—The role of NGOs Breakout Session 4—Community initiatives
15.30—16.00	Tea break
16.00—17.00	Plenary/What next?
17.00	End

第八课　设计培训

本课讲解如何设计一个同传培训课程。到目前为止，本书的内容都是针对希望掌握同传技能的人拟写的，而从本课开始的三课是针对提供同传培训的机构和教师拟写的。不过，第九课里有关如何培训同传技能、技巧的讲解对于希望掌握同传者——无论是跟班学还是自学的学员都很有指导意义。

在设计课程之前，首先需要区分什么叫学习，什么叫培训。两者有本质的区别，不可混淆。学习指的是学习有关同传的知识，培训指的是通过培训，掌握同传的技能、技巧。前者更多的是靠阅读和思考，后者必须靠反复练习。前者培养的是能够研究、讲解同传的人，后者培养的是能够做同传的译员。

打个比方，学习有关武功的知识靠的是阅读和思考。但是如果想成为武功好手，就必须经过长期、艰苦的训练；学习有关高尔夫球的知识，研究高尔夫球要靠阅读和思考，但是要想成为优秀的高尔夫球手就必须经过长期、艰苦的训练，打高尔夫球。

在理想状况下，培训最好是量身定制，根据每个学员或者每组学员的具体情况设计、安排。但是由于写书的局限，本课只能提供原则和参考做法，需要由培训教师或者自学的学员决定适合自己需要的做法。

在此前的各课里有关同传的知识已经有了系统的介绍，可以根据培训课的时间表和培训生的情况安排课文的阅读和讨论，以达到掌握知识的目的。本课将集中精力介绍同传培训的以下三大方面：

- 如何设计同传课程
- 如何使用本教材
- 如何评估培训生的进展和水平

如何设计课程

同传课程的设计至少需要考虑以下问题：

1. 目标
2. 对象
3. 大纲
4. 课时
5. 教师
6. 方法
7. 教材
8. 评估

目标

首先必须明确目标，即这个课程设定的目标是什么，或者说培训生毕业时需要达到什么水准？根据中国目前的同传培训现状来看，基本上可以分成以下三种培训目标：

1. 对同传有一定了解和初步的感觉（有些业余培训班就是这种性质）
2. 能够做一个普通难度会议的同传译员（如同北外、上外、广外这种一流院校的部分课程）
3. 有能力担任多种难度会议的同传译员（上外高翻的精英班和经贸大的欧盟班）

当然，同传课程是否是学位课程也是重要考虑因素。但是在中国现有情况下，是否是学位课程往往是给定的因素，不属于设计的范畴。

本教材是为培训能够担任第一个普通难度会议的译员而编写的，所强调的是“能够做第一个会议”，而不是“能够胜任同传工作”。培训目标必须明确，才能根据目标设计培训内容、方法，才能根据目标衡量培训生是否达到所要求的水平。

对象

确定了培训目标之后就需要确定目标培训对象。由于培训时间有限，所以必须明确入门培训生的最低水平。如果水平不够，就无法在限定时间内达到设定的培训目标。本课以上述第二个目标为例子，即培训目标为“能够做一个普通难度会议的同传译员”。根据笔者历年来的经验，培训生的入门英语水平需要在雅思 7 分左右。雅思 7 分所代表的不仅是英语水平，而且还有英语和英汉双语的一系列技能水平，其中包括自学和自我提高所需的技能水平。

大纲

明确了目标和培训对象之后就可以设计培训大纲，即具体的培训内容。无论是为学位课程，还是业余进修课程设计同传培训，都必须清楚地区分有关译员的培训和有关同传技能的培训。这就要求大纲设计者从概念上清楚地区分什么是同传所需的知识，什么是同传所需的技能。比如，哪个表达法应该译成哪个表达法就属于语言知识，而如何把自己知道的知识表达出来才是技能。

举例：英语里的 inflation rate 在中文里是“通货膨胀率”，这属于知识，不是技能。而如果译员听到 inflation rate 后能够按照所需的速度说出“通货膨胀率”就属于技能。如果译员为了抢时间而说“通胀率”或者根据前面的话已经到位了而决定不译这个词组，也属于技能。

要想成为一名优秀的同传译员就需要拥有三大组能力，这些能力在第三课里有详细的解释，这里仅提供总体示意图供复习：

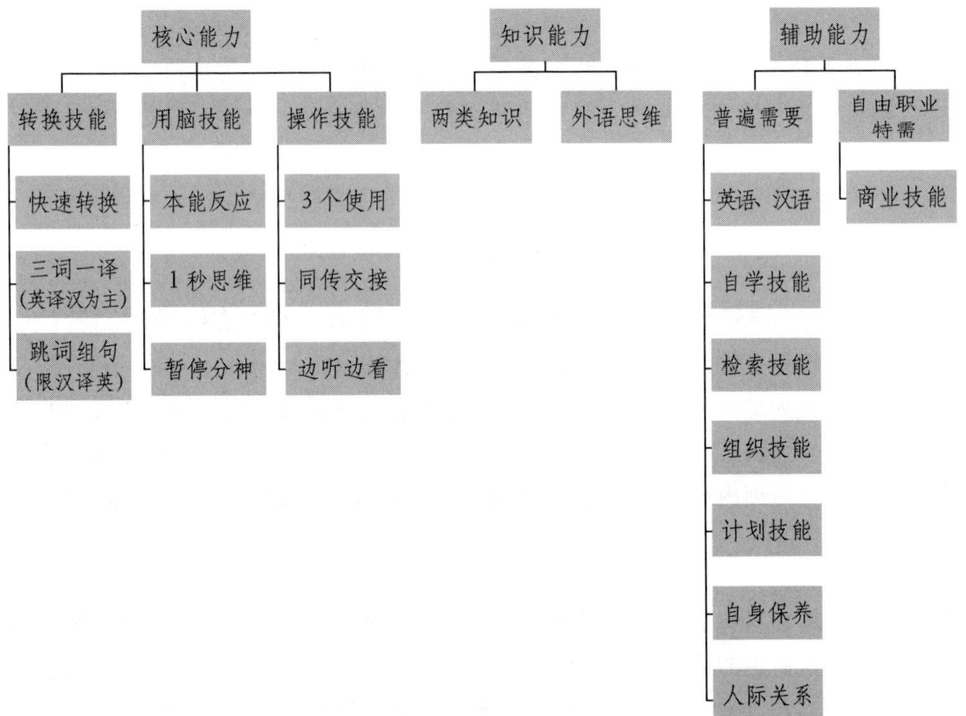

示意图中辅助能力之下的自由职业特需技能里包含了一组商业技能，比如，自由职业译员除了口译周期之外，还需要完成商业周期，即报价、确认、发付款通知、收款、做账、纳税等等。

知识量

同传培训里有个尚未解决的问题，即培训生需要掌握的知识量应该有多大。往往由于课程本身没有明确说明，培训教师也只是说知识越广泛越好，结果导致这个培训中很重要的一个方面几乎完全留给培训生自己去摸索。

造成这种局面的原因之一是很多人都接受这种观点，即优秀译员都必须知识面很广，所以把知识面很广作为同传课程的要求。这里的误区就在于：首先，优秀译员的知识面是多年实践积累的结果，培训生无法在同传课程的有限时间内积累起来；其次，把优秀译员现有知识水平当做目标自然导致培训教师和学生都不知所措。

在确定知识面的时候必须认真区分事业发展的长远目标和同传课程的近期目标。知识面广泛是口译事业发展的长期目标，而当前的同传课程，尤其是那些为本科生或者研究生开设的同传课是入门水平，要想向优秀译员学习就应该参考他们事业发展初期的知识水平。

使用同传的主题领域很多，如果重点不明确，采用常见的尽量广泛的做法就会导致毕业生似乎在培训期间覆盖了很多主题，但是每个主题的知识都极其肤浅，毕业后仍然无法胜任这些主题的同传任务。这是因为走马观花似的覆盖很多主题有个致命的弱点，那就是同传课上了很长时间也不清楚在实战中为同传任务做某个主题的准备时需要达到什么深度。

所以，同传课程的知识量应该根据课程本身的目标，根据同传课上、课下可以使用的时间来界定。与其走马观花似地覆盖很多主题，不如选定其中几个，比较深入地掌握。这种方式的好处在于帮助培训生建立起一个一般性质的同传任务在其相关主题上必须掌握到何种深度的概念。由于不同主题的同传任务所需的技能是一样的，只是所需的主题知识不同，培训生掌握了所需知识深度的概念之后，就可以在今后担任第一个实战同传任务时，运用这种知识，做好这次任务所需知识的准备。

如此界定知识量就可以在大纲里明确列出，在培训期间明确实施，通过考试评估培训生掌握的程度。

课时

在确定了大纲的内容之后就可以设计课时了。由于同传需要以培训为主，学习知识为辅，同传培训大纲的设计必须考虑时间的保证。常规课程安排时间往往采用同样的模式：重要的课一次两节，每节45-50分钟不等，而且每周不超过两次。这种常规做法不适合于同传培训。由于课时太短，培训生刚刚练得有点感觉就下课了，一周以后再上课时几乎是重新开始。这样容易导致进三步退两步半的结局。

解决的办法有两个，一个是压缩，即：把可以安排的课时集中到几周内使用。比如，如果一个学期是20周，每周可以安排2小时，那就可以争取把这40小时压缩到10周内，每周一次，每次4小时，而不要每周2小时分散在20周里。采用压缩式可以为每次课堂的练习效果提供时间上的保证，再加上课堂练习时尽量为培训生多提供机会（稍后有介绍），就可以在很大程度上防止培训生在两次课之间感觉进三步，退两步半。

另外一个办法是加时，即增加分配给同传培训的课时。根据多年来的经验，如果课堂培训法使用得当，每周一次课，每次4小时，达到总数100个小时左右，便可以取得比较令人满意的效果。这当然需要有适当的课下练习作业来补充，以避免两次课期间退步的危险。

教师

接下来需要考虑的是同传培训所需的教师和教材。由于同传在中国是个新兴职业，现有高等院校师资中缺少拥有大量实战经历的教师。一般来说，解决这个问题的办法有三个。首先是引进具有一定同传经历并且喜欢进入高等院校做同传培训的译员，其次是聘请自由职业译员到高等院校兼职，第三是从现有教师队伍里选拔、培养同传教师。

方法

确定了教师之后就必须确定培训方法。国际上对于同传的实证研究很少，对于同传培训方法的实证研究也很少。负责同传培训的教师需要集思广益、博采众长、不断探索、走出自己的道路。本教材提供了建立在笔者理念基础上的全套培训法，可以作为参考、借鉴。

教材

同传教材的选择必须符合培训大纲的要求。不过，很少有某一本教材就能满足某个课程所有需要的理想情况，往往需要担任培训的教师根据具体需要选择不同教材，取各方之长，满足培训中的具体需要。

比如，培训目标比较宏伟的课程，很可能需要在本教材的基础之上，再增加笔者的《实战视译》，为培训生提供更加深入、系统、全面的视译培训。或者增加其他教材，以提供或者丰富某个特需的话题。

以下内容基本上也是以此目标为指南。笔者在多年的实践中探索出一条与众不同的同传培训道路，将在第九和第十课里全面介绍，供培训教师和自学者参考。

评估

大凡评估一般有两种性质，一种是为了检验掌握程度，即对于当前培训的技能掌握得如何。另外一种是检验实际能力，即衡量培训生经过培训所达到的同传水平。无论怎样，评估必须涵盖大纲里规定的主要培训内容，既包括同传技能，也包括所需知识。

具体采用哪种性质的评估方法应该根据同传课程的目标决定。如果培训的目标是能够承担同传任务的译员就必须在课程结束时考察实际水平。如果培训的目标仅限于让培训生对于同传或其中某些技能有一定的了解，就可以只考察掌握程度。

前者的标准可以简化为通过或者没通过，即所做的同传质量可以接受或者不可以接受。这是来自于西欧的理念，认为同传没有完全客观的评价。如果有经验的译员听了觉得可以接受，就基本达到了要求，否则就不能通过。如果是评估培训生是否达到了可以做同传的水平，就必须采用培训生没有预先听过的视频材料，按照任务周期的要求预先做好准备，然后在接近实战的环境和要求下完成同传。当然，所采用的视频材料需要根据大纲的要求确定主题领域及其难度。

后者则可以采用不同手法具体测试某项已经培训过的内容。比如：可以测试限时视译，也可以测试大纲规定的主题知识，或者大纲要求掌握的其他培训内容。如果是测试已经练习过的材料的掌握程度，可以从用过的材料里随机抽选部分内容做测试。

由于同传的培训是技能培训，但往往又课时很有限，所以必须保证培训生课下完成大纲要求的练习量。如果完全靠培训生自觉，就很有可能因为练习量不够而进一步，退大半步，甚至倒退。所以，必须通过大纲规定建立起严谨的日常考核制度。比如，每次上课先简短测试，要求培训生上次课以后必须完成的练习量。具体方法请看第十课里有关如何保证进度的讲解。

如何比较客观地评估同传水平是个缺少研究的领域，而且即使是理论上可以想到的做法也可能由于现实中的条件限制而无法如愿以偿。比如，按理说为了提高客观的程度，应该延长考试时间，评估的译入语应该长一点，还应该加入一些常见的外部因素，比如讲者的口音、速度等等。但是那样做需要大量的资源，一般的培训课程，甚至是大多数大学的学位课程也无法应付，面向全国的证书考试也是这样。所以，同传考试的设计往往是在客观程度和可及资源之间的妥协。有关如何评估的具体方法将于第十课培训手法二里讲解。

本教材的使用

本教材内容由两大部分组成，明显区分知识学习和技能培训。教材的第一部分按照理念阐述的逻辑为顺序，比较全面地讲解了同传所需的各个方面的技能和知识。第二部分为同传技能培训提供了大约一学年所需的练习材料。

第一部分属于知识学习的内容，应该由培训生自己课下阅读，上课时以技能培训的练习为主。当然，在技能培训期间，培训教师可以根据培训生的表现或者出现的问题，使用理念知识部分里的概念解读，提供答案，指导练习，并回答问题。

培训生务必不要在课前看下次上课时将要用于培训的讲稿和参考译入语，也不要自己预先练习。同传培训是为了培训多种技能，如果预先自己练习，比如解决了所有语言问题，就会使课上的练习完全失去有关难点应对方面的培训，导致培训生自己没有得到应有的收获。如果每周如此，势必导致期末考试无法通过，届时将后悔不及。

第二部分由 20 个练习单元组成，英译中和中译英各占一半。每个单元都是一篇模拟实战的讲话稿，供限时视译使用。每个讲稿相当于大约 6.5 分钟的讲话，配有译入语版本供参考。无论哪种语言方向，即无论是英译汉还是汉译英，前两个练习单元的参考译入语都有两个版本，以展示如何在练习限时视译时达到必须有两个方案的要求。

入箱练习和模拟实战的视频、音频材料最好是采用最新的内容，所以本教材没有提供。如今互联网上可以获得的视频、音频材料很多，选择的余地也很多，没有必要以教材方式提供一旦出版就过时的内容。而限时视译的培训目的是语言处理技巧和用脑技能，所用材料的内容时效性不太重要，所以由本教材提供。

参考译入语

每个练习单元附带的参考译入语都是根据同传实战的要求提供的，不过有四点需要说明。首先，由于同传里存在准确幅度（请看第二课）的情况，参考译入语只是笔者认为属于准确幅度之内的诸多可能版本之一，不一定就是最佳版本。培训教师一定不可把参考译入语作为标准答案，应该允许培训生采用任何在准确幅度之内的版本。

第二，参考译入语是根据笔者的理念而专门为同传提供的，完全是按照实战的标准提供的，完全没有经过修饰。同传的版本不可用笔译的标准衡量，那样做是对同传的误解，而且会严重影响同传培训效力。所以，在使用中必须不断提醒培训生以及教师自己：这是同传的版本，不能用阅读的方式来评判。由于大脑作用的原因，如果是在听同传的话，这种版本是很正常的。有关人的大脑对于不同语言来源的反应以及感觉，请看第二课主要议题里的讲解。同传的准确程度主要看当场口译的效果，而不能看之后写下的文字。

第三，笔者对汉译英在同传里的处理有自己的见解，详细论述请参看笔者的《实战笔译》中译英分册。

第四，为了体现实战里的情况，参考译入语不一定保持连贯。比如，同一个概念在一个讲话里的处理就可能不同于在另外一个讲话里的处理，甚至在同一个讲话里也可能有不同处理。同传时讲者持续说话，译员持续口译，如同流水一般。讲者各不相同，话语千变万化。所以，同样的话语有不同的处理版本不仅不可避免，而且是译员能力的重要组成部分。

本课小结

同传课程的设计首先必须明确课程的目标，即培训结束时需要达到的水平。取决同传课程所能达到目标的主要因素有培训生的双语水平、培训教师的资源、可以安排的课时。由于同传是技能培训，所以设计时必须考虑如何避免培训生进三步、退两步从而不断进步。考试的设计必须符合课程目标，必须尽量客观地衡量培训生是否达到了目标规定的水平。

工作坊

由于本课以及下一课的内容都是如何培训同传，所以，工作坊的内容是针对培训教师或者负责同传课程设计者提供的。

假设你在设计一个同传培训课，招生对象是本科四年级非英语专业的学生。课程将持续一个学年，每周不能超过四堂课。请根据上述情况，参照本课的讲解内容草拟一个课程设计大纲。

第九课　如何培训（一）

本课以及下一课详细讲解同传培训手法。这些手法是根据笔者的理念，经过多年在英国培训口译硕士生和公司内的全职译员的反复实践、修改发展起来的方法。在详细讲解之前需要做两点说明。

首先，这些手法与理念紧密相关，如果理念不同或者操作中没有遵循笔者的理念，就有可能起不到预期的效果，甚至没有效果。其次，这些手法往往是在现有条件限制下发展起来的，是目前条件下一组非常实际、非常容易采用的手法。尽管这样，由于尚无实证研究，所以不能声称这些手法最科学、效率最高。采用本教材的培训机构和教师应该争取通过探索和实证研究寻找更加有效或者更加适合于各自需要的培训手法。如果没有条件做更多的探索和研究，则本课提供了一套已经验证的系统。

本课的结构按照笔者在英国设计、主教的口译硕士课程安排，把同传培训分成两大模块，基本上相当于高等院校的两个学期。第一模块培训同传的核心能力，第二模块模拟同传任务的准备和完成。本课内容讲解时都先介绍课堂培训内容和手法，穿插有关这些培训内容和手法具体针对的是哪些核心能力，然后介绍在培训中常见的问题以及解决办法。

本课假定培训生水平为相当于雅思 7 分水平，至少 6.5 分。如果英语水平超出 7 分，可以根据进展加快培训速度、增加内容的难度；如果不到 7 分，就需要根据情况降低每个培训内容的起点、延长练习时间或者降低内容的难度。

笔者主张同传培训从译入语为母语开始，即中国学生从英译汉开始。其主要原因是：首先，译入语为母语时比较容易提高转换的速度，提高译入语的发音质量。其次是英译汉和汉译英时的口译技巧有很大的区别，前者按照原话直译就挺合适的几率大大超过后者。以下培训方法的讲解也按照先讲英译汉，后讲汉译英的顺序。

第一模块

第一模块的焦点是培训同传核心能力里的三组技能，即“转换技能”“用脑技能”“操作能力”，请看示意图：

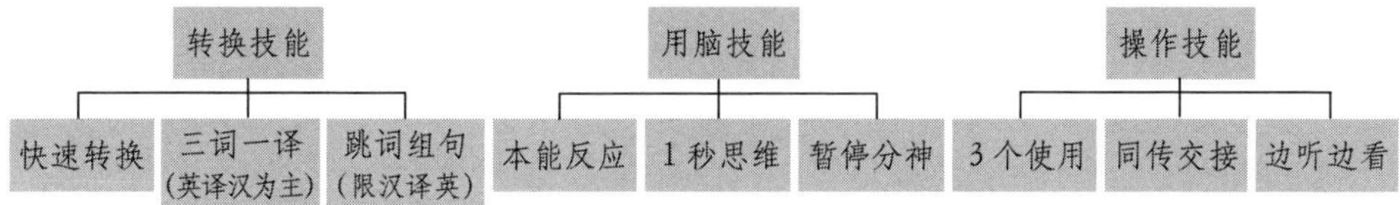

上述这些同传核心能力的训练需要分三个阶段进行：加快速度、限时视译、入箱练习。加快速度分两步：单词、词组。限时视译的培训按照周期进行，每个周期分三步：计时视译、分组讨论、计时视译。请看示意图：

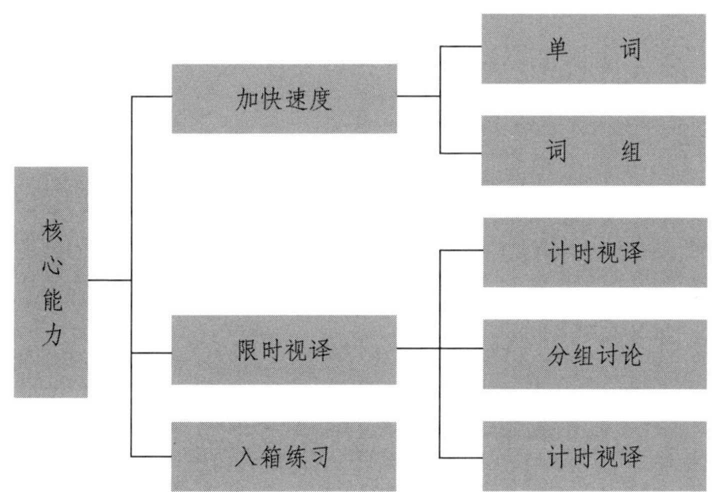

加快速度

加快速度是第一模块的第一阶段，指的是从加快英到汉的转换速度开始。也就是说，先避开生疏词汇或者生疏概念的障碍，从已经熟悉或者相对熟悉的词汇和概念开始加快速度。之所以需要这样做，是因为绝大多数人在开始练习同传之前都没有对自己提过速度的要求，没有在规定时间内说出某个词汇或者概念的经历。第三课里对这种现象有比较详细的说明。

加快速度的培训目的就是要在英到汉的过程里打破从来没有速度要求的老习惯，开始养成以平生最快速度转换的新习惯。然后不断提高速度，使越来越多的词汇转换几乎成为下意识的反应，就像手指碰到很烫的茶壶会马上抽回一样。

加快速度的练习必须兼顾两个技能的培训：快速转换和用脑技能。也就是说，这个阶段虽然主要是培训瞬间说出译入语的能力，但同时也培训瞬间想不起来就立刻把注意力转到下一个单词的能力。即限定大脑分配给每次瞬间思维的时间，绝不停留在某个单词上不停地想。这就是第三课里谈到的流水思维，这是同传的一个要害，是很多人同传无法入门，或即使入门之后水平无法进一步提高的要害。所以，必须从一开始，即从加快单词转换速度时就开始培训，之后还必须贯穿于其他培训内容中。

加快速度的训练可以分两步进行，第一步是从单词开始，由培训教师参照每半个小时需要大约 60 个单词的用量准备。具体单词用量可以根据培训目的、课时长短和培训生现有水平而增减。选定单词之后输入电脑幻灯文件，每张幻灯仅列出一个单词，采用比较大的字号，以便快速识别。上课时用投影仪打出让全班一起练习，也可以在每个座位都配有电脑的语音实验室里，用电脑幻灯程序打出。

单词的选择分成三大类（以下为示例，不同人会有不同感受）：

1. 选择日常很熟悉的单词。比如:morning、afternoon、evening
2. 不是生词，但是转换起来速度不快的单词。比如：planet、terrorism、keyboard
3. 好像认识，但是急切之下又说不准的单词。比如：integration、liberalisation、probability

练习时，每个单词的停留时间控制在 0.5 秒之内，模仿同传时边听、边译的样子不停地进行下去。由于这很可能是绝大多数培训生有生以来第一次被要求快速转换，刚开始练习时可以从打出 5 个单词后就停顿下来，喘口气，培训教师给反馈。然后根据循序渐进的原则，从开始时的 5 个单词进展到 10 个以及更多单词，直至能够 60 个单词一次完成。

以平生最快速度把英语单词转换成汉语单词需要精力非常集中，全神贯注，持续相当一段时间。这也是同传不可或缺的能力，但没有受过培训的人做不到。所以，从同传培训一开始就必须兼顾全神贯注能力的培养。快速转换词汇时一次完成量从少到多就是一种有效的方法。

加快速度练习的第二个阶段采用以两个单词组成的词汇，词汇的选择也分成三大类，以达到循序渐进的目的。以下例子只是说明何为循序渐进，并不是界定哪些词汇属于所有人的感受都完全相同。

1. 日常很熟悉的词汇。比如：
   good morning、business card、football player
2. 并不生疏，但是转换起来速度不快的词汇。比如：
   afternoon report、international terrorism、computer programmer
3. 好像认识，但是急切之下又说不准的词汇。比如：
   inclusive society、corporate governance、management accounting

为了培养不假思索、马上反应的能力，需要把训练融入日常课堂教学与活动。比如，每次提问时都要求培训生马上张口回答。要做到这点，首先培训教师要经常提醒培训生这是同传培训，张口答复的重要性远远超过答复本身的准确性。一旦反应速度提高，准确性本身也会不断提高。相反，如果刚开始就注重质量，势必永远太慢，没说出话来则质量等于零。这个道理类似于开始练英语口语，初期目标必须是张口说，在逐渐熟练过程中纠正语法，提高质量。如果一开始就注重语法和质量势必张不开口。

其次，最好每次都连续要求数个培训生问答同样的问题，造成相互启示、相互示范的气氛，从而加快培训生的进步。这个手法叫"点到开口"，教师点到谁，谁就马上开口回答。教师需要注意的是一定不要在这个阶段去评判答复的对错，那样容易把培训生的注意力吸引到对与错的思考上，导致开不了口。教师应该鼓励培训生通过不断开口的练习，突破一紧张就脑子一片空白的心理障碍。

提高反应速度需要经过一个阶段，需要快而再快。这指的是学员能够不断地强迫自己加快把听到的英语词句转换成汉语的速度。一旦加快速度之后，再强迫自己继续加快。对于大多数初学同传的人来说，这个过程需要反复多次。道理其实也很简单，就像赛跑运动员只有不断挑战自己，跑快一点，再快一点，不断提高速度一样，同传学员也需要不断挑战自己，转换的速度快一点，再快一点，直至达到三词一译所需的速度要求。

加快速度的培训需要持续多长时间，需要覆盖多少词汇是个尚未经过研究的议题。总体来说，无法也没有必要在这个阶段解决所有速度的问题。本阶段的基本目标为：培训生对于为什么需要加快速度、如何加快速度、需要加快到什么程度有了比较清晰的认识，能够做到在绝大多数情况下都能跟得上，由于跟不上而不得不扔掉的词汇为个别现象。

限时视译

限时视译是第一模块的第二个阶段，指的是在限定时间内完成一定长度文字的视译。这个概念有两大组成部分，需要分别说明。

首先是视译，这指的是一边眼看文字，一边说出译入语。其次是限时，由于同传培训所需的视译必须达到和讲者讲话相同的速度才行，这等于在限定的时间内完成视译。由于讲者说话速度有快、有慢，培训初期必须达到大部分讲话人的平均速度才行。这个速度就是平均每秒钟三个英语单词，本书第三课同传技能里对这个问题有比较详细的阐述。

从推理上看，这种在限定时间内把英语的原话转换成汉语的技能最好是通过听译来培训，但是听译作为培训手段有很多局限性。比如，需要很大的工作量才能准备好所需的音频，需要录制、剪辑、制作成文档，还需要相应的设备才能练习。另外，由于音频形式比较固定，缺少课堂培训时所需的灵活程度。课堂培训经常需要根据当时的情况和需要调整培训材料的顺序，或者前后颠倒，或者临时增加或减少。而文字材料无需事先做大量准备工作，从网站上随时可以搜寻所需的话题、难度，接通了互联网就可以马上使用。另外，练习材料可以随身携带，练习的地点不受限制。

虽然看和听的接收途径不同，但是如果按照本书的理念和培训手法，限时视译可以提供同传转换技能和用脑技能所需的练习，培训生过了限时视译关之后，就可以马上进入同传专用的口译箱练习同传。即从视译到同传的听译之间几乎没有感觉得到的差距，限时视译完全可以达到从理论上讲只有听译才能达到的效果。这里需要强调说明的是：视译本身不足以培训出同传所需的核心能力，视译必须达到讲话的平均速度才行，即必须是限时视译才行。

限时视译分三步，每步都有其重点，但同时兼顾其他方面的培训内容，由此形成一个周期。第一步是采用事先没有接触过的材料，其目的有二：一是以视译形式模拟实际同传时边听、边译的情景，培训生必须利用现有能力应对；二是顺便测试培训生目前为止达到的水平。

具体操作方法是选择一篇讲话，分段做视译练习。每段长度可以循序渐进，从 30-40 秒的长度开始，水平提高之后可以延长到 60-70 秒钟。所选材料的长度按照电脑自动统计的字数以每秒三个单词的公式换算即可。

每段视译材料的长度必须合适，太短了反而难度会提高。这是因为回旋的余地小了，被稍微卡住一两次就会无法在限定时间内完成。太长了也不适合初学者，因为视译时必须让目光按照每秒三个单词的速度移动，时间长了眼睛容易产生短期疲劳而导致速度下降。这种与大脑反应无关的因素需要尽量排除。

培训教师需要配备计时的工具，移动电话上的跑秒计时器就很合适、方便。培训教师说开始，同时启动计时器，时间到后叫停。然后请在限定时间内完成的培训生举手，大约掌握一下进展情况。如果虽然没有完成，但是初学者距离这段文字的结尾在 6 个单词之内都可以算基本达到要求。如果大部分人都速度太慢，可以强调一下加快速度的重要，再来一遍。不过，重复视译的次数不要超过两遍，超过了就会增加记忆的因素，失去练习的作用。所以，不管是否有人达到速度要求，在已经视译过两遍之后就应该进入到第二步：分组讨论。

分组讨论有两大注意事项，缺一不可。首先，分组讨论是同传培训的重要手段，不是为了活跃课堂。分组时每组两人效果最好，但是如果培训生是奇数，有一个组是三人也问题不大。分组的重要性在于要达到三词一译的目的，需要采用不同的处理技巧，需要一定的创意思维，而且是瞬间创意思维。两人之间你一句、我一句，你来我往比较容易产生新思路、新办法。一个人自己练，容易出现思路被卡住的情况。而且一旦卡住了就往往停止不前，无法练下去。所以，即使是自学同传，也很有必要找到志同道合的同伴一起练习，相互促进，共同进步。

分组要达到目的必须是两人边口译、边讨论，即：把思路说出来，千万不能自己在脑子里想怎么合适，希望想出方案后再说给同伴听。那样很容易两人都陷入沉默，完全失去两人讨论的益处。正确的做法是两人不停地你来我往地说，现在举个例子。假设有这段话：

I'm very honoured to be here today to speak to such a distinguished audience.

请看以下小组内两个人你来我往、边译边讨论的例子，其关键就在于必须通过你来我往式的讨论把个人脑子里的思路通过说出来与同伴分享，形成两个人的思路相互启发的局面：

甲：我感到很荣幸。

乙：是否可以省掉“感到”，就说“很荣幸”不是更简单？

甲：对对对，“我很荣幸今天到这里来，向如此尊贵的听众”。

乙：等等，如果你说“向如此尊贵的听众”不是要等到这句话说完吗？这不符合三词一译的要求。

甲：那你说怎么办？

乙：能不能说“很荣幸今天到这里来讲话”，后面都扔掉？

甲：那怎么行，扔掉太多了，信息传译得不够。

乙：那你说怎么办？

甲：我们学过一个技巧是把介词处理成动词。能不能把这个 to such a 里的 to 处理成动词呢？

乙：哦，处理成“面对如此尊贵的听众”？不行啊，汉语里怪怪的。

甲：能不能这样讲，“我很荣幸今天到这里来面对如此尊贵的听众讲话”？

…

其次，分组讨论时一定要强调两种选择方案的原则，即每次需要采用三词一译技巧而顺序译时一定要讨论出两个解决方案。这是因为同传要求译员善于瞬间说出译入语，几乎没有思考的时间。在这种情况下，经常由于时间不够而想不起来平常练习时决定采用的某个语言处理技巧。如果平常培训时总是有至少两个方案，就能把瞬间想到解决方案的几率增加一倍。

另外，同传时的情况千变万化。同传事业初期，所需传译的绝大多数内容都会在不同程度上与之前传译过的内容不同。由于后面内容的处理必然受到之前处理方法的制约，所以如果一种语言现象只练习了一个应对技巧，就很容易在实战中由于之前的话与练习时的材料不同导致之后的预备方案用不上。

再举上述例子：I'm very honoured to be here today to speak to such a distinguished audience。这种话至少可以有以下两种处理方法：

- 我很荣幸今天来这里向如此尊贵的听众发表讲话。
- 我很荣幸今天来这里讲话，向如此尊贵的听众发表讲话。

如果平常练习的时候只练第一种，就容易出现在实战中脱口说出：“我很荣幸今天来这里讲话”之后被卡住，一时不知所措的情况。如果平常练习就总是遵循两种方案或者说两个版本的原则，就能在实战时左右逢源，大大增加顺利过关的几率。

分组讨论差不多时，培训教师可以叫停，然后请每个小组分别以比较慢的速度视译一遍，然后抽查他们的第二方案。也可以由其他组提出其他第二、第三方案，以此方法一箭三雕：把握培训生的掌握程度、激发思路、以提出培训生尚未想到的方案的办法帮助他们提高。

分组讨论及其检查、反馈之后，应该给出一点时间，让培训生根据最新的体会再练习一、两遍。接着进入这个周期的最后阶段，即再次计时视译。这次很多培训生都能在限定时间内完成，如果有没有完成者，问相差多少。如果差得太多，比如差一整句甚至更多，就需要让这名培训生单独做一遍，并根据问题所在提出改进办法，或者进入到下一段视译练习，让培训生通过一段时间的训练逐渐提高速度。

五大问题

限时视译阶段常见的问题有五个，前两个问题直接影响培训效果。但是由于它们都是方法上的问题，往往在反复强调、提醒之后就可以解决。后三个问题属于用脑技能和培训生本人习性，必须发现后马上处理，不断改进，争取在入箱练习之前完全克服。以下对这五个问题逐一解释。

分组沉默

这指的是培训教师告诉全班两人一组开始讨论之后，两人都看着讲话文字独立思考，沉默不言，分组讨论变成了分组沉默，完全失去这个练习的作用。解决这个问题不难，首先由培训教师再次强调共同讨论、你来我往的重要性，其次由培训教师或者做得比较好的小组示范一下，一般几个回合之后就能基本解决这个问题。

单一方案

培训教师在抽查时发现培训生在某个句子的讨论中，在三词一译的处理上只有一个解决方案，没有遵循两个方案的原则。这个问题也不难，也是由教师反复提醒，几个回合之后就能基本解决。

多秒思维

这指的是培训生没有做到一秒思维，由于思考如何转换而卡在一个词汇上。一秒思维既是知识，又是技能。从知识的层面上，培训教师需要反复强调其重要性，在培训生的脑子里深深地打上只有一秒余地的烙印。同时告诉培训生，凡是一秒之内没有反应上来的词汇就必须马上扔掉，把注意力立刻转到接下来的话上。扔掉反应不过来的词汇的时候必须坚定、干脆，毫不犹豫、绝不回想。

这种培训方法似乎有些反直觉，很多人会担心这样没有反应上来就扔会导致扔得很多，还有些人会怀疑扔了以后并没有提高译入语的质量。这两种想法都是对同传的误解，必须尽早纠正，否则同传难以入门。

首先，同传如流水一般，讲者不停地说话。卡在一个词汇上想，势必听不见接下来的话，还不如扔掉刚才没有反应上来的词从而听、译接下来的词，没有任何其他选择。其次，这个阶段上是要通过训练获得一秒思维的技能，即要让大脑养成在同传时每次的反应时间自动限制在一秒之内的习惯。果断地扔掉没有反应上来的词汇是一秒思维开始入门的迹象，是需要达到的目标。再次，一旦掌握了一秒思维，就能在三词一译以及其他相应技能的辅助下做到讲者说到哪里，译员就译到哪里。

难免分神

这指的是培训生在做视译的同时还分神评估自己的表现，分神想刚才所说之话的质量，导致没听清讲者接下来的话而且时不时会这样（第三课有详细解释）。难免分神是个常见问题，但是由于这是培训生大脑里的活动，培训教师看不见、摸不着，就连培训生自己也常常没有意识到。这就需要培训教师通过与培训生交谈、询问来了解是否这个原因。基本做法是判断一下刚才听到的内容是否有生词或者难点，如果没有生词或者难点，但又跟得不够紧就有可能是分神了。坚持不分神评估自己也是一个习惯问题，需要培训教师反复强调、培训生有意识的努力，经过一段时间的训练就能逐渐克服。具体做法将在以下入箱练习部分讲解。

缺乏状态

同传所需的是超出平常的速度，所以在练习同传时，培训生必须能够进入这种速度所需的心理和生理状态。这个道理类似于散步和赛跑的关系。散步时没有速度的要求，往往也没有特定的目标。而赛跑则必须竭尽全力奔向特定的目标。赛跑时的心理和生理状态完全不同于散步。

开始练习同传时，绝大多数人的语言处理和表达速度就像散步一样，自己决定速度，自己决定话说成什么样。而同传要求译员语言处理和表达的速度大大超过自己说话时的速度，就像必须从散步突然进入赛跑状态一样。绝大多数人都需要经过一段时间的培训才能练出这种瞬间进入状态的能力。有少数人可能由于生性温和，本来就什么事情都不激动，说话、做事不慌不忙，甚至慢条斯理。这些人不用说无法自己快速进入同传所需的状态，甚至从来都没有出现过有速度思考或者说话的感觉。但这并不是说这种类型的人就无法练会同传，有些人日常说话慢条斯理，但是一到同传时便判若两人，反应和说话速度都很快。

运动员在比赛开始之前都需要做热身运动，目的就是帮助他们接近比赛所需的心理和生理状态，练习同传往往没有这样的热身阶段。培训生可能是刚上完别的课、午休刚睡醒不久、午饭刚吃完不久，在这些情况下练同传就像运动员完全没有热身，马上就开始比赛一样。由于心理和生理都没有进入状态，肯定无法达到最佳速度。

培训教师需要根据情况采取措施，刺激培训生尽快进入状态。培训生没有进入状态的明显迹象之一就是坐姿：松松垮垮，甚至歪歪扭扭，翘着二郎腿等等。所以，第一个办法就是要求培训生坐直了。如果速度还不够快，就必须要求培训生站立练视译。一般情况下，站立之后速度会马上加快，有的培训生的速度甚至可以加快达到三分之一。

如果站立之后速度还是不够快，就需要进一步调动培训生的生理机能。运动员在比赛时需要超常发挥，这都需要肾上腺素的协助。肾上腺素的作用就是大大加快血液循环速度，把更多的氧气输送到身体的各个部分，从而提高体能，提升竞技能力。人在日常生活中也经常借助肾上腺素完成所需完成的任务。比如，急着赶班车时，交活限期快到时，需要推重物时都是这样。如果感觉到热血沸腾，或者哪怕只是感觉到由于激动而浑身微微发热都是受到肾上腺素的影响。很多人在同传课上经过培训教师口头激励就能紧张起来，肾上腺素进入血管，感觉身上微微发热，速度加快。个别培训生由于个性原因不容易激动，就需要培训教师更多的帮助了。

限时视译阶段的目标就是大大提高速度，而培训生速度不够时很直观，马上就能看出速度不够。但是导致速度不够的原因必须诊断准确，否则所开的处方有误会影响疗效，甚至没有疗效，师生双方都干着急。由于视译基本全是脑力活动，看不见、摸不着，需要通过教师询问、培训生反思，共同确定原因。到底是尚未进入状态？遇到比较陌生的词汇或者生词时没有果断扔掉？思维超过一秒？分神了？

有时确定原因需要一段时间，这有些像看病。初步诊断、吃药之后需要复诊，根据疗效调整用药。比如，速度不够是因为经常卡在某个词汇上还是分神，还是激动不起来？

如果正确运用本课的方法，如果培训生英语水平大约雅思 7 分，在一般情况下，经过 50-70 小时的训练，就可以达到新材料也能第一次计时就在限定时间内完成视译的速度。达到这个速度说明培训生无论是在转换技能还是用脑技能方面都已经达到本阶段的要求，可以过渡到下个阶段：入箱练习。

入箱练习

入箱练习是第一模块的第三阶段，指的是培训生进入同传箱用视频材料继续培训转换技能和用脑技能。入箱练习与之前的限时视译除了英语的输入途径不同之外，技能培训的重点也不同。限时视译的重点是三词一译，兼顾一秒思维。入箱练习的重点是一秒思维，兼顾三词一译。

入箱练习必须从有关同传设备及其如何使用的介绍开始，首先介绍译员面前的控制盘如何操作，然后讲解同传时如何交接。有关同传箱里的文明、礼貌（见第三课）也应该同时介绍。这些介绍都属于知识，培训生往往听了就容易忘，需要经过一段时间的反复练习才能掌握，即：实际使用的能力才是技能。

入箱练习需要注意三件事情，首先是材料来源的形式。可以采用的有音频、视频、讲话人直接说话。最理想的材料是视频，不仅仅是因为视频更加接近实战，而且是因为同传时译员的视觉信息渠道非常重要。能看到谁在讲话、有什么形体动作乃至表情、能看到讲话人身后的电脑投影的内容都有助于对讲话人的理解。这就相当于译员必须善于从两个来源接受信息并且让这两个来源相互补充，而不是相互干扰。

自如地兼顾听、看两个信息来源的能力在视译阶段并没有机会培训，因为视译的信息来源只有‘看’这一个。所以，必须在入箱阶段尽早开始培训。刚开始时，有些培训生会感觉受到干扰，因此闭上眼睛。发现这种情况必须马上纠正，不能养成看着讲话人就做不了同传的毛病。

从理论上说，入箱练习时采用讲话人直接说话也是好办法，但是采用讲话人直接说话所需要的资源比较多，而且不容易掌握讲话内容，所以在入箱练习的初级阶段不大合适。如今互联网上的视频材料很多，找到所需的话题以及足够的量不是一件太难的事情。

其次是每次同传练习的持续时间应该从较短逐渐过渡到较长，直至达到每次20分钟。之所以选择20分钟，是因为参照了联合国同传工作量的标准，并不是有经过实证研究的科学。在一线做同传的译员，大多数人遵循联合国的标准，每次做20分钟。但是也有些人偏好每次15分钟后交接，还有些人偏好每次30分钟交接。在特定情况下，有时只有一位译员担任整个活动一小时、甚至更长的任务。

当然，作为初级培训，20分钟比较合适。不过，由于同传要求译员精力十分集中，大多数人在没有经过训练之前都没有这种能力，所以可以从每次5分钟开始，然后增加到10分钟、15分钟，最后增加到20分钟。培训教师可以根据情况，在练习交接几次之后叫停，询问培训生的感受，提供反馈。

最后是培训教师需要建立起自己的监测、反馈体系。由于同传是流水一般，为了让培训生得到所需的练习量，必须让他们在几次交接之后再停下来讨论、提供反馈。另外，还需要在此期间监听多名培训生的情况，以便分别给以反馈。这就要求培训教师有可靠的记录体系，记录所听到的问题。采用录音的方式有很大的局限性，比如事后很难马上找到所需要听的部分。更不用说同传的录音需要是两种语言的，找起来就更费时间，不实用。

最简单的办法就是由培训教师做笔记，先写下听到的相关英语，接着写下培训生的相关译入语。由于这个阶段培训生的常见问题很集中，就是那么几个，而且反馈时需要照顾到全班，每个培训生能够分配到的反馈时间很有限，所以不管记录的是哪一、两个例子，都可以达到培训的目的。

入箱练习初期，需要解决的常见问题有两大类型，首先是操作方面的问题，请看以下清单以及这些常见操作问题的课堂解决办法建议：

同传操作问题	建议
开关话筒时机不对。如开口译时忘了开话筒或者停止口译后忘了关话筒（有些型号的设备是一次只能有一个话筒打开）。	反复强调、反复练习直至问题解决。
话筒距离嘴巴太近，呼吸声太明显或者出现爆音的情况（就是听到噗、噗的声音）。	指导培训生如何开始练习之前调整好话筒，记住话筒位置，养成每次接手之前马上把话筒调整到预定位置的习惯。在练习中，反复提醒直至问题解决。
口译时下意识地用手去调整话筒，导致噪音进入话筒	同上。
接译时没等同伴把句子说完就插了进去。	复习第三课里有关如何交接的讲解，反复强调、反复练习直至问题解决。
接译时迟疑太久，给同伴造成麻烦（不知道是该停止译还是继续译）。	同上。
过早接译，同伴还没有译够规定时间。	同上。
口译时说话声音太大，近乎大声嚷嚷。	指导学生采用卡拉 OK 演唱的形式，靠近话筒尽量降低音量，靠设备而不是本人大声来提供听众所需的音量。

同传操作上的问题比较直观，看到、听到的问题就是问题本身，反复提醒、强调，多加练习就可以解决。但是同传培训里出现的传译技能方面的问题经常被误解，导致应对方法效果不佳。比如，初练同传者几乎所有人都会在不同程度上说自己的最大问题是听和译相互干扰，注意听就影响译、注意译就听不见。

这种现象往往被解释成缺乏分脑能力，其根据是欧洲一名资深译员、同传研究专家对同传的认识。这位专家叫 Daniel Gile，于 20 世纪 70 年代提出：同传译员是四项脑力活动同时进行。边听讲话、边理解、边译、边说，无论哪项活动用脑多了都会影响其他几项。

Daniel Gile 在他的论文里只是对同传译员必须多项脑力活动同时进行这种现象做了描述，但是这个描述被业界以及很多培训机构当做培训的目标，于是产生出对于分脑的培训这种理念。这种理念认为，分脑是同传的关键技能，只有掌握分脑的技能，才能学会同传。反过来说，同传时听与译相互干扰是因为脑力在四项活动之间的分配不合理。为了便于讨论，以下将这种理念简称为“分脑理念”。

遵循分脑理念的培训教师往往把学生听与译相互干扰的现象归咎于缺少分脑能力，因此努力要求培训生调整脑力在听与译以及其他各项任务之间的分配，以求借此获得同声传译的技能。但是，分脑理念面临三个问题。首先，它无法确切说明在实战中四项脑力活动各应分配多少注意力。其次，它无法说明实战中怎样去不断地调整大脑注意力在四项活动之间的分配。再次，从直觉上也可以感觉到要想在不同脑力活动之间调整注意力的分配是很难做到的。比如，怎么才能做到少听一些以便腾出注意力多想一些？或者怎么做到多注意传译时的语言处理，而对于听少注意一些？除了说“尽量这样、那样”以外，很难为培训生提供可以自我感觉到、自我掌控的东西。

比较随心所欲地分脑是译员经过多年的口译实践之后逐渐培养出来的能力，既无法在同传入门阶段掌握，也不是同传入门的必备技能。在入门阶段，基本只能仰赖大脑的自然能力。培训的目标应该是一小组如何充分利用大脑自然能力的技能，掌握了这一小组技能就可以达到同传的要求。快速转换、三词一译、一秒思维就是这样一小组技能，都是为了把需要同时兼顾的脑力活动限制在大脑现有能力的范围之内，以此达到同声传译的目的。

入箱练习阶段常见的传译技能上的问题基本都是在限时视译阶段尚未完全解决的那些，或者在限时视译阶段基本解决了，但是由于采用视频这个不同的来源而导致原来的问题复发。总体说，还是三个方面：三词一译、一秒思维、暂停分神。

培训教师需要在监听时首先注意解决三词一译问题，这个问题最明显的表现就是培训生没有在听到句首的前三个词时就开始译，而是等到三个词以后。英译汉在绝大多数情况下都可以做到才听到三个词就开始译，如果不及时纠正滞后过久的毛病，培训生很快就会逐渐继续推迟至 5–6 个词才开始译。然后会陷入这种格局，无法紧跟讲者，导致很快就出现译一句、漏半句的情况。培训教师必须在发现问题的第一机会提醒培训生必须三词之后马上开口。这样反复练习之后，一般都能解决句首开口晚这个问题。

句首问题在最初解决之后还会复发，所以培训教师不能麻痹。养成三词一译的习惯需要一定的时间，需要及时发现复发的情况，及时提醒、纠正。

接下来就是处理一秒思维和暂停分神问题。如前所述，这些问题导致的表面现象往往是听、译相互干扰。所以，不要为之所迷惑。培训生总是那样说，那是他们的直观感受。而解决办法还在于解决问题的根源。如何判断到底问题是一秒思维还是暂停分神要做两个分析：第一个是请培训生自己回顾、反思一下是哪种情况；第二个是注意观察。

一秒思维问题往往发生在遇到比较生疏的词汇或者概念时。培训教师可以根据自己的语言能力和对培训材料的了解做出这个判断，接着就可以要求学生努力在一瞬间想不起来如何传译时马上放弃刚才的内容，立刻把注意力转到接下来的内容上。

如果所听到的内容并没有明显的生疏词汇或者概念，但又似乎跟讲者跟得不紧，那就有可能是分神问题，即：培训生一边译、一边在听，甚至评估自己的译入语质量。如果怀疑是暂停分神问题，往往一问培训生本人就会得到证实。由于分神是下意识的行为，所以培训生会不知不觉地那样做。但是只要一被问到，往往就会恍然大悟。当然，从意识到纠正还需要一段时间的训练。

除了上述核心能力之外，入箱练习还有其他一些辅助技能需要掌握。最常用的辅助技能之一就是笔记。同传一般不做笔记，但是在听到比较复杂的数字，尤其是数字之后还带有单位的时候，除非译员应对数字的能力很强，否则不得不迅速记下所听到数字，听完之后再根据情况传译过去。这主要有两个原因，一个是英汉数字表述的结构不同，没有听完整个数字无法在汉语里开口。比如，听到 four hundred and thirty six… 不能马上说“四百三十六”，可以笔记下来。等听到 … thousand 再开始说“四十三万六千”。

第二个原因是英汉之间数字和单位的顺序经常相反，只有听完整体才能调整顺序在汉语里正确表达。比如，听到 to reduce rent by 23%…，先说“减少租金”，同时笔记“23%”。等听到 … per square meter 再开始说“每平米减 23%”。

本模块培训最后需要说明的是入箱练习距离同传模拟仅有一步之遥，为了保证培训的实战性质，可以尽早开始为模拟做铺垫，逐渐引入知识能力的培训。有关知识能力的概念在第四课知识能力里有详细讲解，在入箱练习阶段的重点是获得知识的技能，即：在有限时间内快速获得知识的能力。知识能力的其他两个组成部分，无论是预有知识，还是当场现学能力都无法在同传课内解决，必须在英语课和日常学习、生活中积累。有关知识能力如何培训的具体讲解，请看第十课。

本课小结

同传的关键是快速转换和语言的处理，限时视译是克服这两大难关的有效办法。培训生在视译时达到速度和质量的要求之后就可以进入同传箱内练习同传了。

同传培训过程中最常见的问题是听、译、说相互干扰，其原因基本有三个：没有紧跟讲者而达到三词一译的程度、没有遵守一秒思维的约束、不知不觉地分神了。培训教师需要采取类似于医生看病的诊断法确认原因，对症下药，解决问题。

由于本课以及第十课都主要是针对培训教师和培训机构拟写的如何培训同传的内容，不是为教师培训课所写，所以没有教师培训所需要的工作坊。

第十课　如何培训（二）

本课讲解同传培训的第二模块，即：实战模拟如何安排、掌控、评估。注重实战的同传培训项目必须既要有一个学习、练习阶段，还要有一个模拟同传阶段。前一阶段的重点是通过培训教师的讲解，理解同传的理念，并且通过反复练习，初步掌握所需的技能。后一阶段的重点是把前一阶段的知识和技能运用在近乎实际同传的任务中。此外，模拟能产生第一阶段课堂练习时没有的、近乎实战情景中的心理压力。通过模拟，能够让培训生在培训期间明显提高心理素质，做好迎接实战的心理准备。

本课总共有六大内容：

- 内容设计
- 知识能力
- 保证进度
- 反馈指导
- 期末评估
- 如何自学

内容设计

如何设计实战模拟的内容很有讲究。如果培训资源不够，还需要有创意，争取在有限的资源里让培训生在尽量接近于实战的情景下完成同传任务。以下的介绍以比较理想的资源和目标为基础，读者可以根据实际情况和资源能力，参照本课的指导原则和建议而实施。

同传模拟可以分成两种，一种是模拟整个商业同传任务周期，另外一种是仅仅模拟同传任务本身的周期。前者包括接受同传任务之前的商业运作，如接到客户查询、报价、确认细节、发出付款通知或者收款的发票。后者仅仅是同传任务本身，即从如何为同传任务做好准备开始到同传任务结束为止。

模拟同传至少需要一个口译任务来源和一个口译材料来源。口译任务来源可以由培训教师扮演，每周选择一名培训生担任主要联络对象，由培训教师担任客户的角色。如果是模拟整个商业周期，则可以向培训生发出查询函件。培训生答复、报价、接收任务细节、确认。如果是模拟同传任务本身，培训教师可以根据所需难度，先是提前几天，接着是仅提前一天，向培训生发第二天会谈的日程和相关材料。培训生收到材料之后马上转发全班，为口译任务做好准备。

口译材料来源既可以是现成的视频材料，也可以是讲话人现场讲话。第九课里已经就采用视频材料做了说明，这里需要强调的是如果有条件，也应该安排现场讲话。这既可以是一个人做电脑幻灯辅助的演讲，也可以是两人，甚至多人的会谈。如果是培训多语种译员的院校或者机构可以安排国际会议的模拟，由多名讲话人持不同语言讲话，为不同语种的培训生提供模拟国际会议练习的机会。

如果是采用讲话人的方式，其选择也有讲究。比如，英语的讲者既可以全用英语为母语的讲者，也可以使用带有明显口音的英语讲者。所选择的口音可以根据培训生的需要而定。在英国做英汉口译时相对比较常见的口音有：苏格兰、印巴、美国、德国、法国、西班牙和意大利（两个口音相近）。

汉语的讲者可以请其他教师扮演，而由培训生轮流担任也很有好处。既可以深化培训生在特定话题上的知识，锻炼培训生的口才以及交谈时的应变能力，又有助于他们了解将为之翻译的讲者的思路和行为。

每次模拟都必须设计角色说明，角色说明必须包括的内容有：交谈的情景、交谈双方的姓名和身份、交谈的话题、双方的主要论点（必须相反）以及其他需要提醒讲者的事宜。笔者的《实战交传》里也有关于如何设计模拟练习的说明。

同传模拟最理想的状况是在安装了同传设备的房间里进行，可以参照联合国每三名译员一组的做法。不过，如果是每小时之内只能在同传箱里练习 20 分钟，则休息与练习的时间比例不理想。最好是两人一组，但是如果没有足够的同传座位而三人一组，就需要争取其中一人在同传箱外使用听众的耳机听来源语而轻声练习。如果没有同传箱只有语言实验室，也可以基本达到同传的要求，只是无法练习同传设备的使用。

知识能力

知识能力是同传培训里的重要内容，虽然不是同传的核心技能，但是知识能力上的缺陷往往是译员在同传时知识量，包括词汇量不够的最主要原因。所谓知识能力不仅仅指知识本身，还包括在有限时间内快速获得所需知识以及口译现场边译边学的能力。有关知识能力的概念在第四课里有详细讲解。

知识能力的培训应该从上一模块的最后阶段，即入箱练习时开始。由于入箱练习距离同传模拟仅有一步之遥，为了保证培训的实战性质，可以尽早开始为模拟做铺垫，逐渐引入知识能力的培训。

本阶段知识能力的培训需要根据同传任务周期安排，以其为结构。由于每次模拟（以及之前的入箱练习课）都相当于一次同传任务，培训生必须根据接受到的任务说明做好完成同传任务的准备。而这个准备过程就是知识能力的培训过程，每次上课，培训教师可以通过抽查和观察培训生的表现评估知识能力的水平。

知识能力培训的主要内容有：

- 时间管理：如何根据任务的需要高效率地分配、使用时间，在有限的时间内完成同传任务所需的准备。
- 团队协作：小组成员一起商定如何分工，避免重复劳动，提高大家的准备效率。
- 检索归纳：收集背景以及任务材料以供阅读、建立词汇表、收集其他特需信息。
- 限时视译：选定少数核心材料练习限时视译，确保口译时能做到快速反应和一秒思维。

由于课前准备的工作量很大，所以培训生往往感觉时间太少。但是时间量总是相对的，译员在实战中总是在有限的时间里做好完成同传任务所需的准备工作。这就要求译员善于根据每次任务的具体情况，比如自己对任务的熟悉程度，现有材料的多少等等，恰当地分配时间，区分轻重缓急，保证时间使用的效率，保证顺利完成口译任务。由于具体情况千变万化，无法提供如何使用时间的公式，只能由培训生在实践中摸索出适合于自己的时间安排规律。所以，培训生必须充分利用每次模拟（以及之前的入箱练习）的机会，经过反复摸索、验证而为自己积累起所需的知识，同时提高如何获得每次任务所需知识的能力。

培训教师可以根据情况循序渐进，利用掌握提前多少时间通知培训生下次任务主题、提前多少时间提供有限的材料这种方式，培训出能够根据具体情况妥善安排可用时间的能力。可以从刚开始时给比较多的时间逐渐过渡到后来给比较少的时间，从提前 3-4 天逐渐过渡到比如仅仅提前一天。

以下是知识能力培训方面的常见问题及其解决办法建议：

常见问题	办法建议
时间分配不当，有些内容准备过多，有些过少。	让培训生自己分析原因并且提出改进方案。
团队沟通不够，重复劳动或遗漏了本来应该准备的内容。	同上
检索效率低，花了很多时间查找本来不需要那么多时间查找的资料。	请培训生举具体例子以分析效率低的原因，往往知道原因之后就有了解决办法。
视译没有限时，导致同传时知道是什么，但是来不及说。或者内容不陌生，但就是跟不上讲者。	反复强调其重要性，要求下次课前一定要限时。

保证进度

由于同传的培训是技能培训，但往往又课时很有限，所以必须保证培训生课下完成大纲要求的练习量。但是由于培训生通常还有其他课程需要完成，或者属于在职或者业余培训，其他方面的学习、工作或者生活都会与同传练习的所需时间形成竞争。除了少数意志坚定者，如果没有严格的体制约束，大多数培训生都会在不同时期出现没有按质、按量完成练习的情况。这样就会导致由于练习量不够而进一步，退大半步，甚至倒退。所以，同传培训必须通过大纲或者课程质量控制规定建立起严谨的日常考核制度，以此鞭策培训生。

比如，可以在大纲里规定日常测试在毕业考试成绩内所占的比重。如果这个比重规定得比较高，比如 30% 甚至更高，就又可能出现期末考试及格，但是由于平时测试成绩不好而总体不及格的结果。虽然听上去不够公平，其实反而是比较公平地反映出实际水平。由于同传培训必需有一定的量，没有达到临界点所需的量，即使在期末考试的几分钟里质量可以接受，仍然不说明已经有了一定水平。

在大纲或者课程说明里做了规定之后还必须严格执行。如果每周只上一、两次同传课，则每次上课都应该首先进行简短测试，评估培训生是否按照要求完成了指定的练习量并且达到指定的要求。从限时视译使用过的材料里任选一段要求培训生在规定时间内视译完毕就是一个既简单、又省时的测试方法。另外，要求培训生出示准备带入同传箱的词汇表也能看出准备的范围和深度。

反馈指导

由于使用同传的活动各种各样，所以在时间安排上也不尽相同。一般情况下，使用同传的活动往往一个半到两个小时之后就有一次休息，每次半小时左右，午饭一般不少于一小时。模拟课也可以参照这样的时间安排，培训教师可以在休息期间为培训生逐一或者集体提供反馈，指出需要注意的问题和解决方法。

如果模拟练习一段时间之后，培训生已经基本上路，就可以不下课休息，而是由培训生在交接之后的译员休息时间内轮流休息。培训教师也可以在这个时间段分别给培训生提供反馈。这种做法比较适合于本来课时就比较少的同传课。不过，采用这种方法时，培训教师会比较辛苦，往往需要不停地听，不停地为轮到休息的培训生提供反馈。

模拟训练开始后，培训教师监听时的重点仍然是三词一译、一秒思维、暂停分神。虽然在入箱练习阶段的重点类似，但这三大问题需要一定的练习量才能解决。另外，三大问题会由于听到的内容不同、讲者不同，难度不同而反复出现，所以绝大多数培训生仍然需要继续攻克这三关。如果这三关还没有彻底攻克，培训生就会出现跟不上或者漏译的问题。如果这三关都攻克了，则培训生就已经掌握了同传的核心技能，遇到迟疑、停顿或者漏译就基本上全是知识和词汇量的问题，不是同传技能问题。

所以，培训教师听到迟疑、停顿、遗漏时需要判断所听到的语言、概念是否很难。如果是，则为知识问题；如果不是，则为上述的三关问题。三关问题的应对需采用诊断法：首先问培训生刚才在具体某个时候（培训教师必须当时做笔记才能事后帮助培训生回忆起哪一点），为什么迟疑或者停顿。如果培训生说不上来，则提醒问是三个问题中的哪个。一般情况下，培训生都能回忆起来。

让培训生自己回忆的过程很重要，同传时的进程全在培训生的大脑里，培训教师看不见。而且，教师的话重复多遍，不如培训生自己脑子里想一遍更容易产生效果。在培训生回忆之后，培训教师需要重新强调三词一译、一秒思维、暂停分神，要求培训生再努力。如此反复，绝大多数培训生都能逐渐减少由于上述三关引起的迟疑、停顿、遗漏。

期末评估

同传期末考试必须根据大纲或者课程的既定目标而设计。常见的目标有三大类：对于同传有个初步的感性认识、达到能够做第一次同传的水平、胜任一系列同传任务的职业译员。当然还可以根据具体需要或者情况，把目标定在上述三大类之间。以下的介绍以第二类为例，即需要测试培训生是否达到了能够做第一次同传的水平。

由于培训课程总是时间相当有限，只能涵盖部分常见话题，无法涵盖所有话题。另外，除非是为某个话题而设计的培训课，一般性质的学位课程或者培训课都无法预见培训生毕业后的第一次任务会是什么话题。但是，如果按照笔者在本书里讲解的理念和培训方法，则培训的内容既包括同传的核心技能（三词一译、一秒思维、暂停分神），又包括辅助技能，尤其是其中如何为同传任务做准备的技能，而且通过入箱练习和模拟阶段的培训都达到了要求，则培训生就能够接受不熟悉话题的同传任务，把已经熟练掌握的核心技能与通过任务前准备而获得知识的技能结合起来，比较顺利地完成第一次任务。所以，如果课程的目标是能够做第一次同传，则期末考试需要评估的就是能否顺利完成一个不熟悉的话题的同传任务。

但是即使这样，也还需要考虑讲话本身的难度。比如：讲话人的口音、速度、所使用的语言难度都会直接影响到培训生的考试结果。从理想的角度看，最好是考三段讲话，三段的难点分别是讲话人的口音、速度、语言，这样就能比较全面地考核培训生的水平。但是在实践中，这样考试需要很大的资源。如果每个培训生考三段，每段 5 分钟，就是每人 15 分钟。一个班 20 个人就至少需要 5 个小时。另外，要找到三个考试材料分别是难在口音、速度、语言上也很不容易。

有关同传的实证研究很少，有关同传如何考核才算合理、客观、公平就更不用说了。在实践中，一般都根据具体条件和资源情况，采用 5-10 分钟的讲话，而且选择常见的会议讲话速度，没有太重的口音。

如何打分也有一定讲究。欧洲有直接打分的传统，即由考官当场听、当场根据印象打分。其根据是同传的质量就是当场听众的感受，所以，当场的感受是最能直接反应质量的根据。事后听录音总是产生不同的印象，那种印象不是听众的当场感受，所以一些专家认为不可靠。

如果采用当场打分的方法最好能安排两位考官，而且是没有听过培训生练习的考官。这样，考官就相当于听众，这种情况下的考试已经接近于培训生担任第一次同传任务时能够给听众留下的印象了。

无论是当场还是事后打分，具体操作都可以有三种形式：一种是考官戴上两套耳机，一套听来源语，另外一套听培训生的译语，以此判断译语质量；另外一种形式是考官事先熟悉讲话内容，考试时光听译入语，然后判断其质量；第三种形式是考官手持讲稿，既可以是配有参考译入语的版本，也可以光是来源语，然后一边听培训生的口译，一边参照讲稿判断译语质量。

这三种形式各有长短。比如，第一和第三种形式要求考官必须自己会同传，而第二种形式对考官的要求就可以相对低一些。不过，无论哪种形式，现在也都没有实证研究来说明孰优孰劣。

如何自学

口译自学难，同传自学更难。其中的原因比较复杂，但是恐怕最明显的原因就是同传里用脑技能这部分无法像其他技能那样可以看到结果，分析结果。比如，交传的笔记是可以事后分析的，同传的译入语也是可以事后分析的，但是在同传过程中为什么速度不够快，为什么没有做到一秒思维，这些都是一时的大脑活动。自己看不见，摸不着。需要有别人通过监听、观察和你交换看法，才能大概了解到当时是怎么回事。

其次，同传部分核心技能所需的练习量大大超过交传培训里的练习量。比如，交传里笔记的使用大约 30 小时可以过关。而同传里限时视译可能需要 70 个小时、甚至更多，而且练习时对于人的脑力和体力的要求都高于交传。如果完全自学，就必须有非常强的自律能力，能够经受每次几个小时高强度、高要求的训练。一般人都很难做到，往往都在几十分钟之后就泄气，更不要说持续好几个月了。

自学的另外一个难处在于同传的核心技能需要通过改变用脑方式来获得，这是个与绝大多数人目前为止养成的思维习惯完全相反，需要彻底改变思维习惯的过程。期间难免出现自我怀疑，或者有各种各样的疑问的情况。此时如果没有人指导，就很容易迷失方向，达不到培训效果。

尽管这样，同传自学成功的人不在少数，笔者也是其中之一。所以，同传是可以自学的。以下是几点建议供参考。

首先必须评估自己是否适合于自学同传。在评估时一定要尽量客观，扪心自问，不要自欺其人。以下是需要问的几个问题：

1. 我有通过自学而成功的经验吗?
2. 我有不达目的不罢休的先例吗?
3. 我能够做到按照计划完成自学任务，雷打不动吗?
4. 我善于自我分析、反思吗?
5. 我有合适的老师可以偶尔请教的吗?

6. 我有合适的人结成自学同传的对子吗?

如果上述答复都是肯定的，就说明具备了同传自学的一些基本条件。如果有一个答复是否定，恐怕都难以自学。前四个问题是从不同角度看所需的个人条件，后两个是最低限度的外部条件。即使是自学，也需要定期有人指点。另外，两人结伴自学在视译阶段非常重要，很有助于三词一译训练时想出两个方案。而且两人相互掐表计时比较容易相互激励，加快速度。

即使是自学，也可以参照本书的培训结构和手法，只是需要有点创意思维，加以调整以适用于自学。

本课小结

如果同传课程所设计的目标是能够担任首次同传任务或者更高水平，则必须在课程的最后阶段进行模拟同传培训。模拟培训至少需要涵盖同传任务的基本周期，以便培训生真正掌握担任同传译员必须掌握的全套技能。

同传自学很难，但不是不可能。如果自学一定要争取能够结成自学小组以相互帮助，还要有可以咨询的指导老师。

由于本课和第九课一样，是为了培训教师和机构拟写的，所以没有提供教师培训需要的工作坊。

《实战同传》的理念讲解到此结束，请把目前为止讲解的理念和内容运用到此后的练习中，反复练习，严格要求，突破同传的难关。

第二部分　同传练习

英译汉

1. 联合国秘书长潘基文讲话

使用提要

1. 所有练习单元的讲话稿均以两种形式提供。第一种采用常见的讲话稿形式，便于练习限时视译。第二种采用对照、对比形式，便于练习、琢磨三词一译的技巧。
2. 限时视译部分是讲话稿全文，可以根据需要选用。但是在技巧琢磨部分里，只有前半部分的讲话配有参考译入语以保证每个单元的练习长度大体相同。
3. 为了示范如何在视译的讨论阶段达到两个方案的要求，本单元和第二单元的参考译入语都有两个版本。其他单元只有一个版本。
4. 限时视译的速度在前两个单元可以从每秒 2 个英文单词开始，每次大约 40 秒左右的量，即大约 120 个单词。但是在 3 个单元以后必须提高到每秒 3 个单词。这是实战同传必须达到的速度。
5. 在使用或者参照译入语时必须注意：
   - 5.1. 参考译入语只是诸多可能版本之一，不是最佳版本。有些不一定合适的处理是有意保留，而且没有刻意保持连贯一致，即同个表达法在同一讲话里的处理可能各不相同。这些做法都是为了从同传培训一开始就建立作为实战参照的质量标准。如果教材的译入语是经过修饰后的完善版本，这不仅是概念上的误导，而且会导致培训生无法达到教材里的准确度而丧失练习的信心。
   - 5.2. 由于上述原因，一定不可用笔译的准确标准来衡量同传的译入语版本，因为听同传的感觉和阅读文字完全不一样。
   - 5.3. 本教材有意没有提供视译中具体采取的是三词一译所需 10 大技巧中的哪一个，这是为了避免把练习的重点放在讲解技巧的概念上。

英译汉三词一译10大技巧

1. 缺省传译	2. 原话直译	3. 重复谓语	4. 介词转动
5. 先存后译	6. 反话正说	7. 被动变的	8. 点到为止
9. 预测先说	10. 弃卒保车		

限时视译

Pulling Together in Testing Times: Securing a Better Future for All

(*UN Secretary General Ban Ki-moon*)

Mr. President,
Distinguished Heads of State and Government,
Distinguished Delegates,
Ladies and Gentlemen,

Welcome to New York in this beautiful autumn season. And welcome to the opening of this 65th general debate.

Mr. President, congratulations. I look forward to working closely with you in the year ahead, across the full range of challenges facing our community of nations.

Excellencies, Ladies and Gentlemen,

We, the peoples of the United Nations, are bound by certain sacred duties and obligations. To care for the welfare of others. To resolve conflicts peacefully. To act in the world with empathy and understanding. To practice tolerance and mutual respect as a bedrock principle of civilization.

Today, we are being tested. Social inequalities are growing, among nations and within. Everywhere, people live in fear of losing jobs and incomes. Too many are caught in conflict, women and children are bearing the brunt. And we see a new politics at work—a politics of polarization.

We hear the language of hate, false divisions between "them" and "us", those who insist on "their way" or "no way." Amid such uncertainty, so much confusion of purpose, we naturally seek a moral compass. At the United Nations, we find the proper path in community, global cause, fair decisions, mutual responsibility for a destiny we share.

Excellencies, Ladies and Gentlemen,

This is the soul of global governance, the theme of this General Assembly. A collective stand, principled and pragmatic, against forces that would divide us. And that is why the United Nations remains the indispensable global institution for the 21st-century. As we gather today, in solidarity, let us recognize: This is a season for pulling together, for consolidating progress, for putting our shoulder to the wheel and delivering results. Real results, for people most in need, as only the United Nations can do.

Excellencies, Distinguished Delegates,

Together, over the past three years, we embraced an ambitious agenda, framed by three over-arching ideas for our time. A more prosperous world, free of the deepest poverty. A cleaner, greener and more sustainable world for our children. A safer world, free of nuclear weapons. Those are the great challenges of our era. They are not dreams. They are opportunities, within our power to grasp. Together, we have made progress.

We will press ahead — with fresh thinking, fresh approaches, a strong sense of leadership and political will. The Millennium Development Goals Summit showed our collective determination. World leaders came together with concrete national plans to meet the Millennium Development Goals by 2015. They agreed on a responsible and mutually accountable partnership, a partnership that will better the lives of billions of people within our generation.

Our challenge is to deliver on this promise, to turn hopes into realities. We must draw on lessons learned over the past decade: Helping people to help themselves; Investing resources where they have the greatest effect — smart investment in education, decent work, health, smallholder agriculture, infrastructure and green energy; The importance of putting women at the fore.

That is why, at the Summit, I welcomed the endorsement of our Global Strategy for Women and Children's Health. Backed by billions of dollars in new commitments, from governments, business, NGOs and philanthropic organizations, this was a tangible expression of global solidarity.

That is also why, last week, I named a dynamic new head of UN Women. In Michelle Bachelet, the former President of Chile, we found a global leader who can inspire millions of women and girls around the world. We must support her to the utmost. Because, by empowering women, we empower societies.

Ladies and Gentlemen,

Three years ago, we called climate change the "defining challenge" of our era, and so it remains. Clearly, the road toward a comprehensive, binding agreement, in Cancun and beyond ? will not be easy. And yet, we have made progress, and we can make more.

This is a year to build on important areas of agreement—on financing for adaptation and mitigation, on technology transfer, on capacity-building and preventing deforestation. In the longer-term, we face the "50-50-50 challenge." By 2050, the world's population will grow by 50 percent.

To keep climate change in check, we will need to cut greenhouse gas emissions by 50 percent by then. The world looks to us for creative solutions. And that is why, on Sunday, we hosted the first meeting of our high-level Panel on Global Sustainability. I am confident that it will stimulate new thinking as we work toward Rio+20 in 2012.

On nuclear disarmament, as well, we see new momentum: A new START agreement, the Summit on Nuclear Security, a successful NPT review conference. Our role is to keep pushing, to find a path to bring the Comprehensive Test Ban Treaty into force, to realize agreements on fissile materials and securing nuclear materials and facilities.

Tomorrow, we are hosting a high level meeting to rejuvenate the Conference on Disarmament. I believe the next few years will be critical. Will we advance our work on non-proliferation and disarmament, or will we slide back? It is up to us.

Excellencies, Ladies and Gentlemen,

As always, over the past year, we were there for those in urgent need: The people of Pakistan, coping with epic floods and the monumental task of reconstruction; The people of Haiti, where the work of rebuilding goes on, and where so many lost their lives, including 101 of our colleagues; The people of Somalia, Sudan, Niger, Gaza.

As always, we continue to work for peace and security.

Three years ago, in partnership with the African Union, we deployed the first peacekeeping force in Darfur. During the coming year, the United Nations will be critical to keeping a larger peace as north and south Sudan decide their future. Tomorrow's High-Level Meeting on Sudan will help chart that path.

In the Democratic Republic of the Congo, we have adapted our mission to new and changing circumstances. We have worked closely with the African Union in Somalia. We have seen victories for preventive diplomacy, as well. In Iraq, we helped broker the compromises that kept this year's elections on track.

In Guinea, we stand with regional partners in insisting on democracy. In Sierra Leone, we helped defuse confrontations and keep peace moving forward. Quick-footed diplomacy helped contain the troubles in Kyrgyzstan. In Afghanistan, we carry on our work despite exceptionally difficult security and humanitarian conditions.

We will seek to reduce tensions on the Korean Peninsula and encourage the Democratic People's Republic of Korea to return to the Six-Party Talks. On Iran, we continue to urge the government to engage constructively with the international community and comply fully with the relevant Security Council resolutions.

In the Middle East, we see encouraging movement toward a comprehensive peace. Working with the Quartet, we will do everything possible to help bring negotiations to a successful conclusion. I strongly discourage either side from any action that would hold back progress.

In all we do, human rights are at the core. There can be no peace without justice. The global community has worked hard and long to usher in a new "age of accountability." In our modern era, let us send a clear message: No nation, large or small, can violate the rights of its citizens with impunity.

Excellencies, Distinguished Delegates, Ladies and Gentlemen,

Let me close on a theme that has defined our work together: building a stronger UN for a better world. The renovation of our Secretariat is on track, on schedule, on budget. Organizational changes introduced over the past few years are bearing fruit. Among them: the "New Horizons" initiative to streamline peacekeeping operations. In consultation with the Member States and our staff, we will do all in our power to create a faster, more modern, flexible and effective UN workforce, to recruit the best talent of tomorrow.

Heads of State and Government, Distinguished Ministers, Ladies and Gentlemen,

Today and in the months ahead, we will speak of many things — important issues, affecting all humankind. Let us remember, in these difficult times: we are being tested. Let us remember: the many lives lost in service to our ideals. Let us remember: the world still looks to the United Nations for moral and political leadership.

The great goals are within reach. We can achieve them by looking forward, pulling together, uniting our strength as a community of nations, in the name of the larger good. Thank you very much, and I count on your leadership and commitment. Thank you.

技巧琢磨

Mr. President, Distinguished Heads of State and Government, Distinguished Delegates, Ladies and Gentlemen,

Welcome to New York in this beautiful autumn season.

And welcome to the opening of this 65th general debate.

❶ 主席先生、尊敬的国家与政府首脑们、尊敬的来宾们、女士们、先生们，欢迎来到纽约，在美丽的秋季来纽约。欢迎出席开幕式，第65届联大辩论开幕式。

❷ 主席先生、尊敬的首脑们、来宾们、女士们、先生们，欢迎来到纽约。欢迎参加第65届联大辩论的开幕式。

Mr. President, congratulations. I look forward to working closely with you in the year ahead, across the full range of challenges facing our community of nations.

Excellencies, Ladies and Gentlemen,

We, the peoples of the United Nations, are bound by certain sacred duties and obligations.

❶ 主席先生，祝贺你。我期待着与您在今后一年合作，应对所有挑战，我们联合国面临的挑战。阁下们，女士们、先生们，我们——联合国的人们，联系的原因是神圣的职责和义务。

❷ 主席先生，祝贺你。我期待着与您合作，在今后一年里应对所有挑战。阁下们、女士们、先生们，我们——联合国的人们，由神圣的职责和义务联系起来。

To care for the welfare of others. To resolve conflicts peacefully. To act in the world with empathy and under-standing. To practice tolerance and mutual respect as a bedrock principle of civilization.

Today, we are being tested. Social inequalities are growing, among nations and within.

❶ 关心他人的福利。解决冲突，和平地解决。行动有同理心和理解。实践容忍和相互尊重，以此为文明的原则。

今天，我们正在接受考验。社会不平等在增加，国家之间和之内都如此。

❷ 关心他人，和平地解决冲突。行动时富有同理心和理解，容忍并相互尊重，以此作为基本原则。

今天，我们正被考验。社会不平等在增加。

Everywhere, people live in fear of losing jobs and incomes. Too many are caught in conflict, women and children are bearing the brunt. And we see a new politics at work—a politics of polarization. We hear the language of hate, false divisions between "them" and "us", those who insist on "their way" or "no way." Amid such uncertainty, so much confusion of purpose, we naturally seek a moral compass.

❶ 无论何处，人们都害怕失去工作和收入。太多人陷入冲突，女人和儿童首当其冲。我们看到新的政治出现：两极分化的政治。我们听到的语言有憎恨，错误地区分他们和我们，那些人坚持他们的路，否则无路可走。这种不确定中，太多目的的困惑，我们自然寻求道德指南针。

❷ 无论哪里，人们都在担心失业。太多人陷入冲突，女人和儿童尤其遭殃。我们看到新的政治：两极分化。我们听到仇恨的语言，错误地区分他们和我们，那些人坚持不依他们不行。如此不确定、困惑，分不清目的，我们当然要寻找指南针。

At the United Nations, we find the proper path in community, global cause, fair decisions, mutual responsibility for a destiny we share. Excellencies, Ladies and Gentlemen, This is the soul of global governance, the theme of this General Assembly.

❶ 在联合国，我们找到合适的道路，社区、全球事业、公平决定、共同责任、共同的命运。阁下们、女士们、先生们，这是灵魂，全球治理的灵魂，是主题，本届大会的主题。

❷ 在联合国，我们找到合适的道路，即社区、全球事业、公平决定、共担责任、休戚与共。阁下们、女士们、先生们，这是全球治理的灵魂，本届大会的主题。

A collective stand, principled and pragmatic, against forces that would divide us. And that is why the United Nations remains the indispensable global institution for the 21st-century.

❶ 集体立场，讲原则，重实效，反对那些分裂我们的力量。这就是为何联合国仍然是不可缺少的全球机构，21 世纪不可缺少。

As we gather today, in solidarity, let us recognize: this is a season for pulling together, for consolidating

我们今天聚集一堂，团结起来，让我们认识到：现在要共同努力，巩固进展，把肩膀顶到车轮上，实现结果。真实的结果，为了最需要的人民，只有联合国才能做到。

progress, for putting our shoulder to the wheel and delivering results. Real results, for people most in need, as only the United Nations can do.

Excellencies, Distinguished Delegates,

Together, over the past three years, we embraced an ambitious agenda, framed by three overarching ideas for our time. A more prosperous world, free of the deepest poverty. A cleaner, greener and more sustainable world for our children. A safer world, free of nuclear weapons.

Those are the great challenges of our era. They are not dreams. They are opportunities, within our power to grasp. Together, we have made progress. We will press ahead—with fresh thinking, fresh approaches, a strong sense of leadership and political will. The Millennium Development Goals Summit showed our collective determination. World leaders came together with concrete national plans to meet the Millennium Development Goals by 2015.

团结、原则、务实、反对分裂我们的力量。为此，联合国仍然不可缺，在21世纪仍然很重要。

我们聚集一堂，团结一致，认识到：现在需要一起使劲，巩固进展，挽起袖子，做出成果。真正的成果，为最需要帮助的人提供，只有联合国才能做到。

阁下们、尊敬的代表们，过去三年，我们拥抱雄心勃勃的议程，框架里有三个总体信念，是我们时代的：一个更繁荣的世界，没有赤贫的世界；一个更清洁、更环保、更可持续的世界，为了后代的世界；一个更安全、无核武器的世界。

阁下们、代表们，过去三年，我们一起致力于雄心勃勃的议程，框架里有三个总体的，我们时代的信念：一个更繁荣的世界，无赤贫；更清洁、更环保、更可持续、造福后代的世界；一个更安全、没有核武器的世界。

这些是巨大挑战，我们时代的挑战。它们不是梦想，是机遇，我们的力量可以抓住。我们共同取得了进步。我们将推进，用新思维、新做法、强大的领导意识和政治意愿推进。千年发展目标高峰会显示了我们的集体决心。世界领袖齐聚一堂，以具体的国家计划，旨在实现千年发展目标，2015年之前实现。

这些是巨大挑战，不是梦想，是机遇，我们可以抓住。我们携手取得进步。我们将继续努力，要有新思维、新做法、强烈的领导意识和政治意愿。千年发展目标高峰会显示了我们的决心。世界领导人带来了国家计划，以实现千年发展目标，不迟于2015年。

They agreed on a responsible and mutually accountable partnership, a partnership that will better the lives of billions of people within our generation. Our challenge is to deliver on this promise, to turn hopes into realities. We must draw on lessons learned over the past decade: Helping people to help themselves; Investing resources where they have the greatest effect—smart investment in education, decent work, health, smallholder agriculture, infrastructure and green energy;

❶ 他们商定了一个负责、互相问责的伙伴关系，将改善生活，惠及数十亿人，在我们这代人实现。我们的挑战是实现这个承诺，变希望为现实。我们必须吸取教训，过去十年的教训。帮助人们自助；投资资源到有最大效果之处，明智地投资于教育、体面的工作、保健、小户农业、基础设施和绿色能源；

❷ 他们商定了一个负责、互相问责的伙伴关系，这将改善数亿人的生活。我们的挑战是实现承诺，让希望成真。我们必须吸取过去十年的教训。帮助人们自助；投资资源，以获得最大效果，明智地投资于教育、就业、卫生、小农业、基础设施和绿色能源；

The importance of putting women at the fore. That is why, at the Summit, I welcomed the endorsement of our Global Strategy for Women and Children's Health. Backed by billions of dollars in new commitments, from governments, business, NGOs and philanthropic organizations, this was a tangible expression of global solidarity. That is also why, last week, I named a dynamic new head of UN Women. In Michelle Bachelet, the former President of Chile, we found a global leader who can inspire millions of women and girls around the world. We must support her to the utmost. Because, by

❶ 重要的是让妇女成为重点。因此在峰会上，我欢迎赞同我们的全球战略——妇女和儿童的保健战略。支持来自数十亿美元的新承诺，来自政府、企业、非政府组织和慈善组织，这是具体表现——全球团结的表现。这也是为何上周我任命了一位充满活力的新领导人，联合国妇女署的领导人。米歇尔·巴舍莱是智利前总统，我们找到了一位全球领导人，她能激励数以百万计的妇女和女孩，在全世界都有影响。我们必须支持她，全力支持。因为，给以妇女力量，我们就能增强社会的力量。

❷ 必须让妇女成为重点。因此在峰会上，我很高兴，我们的全球妇女和儿童保健战略得到了赞同。提供支持的数十亿

empowering women, we empower societies.

美元都是新承诺，来自政府、企业、非政府组织和慈善组织，这些都具体地表现出全球的团结。为此，上周，我任命了一位充满活力的人来领导联合国妇女署。在米歇尔·巴舍莱这位智利前总统身上，我们看到了一位全球领导人，她能激励数以百万计的妇女和女孩，无论在哪个国家。我们必须支持她。因为，给了妇女力量，就是给予社会力量。

Ladies and Gentlemen,

Three years ago, we called climate change the "defining challenge" of our era, and so it remains.

Clearly, the road toward a comprehensive, binding agreement, in Cancun and beyond will not be easy.

And yet, we have made pro-gress, and we can make more. This is a year to build on important areas of agreement—on financing for adaptation and mitigation, on technology transfer, on capacity-building and preventing deforestation. In the longer-term, we face the "50-50-50 challenge."

① 女士们、先生们，三年前，我们称气候变化为“定义式的挑战”，它依然如此。显然，道路，达成全面、有约束力的协议的道路，在坎昆会议及以后都不易。但是，我们已经取得了进展，而且可以取得更多。今年，要达成在协议重要领域的共识，包括资助适应和减缓气变、技术转让、能力建设、防止毁林。从长远来看，我们面临着“50-50-50 挑战”。

② 女士们、先生们，三年前，我们称气候变化为“定义式的挑战”，现在还是。显然，一个全面、有约束力的协议在坎昆及其后都不易达成。但我们已经有进展了，还能继续进展。今年，重要领域需要有共识，比如资助适应和减缓气变、技术转让、能力建设、防止毁林。长远看，我们面临“50-50-50 挑战”。

By 2050, the world's population will grow by 50 percent. To keep climate change in check, we will need to cut greenhouse gas emissions by 50 percent by then. The world looks to us for creative solutions. And that is why, on

① 到 2050 年，世界人口将增加 50%。为了保证气候变化受控制，我们需要减少温室气体排放达 50%。世界期待我们找出具有创意的解决方案。正因如此，周日，我们举行了全球可持续性高级小组首次会议。我相信，它将激发新思维，伴

Sunday, we hosted the first meeting of our high-level Panel on Global Sustainability. I am confident that it will stimulate new thinking as we work toward Rio+20 in 2012. On nuclear disarmament, as well, we see new momentum: A new START agreement, the Summit on Nuclear Security, a successful NPT review conference.

随我们走向“里约 +20”这个 2012 年的会议。在核裁军方面，我们也看到了新的势头：新的裁武协定、核安全峰会、成功的《不扩散条约》回顾大会。

2050 年，人口将增加 50%。为了保持气候，需要减排 50%，不迟于 2050 年。世界等着我们找到创造性的方案。为此，我们周日举行了第一次全球可持续性高级小组会议。我相信，这将激发新思维，我们的“里约 +20”会议将于 2012 年召开。核裁军也有了新势头：新的裁武协定、核安全首脑会议、成功举行《不扩散条约》回顾大会。

Our role is to keep pushing, to find a path to bring the Comprehensive Test Ban Treaty into force, to realize agreements on fissile materials and securing nuclear materials and facilities. Tomorrow, we are hosting a high level meeting to rejuvenate the Conference on Disarmament. I believe the next few years will be critical. Will we advance our work on non-proliferation and disarmament, or will we slide back? It is up to us.

我们的作用是不断推动，找到途径，促使《全面禁止核试验条约》生效，达成协定，关于裂变材料和保护核材料与设施的协定。明天，我们将举行高级别会议，以重振裁军大会。我相信，今后几年将至关重要。我们推进工作，促进不扩散和裁军？还是我们将倒退？这取决于我们。

我们的作用是不断推动，找到途径，促使《禁止试验条约》生效，达成有关裂变材料和保护核材料与核设施的协议。我们将举行高级别会议，重振裁军大会。今后几年至关重要。我们将推进不扩散和裁军还是倒退？要看我们的。

Excellencies, Ladies and Gentlemen,

As always, over the past year, we were there for those in urgent need: The people of Pakistan, coping with

各位阁下、女士们、先生们，一如既往，过去一年来，我们在那里，帮助迫切需要帮助的人们：巴基斯坦人遇到特大洪水、面临艰巨任务，需要重建；海地人，在那里的重建正在进行，有很多

epic floods and the monumental task of reconstruction; The people of Haiti, where the work of rebuilding goes on, and where so many lost their lives, including 101 of our colleagues; The people of Somalia, Sudan, Niger, Gaza. As always, we continue to work for peace and security. Three years ago, in partnership with the African Union, we deployed the first peacekeeping force in Darfur.

人丧生，包括101位我们的同事；索马里人、苏丹人、尼日尔人、加沙人。一如既往，我们继续为和平与安全工作。三年前，在与非洲联盟的合作下，我们部署了第一支维和部队——在达尔富尔。

❷ 阁下们、女士们、先生们，一如既往，过去一年来，我们在帮助迫切需要帮助的人：巴基斯坦人正在应对特大洪水和艰巨的重建任务；海地人正在重建家园，有很多人丧生，包括101位我们的同事；还有索马里人、苏丹人、尼日尔人和加沙人。一如既往，我们继续工作，推动和平与安全。三年前，与非洲联盟合作，我们部署了首支维和部队——在达尔富尔。

During the coming year, the United Nations will be critical to keeping a larger peace as north and south Sudan decide their future. Tomorrow's High-Level Meeting on Sudan will help chart that path. In the Democratic Republic of the Congo, we have adapted our mission to new and changing circumstances. We have worked closely with the African Union in Somalia. We have seen victories for preventive diplomacy, as well. In Iraq, we helped broker the compromises that kept this year's elections on track. In Guinea, we stand with regional partners in insisting on democracy. Quick-footed diplomacy helped contain the troubles in Kyrgyzstan.

❶ 明年，联合国将至关重要，要维持更大范围的和平，因为北、南苏丹要决定自己的未来。明天的高级别会议将讨论苏丹问题，帮助规划道路。在刚果民主共和国，我们调整了任务，以适应新的和变化的情况。我们密切合作，与非洲联盟合作，在索马里合作。我们看到了预防性外交的胜利。在伊拉克，我们帮助达成妥协，使今年的选举能如期进行。在几内亚，我们与区域合作伙伴合作，坚持民主。迅速的外交帮助控制了吉尔吉斯斯坦的骚乱。

❷ 明年，联合国将要维持更大范围的和平，因为北、南苏丹要决定他们的未来。明天的会议将帮助制定前进的道路。在刚果民主共和国，我们调整了任务，以适应新情况。我们与非洲联盟密切合作，在索马里工作。我们看到了胜利，预

防性外交的胜利。在伊拉克，我们促成妥协，保证了今年的选举。在几内亚，我们与区域伙伴合作，坚持民主。迅速的外交帮助控制了骚乱，稳定了吉尔吉斯斯坦。

In Sierra Leone, we helped defuse confrontations and keep peace moving forward. In Afghanistan, we carry on our work despite exceptionally difficult security and humanitarian conditions. We will seek to reduce tensions on the Korean Peninsula and encourage the Democratic People's Republic of Korea to return to the Six-Party Talks. On Iran, we continue to urge the government to engage constructively with the international community and comply fully with the relevant Security Council resolutions.

❶ 在塞拉利昂，我们帮助化解了对抗，使和平进程向前。在阿富汗，我们继续工作，尽管异常艰难的安全和人道主义条件很不利。我们将力求减少紧张局势，朝鲜半岛的紧张局势，鼓励朝鲜民主主义人民共和国重返六方会谈。在伊朗问题上，我们继续敦促伊朗政府建设性地接触国际社会，全面遵守相关的安理会决议。

❷ 在塞拉利昂，我们化解对抗，推动和平进程。在阿富汗，我们继续工作，不顾非常严峻的安全和人道主义环境。我们将力求减少紧张，稳定朝鲜半岛，鼓励北朝鲜重返六方会谈。在伊朗问题上，我们继续敦促其政府以建设性态度与国际社会接触，遵守安理会决议。

In the Middle East, we see encouraging movement toward a comprehensive peace. Working with the Quartet, we will do everything possible to help bring negotiations to a successful conclusion. I strongly discourage either side from any action that would hold back progress. In all we do, human rights are at the core. There can be no peace without justice. The global community has worked hard and long to usher in a

❶ 在中东，我们看到了令人鼓舞的动向，实现全面和平的动向。与四方合作，我们将尽力促使谈判取得圆满成功。 我力劝任何一方不要采取任何行动，阻碍进展的行动。在我们的所有工作中，人权都是核心。要有和平，就要有正义。国际社会努力地长期工作，是为迎来一个新的“问责制时代”。

❷ 在中东，我们看到了令人鼓舞的动向，有助于全面和平。我们与四方合作，尽力促成谈判。 我力劝各方不要采取

new "age of accountability."

行动阻碍进展。我们的工作中，人权是核心。要有和平，就要有正义。国际社会长期的努力就是为迎来一个新的"问责制时代"。

In our modern era, let us send a clear message: No nation, large or small, can violate the rights of its citizens with impunity. Excellencies, Distinguished Delegates, Ladies and Gentlemen, Let me close on a theme that has defined our work together: building a stronger UN for a better world. The renovation of our Secretariat is on track, on schedule, on budget. Organizational changes introduced over the past few years are bearing fruit. Among them: the "New Horizons" initiative to streamline peacekeeping operations.

❶ 在现代社会，让我们发出明确信息：任何国家，不论大小，都不可侵犯其公民的权利而不受惩罚。阁下们、尊敬的代表们、女士们、先生们，最后，我要说的主题定义了我们的共同工作：建设一个更强大的联合国，建设一个更好的世界。翻修联合国秘书处的工作在按计划、按时、按预算进行。组织改革在过去几年的推行，正在日益见效。其中有"新地平线"倡议，以精简维持和平行动。

❷ 在当今时代，让我们发出明确信息：任何国家，不论大小，都不可侵犯公民的权利而不受惩罚。各位阁下，代表们，女士们，先生们，最后，我要说的正是我们共同工作的内容：建设一个更强大的联合国，以实现一个更美好的世界。装修秘书处的工作在顺利、按时、按预算进行。组织改革的推行是几年前开始的，已经见效。其中的"新地平线"倡议是为了精简维持和平行动。

In consultation with the Member States and our staff, we will do all in our power to create a faster, more modern, flexible and effective UN workforce, to recruit the best talent of tomorrow. Heads of State and Government, Distinguished Ministers, Ladies and Gentlemen, Today and in the months ahead, we

❶ 在与会员国和工作人员协商后，我们将尽力建设一个更快、更现代化、更灵活和更有效的联合国工作队伍，征聘未来最优秀的人才。国家与政府首脑们、尊敬的部长们、女士们，先生们，今天以及今后几个月，我们将要讨论许多事情——重要议题，关乎全人类。让我们记住，在这艰难的时期：我们正经受考验。

will speak of many things—important issues, affecting all humankind. Let us remember, in these difficult times: we are being tested.

与会员国和工作人员磋商，我们将尽力建立更快、更现代化、更灵活和更有效的联合国队伍，招聘最优秀的人才。首脑们、部长们、女士们、先生们，今天及今后几个月，我们将要讨论许多事情——重要的关乎全人类的议题。别忘记，在这艰难的时候：我们正经受考验。

Let us remember: the many lives lost in service to our ideals. Let us remember: the world still looks to the United Nations for moral and political leadership. The great goals are within reach. We can achieve them by looking forward, pulling together, uniting our strength as a community of nations, in the name of the larger good.

Thank you very much, and I count on your leadership and commitment. Thank you.

我们不能忘记：许多人丧生，是为了我们的理想。

我们不能忘记：世界仍然期待联合国提供道义支持和政治领导。宏伟目标是可实现的。我们能够实现目标，通过放眼未来，共同努力，团结力量，形成国际社区，为了更广泛的利益努力。

谢谢，我仰赖你们的领导力和承诺。谢谢。

让我们记住：许多人丧生，为了我们的理想丧生。让我们记住：世界仍然期待联合国发挥领导作用。宏伟目标是可实现的。我们能够实现目标，只要我们放眼未来，共同努力，团结力量，形成国际社区，就能做到。

谢谢，我仰赖各位了。谢谢。

2.美国总统奥巴马讲话

使用提要

1. 所有练习单元的讲话稿均以两种形式提供。第一种采用常见的讲话稿形式，便于练习限时视译。第二种采用对照、对比形式，便于练习、琢磨三词一译的技巧。
2. 限时视译部分是讲话稿全文，可以根据需要选用。但是在技巧琢磨部分里，只有前半部分的讲话配有参考译入语以保证每个单元的练习长度大体相同。
3. 为了示范如何在视译的讨论阶段达到两个方案的要求，本单元和第一单元的参考译入语都有两个版本。其他单元只有一个版本。
4. 限时视译的速度在这个单元还可以是每秒 2 个英文单词，每次大约 40 秒左右的量，即大约 80 个单词。但是在 3 个单元以后必须提高到每秒 3 个单词，这是实战同传必须达到的速度。
5. 在使用或者参照译入语时必须注意：

   5.1. 参考译入语只是诸多可能版本之一，不是最佳版本。有些不一定合适的处理是有意保留，而且没有刻意保持连贯一致，即同个表达法在同一讲话里的处理可能各不相同。这些做法都是为了从同传培训一开始就建立作为实战参照的质量标准。如果教材的译入语是经过修饰后的完善版本，这不仅是概念上的误导，而且会导致培训生无法达到教材里的准确度而丧失练习的信心。

   5.2. 由于上述原因，一定不可用笔译的准确标准来衡量同传的译入语版本，因为听同传的感觉和阅读文字完全不一样。

   5.3. 本教材有意没有提供视译中具体采取的是三词一译所需 10 大技巧中的哪一个，这是为了避免把练习的重点放在讲解技巧的概念上。

英译汉三词一译10大技巧

1. 缺省传译	2. 原话直译	3. 重复谓语	4. 介词转动
5. 先存后译	6. 反话正说	7. 被动变的	8. 点到为止
9. 预测先说	10. 弃卒保车		

限时视译

Remarks at United Nation's Climate Change Summit

(*US President Barack Obama*)

Thank you very much. Good morning. I want to thank the Secretary General for organizing this summit, and all the leaders who are participating. That so many of us are here today is a recognition that the threat from climate change is serious, it is urgent, and it is growing. Our generation's response to this challenge will be judged by history, for if we fail to meet it—boldly, swiftly, and together—we risk consigning future generations to an irreversible catastrophe.

No nation, however large or small, wealthy or poor, can escape the impact of climate change. Rising sea levels threaten every coastline. More powerful storms and floods threaten every continent. More frequent droughts and crop failures breed hunger and conflict in places where hunger and conflict already thrive. On shrinking islands, families are already being forced to flee their homes as climate refugees. The security and stability of each nation and all peoples—our prosperity, our health, and our safety—are in jeopardy. And the time we have to reverse this tide is running out.

And yet, we can reverse it. John F. Kennedy once observed that "Our problems are man-made, therefore they may be solved by man." It is true that for too many years, mankind has been slow to respond or even recognize the magnitude of the climate threat. It is true of my own country, as well. We recognize that. But this is a new day. It is a new era. And I am proud to say that the United States has done more to promote clean energy and reduce carbon pollution in the last eight months than at any other time in our history.

We are making our government's largest ever investment in renewable energy—an investment aimed at doubling the generating capacity from wind and other renewable resources in three years. Across America, entrepreneurs are constructing wind turbines and solar panels and batteries for hybrid cars with the help of loan guarantees and tax credits—projects that are creating new jobs and new industries. We're investing billions to cut energy waste in our homes, our buildings, and appliances—helping

American families save money on energy bills in the process.

We've proposed the very first national policy aimed at both increasing fuel economy and reducing greenhouse gas pollution for all new cars and trucks — a standard that will also save consumers money and our nation oil. We're moving forward with our nation's first offshore wind energy projects. We're investing billions to capture carbon pollution so that we can clean up our coal plants. And just this week, we announced that for the first time ever, we'll begin tracking how much greenhouse gas pollution is being emitted throughout the country.

Later this week, I will work with my colleagues at the G20 to phase out fossil fuel subsidies so that we can better address our climate challenge. And already, we know that the recent drop in overall U.S. emissions is due in part to steps that promote greater efficiency and greater use of renewable energy.

Most importantly, the House of Representatives passed an energy and climate bill in June that would finally make clean energy the profitable kind of energy for American businesses and dramatically reduce greenhouse gas emissions. One committee has already acted on this bill in the Senate and I look forward to engaging with others as we move forward.

Because no one nation can meet this challenge alone, the United States has also engaged more allies and partners in finding a solution than ever before. In April, we convened the first of what have now been six meetings of the Major Economies Forum on Energy and Climate here in the United States. In Trinidad, I proposed an Energy and Climate Partnership for the Americas. We've worked through the World Bank to promote renewable energy projects and technologies in the developing world. And we have put climate at the top of our diplomatic agenda when it comes to our relationships with countries as varied as China and Brazil; India and Mexico; from the continent of Africa to the continent of Europe.

Taken together, these steps represent a historic recognition on behalf of the American people and their government. We understand the gravity of the climate threat. We are determined to act. And we will meet our responsibility to future generations.

But though many of our nations have taken bold action and share in this determination, we did not come here to celebrate progress today. We came because there's so much more progress to be made. We came because there's so much more work to be done.

It is work that will not be easy. As we head towards Copenhagen, there should be no illusions that the hardest part of our journey is in front of us. We seek sweeping but necessary change in the midst of a global recession, where every nation's most immediate priority is reviving their economy and putting their people back to work. And so all of us will face doubts and difficulties in our own capitals as we try to reach a lasting solution to the climate challenge.

But I'm here today to say that difficulty is no excuse for complacency. Unease is no excuse for inaction. And we must not allow the perfect to become the enemy of progress. Each of us must do what we can when we can to grow our economies without endangering our planet—and we must all do it together. We must seize the opportunity to make Copenhagen a significant step forward in the global fight against climate change.

We also cannot allow the old divisions that have characterized the climate debate for so many years to block our progress. Yes, the developed nations that caused much of the damage to our climate over the last century still have a responsibility to lead—and that includes the United States. And we will continue to do so—by investing in renewable energy and promoting greater efficiency and slashing our emissions to reach the targets we set for 2020 and our long-term goal for 2050.

But those rapidly growing developing nations that will produce nearly all the growth in global carbon emissions in the decades ahead must do their part, as well. Some of these nations have already made great strides with the development and deployment of clean energy. Still, they need to commit to strong measures at home and agree to stand behind those commitments just as the developed nations must stand behind their own. We cannot meet this challenge unless all the largest emitters of greenhouse gas pollution act together. There's no other way.

We must also energize our efforts to put other developing nations—especially the poorest and most vulnerable—on a path to sustained growth. These nations do not have the same resources to combat climate change as countries like the United States or China do, but they have the most immediate stake in a solution. For these are the nations that are already living with the unfolding effects of a warming planet—famine, drought, disappearing coastal villages, and the conflicts that arise from scarce resources. Their future is no longer a choice between a growing economy and a cleaner planet, because their survival depends on both. It will do little good to alleviate poverty if you can no longer harvest your crops or find drinkable water.

And that is why we have a responsibility to provide the financial and technical assistance needed to help these nations adapt to the impacts of climate change and pursue low-carbon development.

What we are seeking, after all, is not simply an agreement to limit greenhouse gas emissions. We seek an agreement that will allow all nations to grow and raise living standards without endangering the planet. By developing and disseminating clean technology and sharing our know-how, we can help developing nations leap-frog dirty energy technologies and reduce dangerous emissions.

Mr. Secretary, as we meet here today, the good news is that after too many years of inaction and denial, there's finally widespread recognition of the urgency of the challenge before us. We know what needs to be done. We know that our planet's future depends on a global commitment to permanently reduce greenhouse gas pollution. We know that if we put the right rules and incentives in place, we will unleash the creative power of our best scientists and engineers and entrepreneurs to build a better world. And so many nations have already taken the first step on the journey towards that goal.

But the journey is long and the journey is hard. And we don't have much time left to make that journey. It's a journey that will require each of us to persevere through setbacks, and fight for every inch of progress, even when it comes in fits and starts. So let us begin. For if we are flexible and pragmatic, if we can resolve to work tirelessly in common effort, then we will achieve our common purpose: a world that is safer, cleaner, and healthier than the one we found; and a future that is worthy of our children.

Thank you very much.

技巧琢磨

Thank you very much. Good morning.

I want to thank the Secretary General for organizing this summit, and all the leaders who are participating. That so many of us are here today is a recognition that the threat from climate change is serious, it is urgent, and it is growing. Our generation's response to this challenge will be judged by history, for if we fail to meet it — boldly, swiftly, and together — we risk consigning future generations to an irreversible catastrophe.

感谢各位。早上好。我想谢谢秘书长组织此次峰会。谢谢所有领导人的参加。我们这么多人都来了，表明我们认识到气候变化的威胁很严峻、急迫，并且越来越大。我们这一代人的回应，对于挑战的回应会被评判，由历史评判。如果失败了，没有大胆的、迅速的、共同的应对，我们就有可能将子孙后代置于不可逆转的灾难。

感谢各位。早上好。我想感谢秘书长组织此次峰会。谢谢所有领导人的参加。我们这么多人都来了，表明我们认识到了气候变化的威胁很严峻、急迫，并且越来越大。我们这代人回应挑战的评判将由历史做出。如果没有成功，不能大胆、迅速、共同地行动，我们就会将后代置于不可逆转的灾难。

No nation, however large or small, wealthy or poor, can escape the impact of climate change. Rising sea levels threaten every coastline. More powerful storms and floods threaten every continent. More frequent droughts and crop failures breed hunger and conflict in places where hunger and conflict already thrive. On shrinking islands, families are already being forced to flee their homes as climate

任何国家，不论大小贫富，都不能逃离影响——气候变化的影响。上升的海平面威胁着所有海岸。更强大的风暴与洪水威胁着每个大陆。更频繁的干旱，作物歉收带来饥饿与冲突，而这些地方的饥饿与冲突本来就很严重。不断缩小的岛屿上，许多家庭已经被迫逃离家园，成了气候难民。安全与稳定，每个国家和人民的安全与稳定、繁荣、健康和安全都受到了威胁。我们的时间，想要逆转这个潮流的时间已经不多了。

refugees. The security and stability of each nation and all peoples — our prosperity, our health, and our safety — are in jeopardy. And the time we have to reverse this tide is running out.

②国家不论大小贫富，都不能逃离气候变化的影响。上升的海平面威胁着所有海岸。更大的风暴与洪水威胁着每个大陆。更加频繁的干旱、作物歉收导致了本来充满饥饿与冲突的地区饥饿、冲突频繁。不断缩小的岛屿上，许多家庭已经被迫逃离。安全与稳定无论哪个国家和人民，我们的繁荣、健康和安全都面临威胁。我们的时间，要想逆转这一趋势，越来越紧迫了。

And yet, we can reverse it. John F. Kennedy once observed that "Our problems are manmade, therefore they may be solved by man." It is true that for too many years, mankind has been slow to respond or even recognize the magnitude of the climate threat. It is true of my own country, as well. We recognize that. But this is a new day. It is a new era. And I am proud to say that the United States has done more to promote clean energy and reduce carbon pollution in the last eight months than at any other time in our history.

①但是，我们可以逆转潮流。肯尼迪曾经说到："我们的问题是人为的，所以问题的解决靠人。"确实，多年来，人类都很慢地回应，甚至不承认程度——气候变化的程度。我自己的国家也是如此。我们承认这点。但，这是新的一天，新的时代。我自豪地说，美国已经做了很多，宣传清洁能源，减少碳污染，过去8个月做的超过了以往。

②但是，我们可以做到。肯尼迪说过："我们的问题是人为的，所以解决要靠人。"多年来，人类速度慢，没有快速地回应，甚至不承认气候变化的程度。我自己的国家也是如此。我们承认这点。但，这是新的一天，新时代。我自豪地说，美国努力宣传清洁能源，减少碳污染，过去8个月的努力超过历史其他时期。

We are making our government's largest ever investment in renewable energy — an investment aimed at doubling the generating capacity from wind and other renewable resources in three

①我们正在做政府有史以来最大的投资，发展可再生能源，旨在增加一倍的发电能力，把风能和其他可再生能源发电增加一倍——这是三年的项目。美国的创业家正在建设风力涡轮机、太阳能板和电池，

years. Across America, entrepreneurs are constructing wind turbines and solar panels and batteries for hybrid cars with the help of loan guarantees and tax credits—projects that are creating new jobs and new industries. We're investing billions to cut energy waste in our homes, our buildings, and appliances—helping American families save money on energy bills in the process.

用于混合动力汽车，还得到了贷款担保和税收优惠，这些项目正在创造新的就业机会和新的产业。我们投资数十亿，减少能源浪费，家庭的浪费、建筑和电器的浪费，帮助美国家庭省钱——省能源账单的钱。

❷ 我们正在做出有史以来最大的投资，投入可再生能源，旨在增加发电能力，把风能和其他可再生能源翻一番，在三年后完成。美国的创业家正在建设风力涡轮机、太阳能板和电池，用于混合动力汽车，再加上贷款担保和税收优惠，这些项目创造新的就业机会和产业。我们投资数十亿，减少来自家庭、建筑和电器上的能源浪费，帮助美国家庭减少能源开支。

We've proposed the very first national policy aimed at both increasing fuel economy and reducing greenhouse gas pollution for all new cars and trucks—a standard that will also save consumers money and our nation oil. We're moving forward with our nation's first offshore wind energy projects. We're investing billions to capture carbon pollution so that we can clean up our coal plants. And just this week, we announced that for the first time ever, we'll begin tracking how much greenhouse gas pollution is being emitted throughout the country.

❶ 我们已经提议了第一个国家政策，节约燃料、减少温室气体污染的政策，减少所有新车的污染，这一标准还将节约消费者的钱和全国的油。我们正在推进美国第一个海上风能项目。我们投资数十亿来捕捉碳，让煤电厂更清洁。本周，我们宣布了，我们将首次开始跟踪温室气体排放全国有多少。

❷ 我们提出了国家政策，旨在节约燃料、减少所有新车的温室气体污染，新标准还能为消费者省钱，为美国省油。我们正推进美国的海上风能项目。我们投资数十亿来捕捉碳，从而清理我们的煤电厂。就在本周我们宣布将开始跟踪温室气体在美国的排放量。

Later this week, I will work with my colleagues at the G20 to phase out fossil fuel subsidies so that we can better address our climate challenge. And already, we know that the recent drop in overall U.S. emissions is due in part to steps that promote greater efficiency and greater use of renewable energy.

❶ 本周稍晚，我将和同事们一起在G20逐步淘汰化石燃料补贴，从而可以更好地处理气候变化问题。我们知道最近的减少——美国总排放的减少的部分原因就是我们宣传更高的效率，更多的使用可再生能源。

❷ 本周稍晚，我将和同事们在G20分期结束化石燃料补贴，以便更好地应对气变。我们知道，近来美国总排放减少的部分原因是我们倡导提高效率，多使用可再生能源。

Most importantly, the House of Representatives passed an energy and climate bill in June that would finally make clean energy the profitable kind of energy for American businesses and dramatically reduce greenhouse gas emissions. One committee has already acted on this bill in the Senate and I look forward to engaging with others as we move forward.

❶ 更重要的是，众议院通过了一个能源与气候法案，6月通过的，这最终将使清洁能源变成有利可图的能源，让美国公司能赚钱并且大幅减少温室气体排放。一个委员会已经开始行动——在参议院开展行动，我期待参与，一起向前。

❷ 更重要的是，众议院通过了一个能源与气候法案，这将使清洁能源最终有利可图，让美国公司愿意做，同时大幅减少温室气体排放。有个委员会已经采取行动，在参议院努力，我期待能与其他人一起推进此事。

Because no one nation can meet this challenge alone, the United States has also engaged more allies and partners in finding a solution than ever before. In April, we convened the first of what have now been six meetings of the Major Economies Forum on Energy and Climate here in the United States.

❶ 因为没有一个国家能够解决这一挑战，单打独斗不行，美国已经联合了很多同盟和伙伴方一起寻找解决方案，阵容超过以往。4月，我们召开了首次会议，现在已经开了6次，是主要经济国的能源与气候论坛。在特立尼达，我提议了建立能源与气候伙伴关系，由美洲国家参加。我们与世行合作，促进可再生能

In Trinidad, I proposed an Energy and Climate Partnership for the Americas. We've worked through the World Bank to promote renewable energy projects and technologies in the developing world. And we have put climate at the top of our diplomatic agenda when it comes to our relationships with countries as varied as China and Brazil; India and Mexico; from the continent of Africa to the continent of Europe.

源项目和技术在发展中国家的发展。我们把气候放在首位，外交议程的首位，我们与其他国家的关系，比如中国和巴西、印度和墨西哥、非洲大陆和欧洲大陆等等都注重气变。

❷ 因为没有哪个国家能够自己解决这一挑战。美国联合了很多联盟和伙伴方一起寻找解决方案。4 月，我们召开了第 6 次会议，主要经济体能源与气候论坛，就在美国举行。在特立尼达岛，我提议的能源与气候伙伴关系是为全美洲考虑的。我们通过世行促进可再生能源项目和技术在发展中国家的发展。我们把气候放在外交议程的首位，以此发展我们与其他国家的关系，比如中国、巴西、印度、墨西哥、非洲大陆、欧洲大陆等等。

Taken together, these steps represent a historic recognition on behalf of the American people and their government. We understand the gravity of the climate threat. We are determined to act. And we will meet our responsibility to future generations.

But though many of our nations have taken bold action and share in this determination, we did not come here to celebrate progress today. We came because there's so much more progress to be made. We came because there's so much more work to be done.

❶ 总体来看，这些步骤代表了历史性的认知，美国人民与政府都理解气候威胁的严重性。我们决意行动，担负起责任，为后代负责。但是，尽管许多国家采取了大胆的行动、拥有这一决心，但是我们不是来这里庆祝进展的，我们来这里是因为还需要取得更大的进展，因为还有许多工作要做。

❷ 这些步骤代表了历史性的认知，美国人民与政府认识到，气候威胁很严重。我们决意行动，担负起后代的责任。但是，虽然许多国家采取了大胆的行动，拥有同样的决心，但是我们来这里不是庆祝进展，而是还有很多进展有待取得，还有很多工作要做。

It is work that will not be easy. As we head towards Copenhagen, there should be no illusions. The hardest part of our journey is in front of us. We seek sweeping but necessary change in the midst of a global recession, where every nation's most immediate priority is reviving their economy and putting their people back to work. And so all of us will face doubts and difficulties in our own capitals as we try to reach a lasting solution to the climate challenge.

❶ 这些工作绝不轻松。随着哥本哈根大会的临近，不能有错觉，最艰难的行程正在前方。我们寻求彻底而又必要的改变，在全球衰退中寻求，现在每个国家最迫切的重点就是振兴经济、让人们找到工作。所以，我们所有人都会遭遇疑问和困难。我们会努力找到持久的解决方案，以此应对气变带来的困难。

❷ 这些工作很不容易。我们快要召开哥本哈根大会了，必须清楚地认识到最艰难的旅程就在眼前。我们寻求大规模的、但是必要的改变，每个国家当前最迫切的重点是重振经济，让人们重新就业。所以，我们都将面临怀疑和困难，各国政府无一例外，需要持久的解决方案。

But I'm here today to say that difficulty is no excuse for complacency. Unease is no excuse for inaction. And we must not allow the perfect to become the enemy of progress. Each of us must do what we can when we can to grow our economies without endangering our planet—and we must all do it together. We must seize the opportunity to make Copenhagen a significant step forward in the global fight against climate change.

❶ 但我今天是想说困难不是懈怠的借口，不安不是不作为的借口。我们不能允许完美变成进步的敌人。我们大家都必须尽力而为，促进经济发展，而不危害我们的星球。我们必须一起努力、抓住机遇，将哥本哈根大会变成重要的一步，全球应对气变过程中的重要一步。

❷ 但我在这里是说困难不是借口，懈怠不是理由，不安不是借口，不能不作为。我们不能让完美变成敌人，阻碍进步。我们必须尽力而为，促进经济发展，而不危害环境。我们必须一起努力、抓住机遇，让哥本哈根大会变成重要的一步，以此推动全球应对气变的进展。

We also cannot allow the old divisions that have characterized the climate debate for so many years to block our progress. Yes, the developed nations that caused much of the damage to our climate over the last century still have a responsibility to lead—and that includes the United States. And we will continue to do so—by investing in renewable energy and promoting greater efficiency and slashing our emissions to reach the targets we set for 2020 and our long-term goal for 2050.

❶ 我们也不能允许旧的分歧——形成气候辩论特征的分歧，多年来一直阻碍我们的进步。是的，发达国家造成了很多破坏，破坏了气候，过去一个世纪都是如此。他们仍然有责任率先行动，这也包括美国。我们会继续这样做，投资于可再生能源、提高效率、大幅减排，以达到2020年的目标和长期的2050年的目标。

❷ 我们不能允许旧的分歧继续影响气候辩论，阻碍进展。是的，发达国家是破坏气候的主要原因。他们仍然有责任率先行动，这也包括美国。我们会继续这样做，投资于可再生能源、提高效率、大幅减排，以达到2020年目标和长期的2050年目标。

But those rapidly growing developing nations that will produce nearly all the growth in global carbon emissions in the decades ahead must do their part, as well. Some of these nations have already made great strides with the development and deployment of clean energy. Still, they need to commit to strong measures at home and agree to stand behind those commitments just as the developed nations must stand behind their own. We cannot meet this challenge unless all the largest emitters of greenhouse gas pollution act together. There's no other way.

❶ 但是，那些快速增长的发展中国家将造成几乎所有的增长——全球碳排放的增长，未来几十年都这样。他们也必须尽力。有些国家已经大步骤地发展、部署清洁能源。然而，他们仍然需要采取有力措施，在本国采取并且同意支持这些承诺，就像发达国家必须支持自己的承诺一样。我们解决这些挑战必须靠所有大排放国一起行动，别无它法。

❷ 但那些快速增长的发展中国家会带来所有的、全球碳排的增长，持续几十年。他们必须尽力。其中有些已经大步地发展、部署清洁能源。然而，他们仍需要采取有力措施，在本国实施，并且愿意支持这些承诺，如同发达国家必须坚守承诺一样。应对挑战需要所有的排放大国一起行动，别无它法。

We must also energize our efforts to put other developing nations — especially the poorest and most vulnerable — on a path to sustained growth. These nations do not have the same resources to combat climate change as countries like the United States or China do, but they have the most immediate stake in a solution. For these are the nations that are already living with the unfolding effects of a warming planet—famine, drought, disappearing coastal villages, and the conflicts that arise from scarce resources. Their future is no longer a choice between a growing economy and a cleaner planet, because their survival depends on both. It will do little good to alleviate poverty if you can no longer harvest your crops or find drinkable water.

❶ 我们必须强化努力，让其他发展中国家，尤其是最穷、最弱的国家迈上持续增长的道路。这些国家的资源，在应对气候变化方面不如美国、中国，但是他们有着最迫切攸关的利益，急需解决方案。这些国家的生活已经受到渐渐显露的影响——来自星球变暖的影响，饥荒、干旱、逐渐消失的沿海村庄、稀缺资源的冲突等。未来不是选择，无法在经济增长和干净的星球之间选择。他们的生存仰赖于两者。要想扶贫就必须有收成，有饮用水。

❷ 我们必须更加努力，让其他发展中国家，尤其是最穷、最弱的国家迈上持续增长的道路。这些国家没有同样的资源，应对气变时无法像美国或中国那样，但是他们有最直接的利益，需要解决方案。这些国家的生活环境受到了渐渐显露的、全球变暖带来的影响：饥荒、干旱、消失的沿海村庄、冲突等。未来不再是做选择，不是选经济增长还是干净的地球的问题。两者对生存都必不可少。要想扶贫，收成和饮用水都是必须的。

And that is why we have a responsibility to provide the financial and technical assistance needed to help these nations adapt to the impacts of climate change and pursue low-carbon development.

What we are seeking, after all, is not simply an agreement to limit greenhouse gas emissions. We seek

❶ 为此，我们有责任提供资金与技术援助，帮助这些国家适应影响，应对气变，寻求低碳发展。我们寻求的并不是简单的同意限制温室气体排放，而是所有国家都要增长，提高生活标准，并且不危害地球。通过发展、传播清洁技术，分享专门知识，我们可以帮助发展国家实现蛙跃，淘汰肮脏的能源技术，减少危险的排放。

an agreement that will allow all nations to grow and raise living standards without endangering the planet. By developing and disseminating clean technology and sharing our know-how, we can help developing nations leap-frog dirty energy technologies and reduce dangerous emissions.

❷ 为此，我们有责任提供资金与技术援助，帮助这些国家适应气变，发展低碳经济。我们要的不是简单的协议，限制排放，而是要让所有国家都能增长，提高生活标准而不危害地球。通过发展、传播清洁技术，分享我们的专门知识，帮助发展国家跳过肮脏的能源技术、减少危险的排放。

Mr. Secretary, as we meet here today, the good news is that after too many years of inaction and denial, there's finally widespread recognition of the urgency of the challenge before us. We know what needs to be done. We know that our planet's future depends on a global commitment to permanently reduce greenhouse gas pollution. We know that if we put the right rules and incentives in place, we will unleash the creative power of our best scientists and engineers and entrepreneurs to build a better world. And so many nations have already taken the first step on the journey towards that goal.

❶ 秘书长先生，我们今天在这里，好消息是在多年以来的不行动与否认之后，终于，我们都已普遍认识到挑战的紧急性。我们知道需要做什么，知道我们的地球的未来依靠一个全球的承诺，即永远减少温室气体污染。我们知道，如果我们把合适的规则和激励措施制定到位，就能释放创造力，让最好的科学家、工程师、创业家来建造一个更美好的世界。许多国家已经走出了第一步，朝着目标迈进。

❷ 秘书长先生，我们的好消息是：多年以来的不行动与否认已是过去，人们终于普遍认识到紧急的挑战就在当前。我们知道需要做什么，知道地球的未来依靠全球的承诺，要永远减少温室气体。我们知道，如果有合适的规则和激励措施，就能释放创造力，让最好的科学家、工程师、创业家发挥创意，建造更美好的世界。许多国家已经迈出第一步，朝着目标前进。

But the journey is long and the journey is hard. And we don't have much time left to make that journey. It's a journey that will require each of us to persevere

❶ 但是这个旅程很长、很艰辛。我们没有很多时间完成这一旅程。旅程要求我们大家都坚持不懈，奋争每一寸进展，哪怕走走停停。让我们开始吧。如果我们灵活且务实，决心不畏劳苦、共同努

through setbacks, and fight for every inch of progress, even when itcomes in fits and starts. So let us begin. For if we are flexible and pragmatic, if we can resolve to work tirelessly in common effort, then we will achieve our common purpose: a world that is safer, cleaner, and healthier than the one we found; and a future that is worthy of our children.

力，就能达成共同的目的，让世界更加安全、干净、健康，比现在更好；让未来适合孩子们的成长。

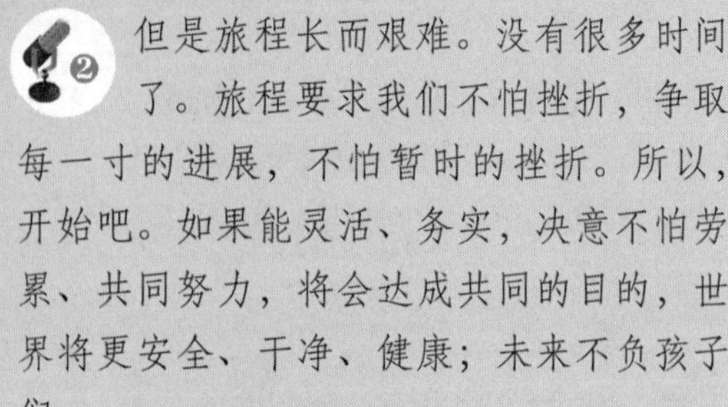

但是旅程长而艰难。没有很多时间了。旅程要求我们不怕挫折，争取每一寸的进展，不怕暂时的挫折。所以，开始吧。如果能灵活、务实，决意不怕劳累、共同努力，将会达成共同的目的，世界将更安全、干净、健康；未来不负孩子们。

Thank you very much.

谢谢各位。

非常感谢。

3. 欧盟贸易专员德古赫特的讲话

使用提要

1. 本单元的讲话稿仍然以两种形式提供：限时视译和技巧琢磨。但是目前为止应该已经掌握了两个版本的原则，所以参考译入语只提供一个版本。
2. 限时视译每次的长短仍然可以是每秒 2 个英文单词，即大约 80 个单词。
3. 在使用或者参照译入语时必须注意：

   3.1. 参考译入语只是诸多可能版本之一，不是最佳版本，而且故意保留了一些不完美的地方。这些做法都是为了从同传培训一开始就建立作为实战参照的质量标准。如果教材的译入语是经过修饰后的完善版本，这不仅是概念上的误导，而且会导致培训生无法达到教材里的准确度而丧失练习的信心。

   3.2. 由于上述原因，一定不可用笔译的准确标准来衡量同传的译入语版本，因为听同传的感觉和阅读文字完全不一样。

   3.3. 本教材有意没有提供视译中具体采取的是三词一译所需 10 大技巧中的哪一个，这是为了避免把练习的重点放在讲解技巧的概念上。

英译汉三词一译10大技巧

1. 缺省传译 2. 原话直译 3. 重复谓语 4. 介词转动
5. 先存后译 6. 反话正说 7. 被动变的 8. 点到为止
9. 预测先说 10. 弃卒保车

限时视译

EU-ASEAN Trade and Investment

(*EU Commissioner Karel De Gucht*)

Prime Minister Hun,
Dr Pitsuwan,
Vice Prime Ministers, Ministers,
Minister Cham,
Business leaders,
Ladies and Gentlemen,

I am delighted to be here in Phnom Penh to speak to you this morning. I am very grateful to you Prime Minister Hun Sen and to Minister Cham Prasidh for hosting this event. And I thank also the many business organisations that have put in the practical work needed to bring us all here together.

As I understand it, mine is the first visit by a European Commissioner to Cambodia for some time. And it comes at a good moment. At the end of last year the European Union celebrated a significant milestone in its relations with Cambodia by upgrading our delegation here to the status of a full diplomatic mission.

That change is a recognition of how seriously Europe takes our relations with Cambodia. And I know it will mark the beginning of closer friendship between our people. But it is also a sign of how the whole South East Asian region is seen as crucial in Brussels and other European capitals.

We are celebrating 35 years of EU-ASEAN cooperation this year. That is a long time. But let me assure you that in Europe we feel no fatigue, only a strong appetite to deepen our ties even further.

That is why events such as the EU-ASEAN Business Summit are so important. Because by bringing our businesspeople closer together we bring our economies and societies closer together. And that is vital for the future success of both our regions.

I'd like to take a few minutes this morning to talk to you about why the EU ASEAN economic relationship is so important, about what we are doing in government to encourage further cooperation, and about your crucial role as businesspeople in that process.

Let me start by explaining how trade and investment fits in with our overall strategy for jobs and growth in Europe. In Europe we know that in future 90% of economic growth in the world will happen outside our borders. A huge proportion of that growth will happen in the ASEAN region. Far from seeing this as a threat, we Europeans see the stunning growth figures in Asia as part of the solution to our economic challenges.

First, because European companies are already intimately connected to that growth. We know, for instance, that the European economy is already 36 million jobs better off as a result of our open trade policy.

And second, because we have the opportunity to strengthen those connections even further through engagement with regions like ASEAN. At €160 billion per year, Europe accounts for over 10% of ASEAN's total trade in goods. The percentage for services is even higher—at 13% of the total.

These figures probably underestimate the total trade between our two regions as today's global supply chains mean that of ASEAN's exports to China often end up in products eventually shipped to Europe. On top of this, stocks of bilateral investment stand at 260 billion euro and bilateral investment flows were over 31 billion euro in 2010. European investment in ASEAN accounts for a quarter of the yearly total.

Our trade and investment relationship already contributes to growth in both our economies.

As a result, some of you might be concerned about the economic news from Europe in recent months. Let me reassure you. There is no doubt that some parts of Europe face serious challenges at present. But Europe as a whole is doing much better than you might think.

Sure, parts of the euro zone, particularly the south of Europe, are going through a tough time. A painful adjustment process is needed to work off excesses built up before 2007. The shock of the financial crisis has also raised the spectre of default in some European countries, which would have grave consequences for the international financial system.

These problems are very serious. However, the European Union has made good progress towards solving them. We have enhanced budget discipline through the European Fiscal Compact and we have put in place significant financial firewalls to prevent any backsliding.

We are also moving forward on our strategy to kick-start economic growth. In fact, the crisis is allowing governments to finally grasp the nettle and carry out many difficult but vital structural reforms. As I mentioned, our open international trade and investment policy is also a key part of those efforts.

But beyond this good progress, I feel I must point out that even today we are in pretty good health, despite initial appearances. The EU remains the world's biggest trading power. Our goods exports rose by almost 60%—to 1.3 trillion euro—in the decade to 2010. Imports rose by 51% to 1.5 trillion euro. While we do have a trade deficit, it is largely caused by our significant oil and gas bill. In manufactured goods our significant surplus of almost 190 billion euros has trebled over the last decade.

The EU's share of world exports has remained stable at around 20% of the total over the last decade. Over the same period, the US and Japanese shares fell by six percentage points each to hit 12% and 6%, respectively. The EU also maintains its global leadership in high-value-added products—we account for 30% of total exports—and high-tech products—where our share was 17% in 2007.

More fundamentally, it is just plain wrong to say that Europe as a whole has a problem of competitiveness or that we live beyond our means. Just look at our current account, which is, by a small amount, in surplus. In addition, the euro remains and will stay the second reserve currency in the world.

Rest assured, then, Europe remains a strong and, dare I say it, vital partner for South East Asia. That is good news, because the European Union and ASEAN have a great deal of work to do together. We need a comprehensive, 21st century free trade agreement between our two regions. It should tackle the full range of barriers that obstruct flows of goods, services and investment between our regions.

That means not only eliminating tariffs, but also: tackling regulations that block trade in goods and services, improving the protection of intellectual property rights and securing access to markets for government procurement; all within a legally binding framework.

You may say thȧt that sounds like a tall order. And indeed it will take some time.

But I am happy to tell you that we are making concrete progress towards that objective:

Our bilateral negotiations with Singapore are close to conclusion we are making good progress with Malaysia. I am also happy to announce that here in Phnom Penh we decided with my Vietnamese colleague Minister Hoang to launch FTA negotiations after having concluded the scoping exercise last week. And I hope that we can advance discussions also with other ASEAN partners in the coming months.

But I want to make very clear that as we engage in these negotiations our overarching goal of regional integration remains clear. That goal is made even more important by the programme to build an ASEAN Economic Community by 2015, which we fully support. We have momentum now. I hope we can use it to get to the critical mass that will allow us to come back to the regional process very soon.

But of course no matter what we policymakers achieve together, we will have very little impact without an active private sector. I am a liberal by political conviction. I strongly believe that the role of government in economic policymaking is to remove barriers so that business can generate growth and jobs. That is what we do in trade negotiations—we try to get governments out of the way as much as possible.

And that is why today's business summit is so important.

Of course it is a good opportunity for policymakers like me to hear your advice on what we can do better. And I look forward to hearing the recommendations you have for us. But what are much more significant are the discussions you have with each other. Because it is you as business leaders who build our economic relationship.

The commercial relationships you create deliver the jobs and growth our countries and regions both need.

So I hope that you understand that responsibility and take it with you in today's important discussions. I, for one, look forward to a lively and stimulating debate.

技巧琢磨

Prime Minister Hun,
Dr Pitsuwan,
Vice Prime Ministers, Ministers,
Minister Cham,
Business leaders,
Ladies and Gentlemen,

I am delighted to be here in Phnom Penh to speak to you this morning. I am very grateful to you Prime Minister Hun Sen and to Minister Cham Prasidh for hosting this event. And I thank also the many business organisations that have put in the practical work needed to bring us all here together.

洪森首相，
素林博士，
副首相，
大臣们，
占蒲拉西大臣，
商业领袖，

女士们，先生们，我非常高兴来到金边发表演讲。我非常感谢洪森首相和占蒲拉西大臣举办本活动。我还要感谢很多商业组织，他们投入实际工作，把我们聚到了一起。

As I understand it, mine is the first visit by a European Commissioner to Cambodia for some time. And it comes at a good moment. At the end of last year the European Union celebrated a significant milestone in its relations with Cambodia by upgrading our delegation here to the status of a full diplomatic mission.

据我了解，我的首次访问也是由欧盟委员首次访问柬埔寨，在一段时间里没有过。访问时机很好。去年年底，欧盟庆祝了一个显著的里程碑——庆祝与柬埔寨的关系，升级我们的代表团使之成为全面外交使团。

That change is a recognition of how seriously Europe takes our relations with Cambodia. And I know it will mark the beginning of closer friendship between our people. But it is also a sign of how the whole South East Asian region is seen as crucial in Brussels and other European capitals.

这个变化反映出欧洲在很认真地对待与柬埔寨的关系。我知道这将标志着开启更亲密的友谊，人民之间的友谊。它还标志着整个东南亚区域的重要性，布鲁塞尔和其他欧洲国家都很重视。

We are celebrating 35 years of EU-ASEAN cooperation this year. That is a long time. But let me assure you that in Europe we feel no fatigue, only a strong appetite to deepen our ties even further.

我们将庆祝35年的欧盟-东盟合作。这是很长的时间。但是我保证，在欧洲，我们没有感到疲劳，只有强烈的欲望，希望深化我们的联系。

That is why events such as the EU-ASEAN Business Summit are so important. Because by bringing our business-people closer together we bring our economies and societies closer together. And that is vital for the future success of both our regions.

因此，诸如欧盟-东盟商业峰会这样的活动非常重要。因为通过让我们的商界人士更加紧密，我们的经济和社会也会更加紧密。这非常重要，对未来的成功，两个区域的成功都如此。

I'd like to take a few minutes this morning to talk to you about why the EU-ASEAN economic relationship is so important, about what we are doing in government to encourage further cooperation, and about your crucial role as businesspeople in that process.

我想用几分钟谈谈为何欧盟东盟经济关系如此重要，谈谈我们做了什么，我们政府是怎样鼓励进一步合作的，谈谈你们的重要角色，即商界人士在这个过程中的地位。

Let me start by explaining how trade and investment fits in with our overall strategy for jobs and growth in Europe. In Europe we know that in future 90% of economic growth in the world will happen outside our borders. A huge proportion of that growth will happen in the ASEAN region.

我首先解释贸易和投资如何与我们的整体战略一致，即就业和经济增长的欧洲战略。我们欧洲知道未来90%的经济增长将发生在我们的边界以外，很大部分将发生在东盟区域。

Far from seeing this as a threat, we Europeans see the stunning growth figures in Asia as part of the solution to our economic challenges.

远非视这点为威胁，我们欧洲人看到的惊人的增长数字——这些亚洲的数字是解决方案，有助于解决欧洲经济面临的挑战。

First, because European companies are already intimately connected to that growth. We know, for instance, that the European economy is already 36 million jobs better off as a result of our open trade policy.

第一，因为欧洲公司已经密切地联系于这一增长。我们知道，例如，欧洲经济已经有3600万工作岗位得益于我们开放的贸易政策。

And second, because we have the opportunity to strengthen those connections even further through engagement with regions like ASEAN.

第二，因为我们有机会加强这些联系，方法是接触东盟这样的区域。

At €160 billion per year, Europe accounts for over 10% of ASEAN's total trade in goods. The percentage for services is even higher—at 13% of the total.

以1600亿每年，欧洲占了10%以上的东盟货物贸易量。服务业的百分比更高，占13%。

These figures probably underestimate the total trade between our two regions as today's global supply chains mean that of ASEAN's exports to China often end up in products eventually shipped to Europe.

这些数据可能低估了我们两个区域的总贸易量，因为今天的全球供应链意味着东盟出口到中国的产品经常最终又运往了欧洲。

On top of this, stocks of bilateral investment stand at 260 billion euro and bilateral investment flows were over 31 billion euro in 2010. European investment in ASEAN accounts for a quarter of the yearly total.

除此之外，双边投资存量达2600亿欧元，双边投资流量超过310亿欧元，2010年如此。欧洲对东盟的投资占四分之一的年总量。

Our trade and investment relationship already contributes to growth in both our economies.

我们的贸易和投资关系已经有助于双方经济的增长。

As a result, some of you might be concerned about the economic news from Europe in recent months.

因此，各位中有些人可能担忧经济新闻里有关欧洲近几个月的情况。

Let me reassure you.

There is no doubt that some parts of Europe face serious challenges at present. But Europe as a whole is doing much better than you might think.

请放心。

毫无疑问，有些欧洲地区面临严峻挑战。但是欧洲整体的表现不错，比大家的想象要好。

Sure, parts of the euro zone, particularly the south of Europe, are going through a tough time. A painful adjustment process is needed to work off excesses built up before 2007. The shock of the financial crisis has also raised the spectre of default in some European countries, which would have grave consequences for the international financial system.

These problems are very serious.

当然，部分欧元区，尤其是南部欧洲，正经历艰难时刻。痛苦的调整过程是必须的，以消除累积的过剩，这些是2007年以前累积起来的。金融危机也引起了恐慌，人们害怕有些欧洲国家违约，这将导致严重后果，影响国际金融系统。

这些问题很严峻。

However, the European Union has made good progress towards solving them. We have enhanced budget discipline through the European Fiscal Compact and we have put in place significant financial firewalls to prevent any backsliding.

但是，欧盟取得了很好的进展，以解决问题。我们加强了预算纪律，通过欧洲财政契约实现。我们实施了相当量的财务防火墙，防止滑坡。

We are also moving forward on our strategy to kick-start economic growth. In fact, the crisis is allowing governments to finally grasp the nettle and carry out many difficult but vital structural reforms. As I mentioned, our open international trade and investment policy is also a key part of those efforts.

我们正在推进战略，以刺激经济增长。金融危机使政府迎难而上，实施许多艰难但是重要的结构改革。我说过，开放的国际贸易和投资政策也是这些努力的核心。

But beyond this good progress, I feel I must point out that even today we are in pretty good health, despite initial appearances.

但是除了进步，我认为必须指出，即使今天，我们也还处于健康状态，不论最初的迹象如何。

The EU remains the world's biggest trading power. Our goods exports rose by almost 60%—to 1.3 trillion euro—in the decade to 2010. Imports rose by 51% to 1.5 trillion euro. While we do have a trade deficit, it is largely caused by our significant oil and gas bill. In manufactured goods our significant surplus of almost 190 billion euros has trebled over the last decade.

欧盟仍是世界上最大的贸易力量。我们的货物出口增加了近60%，达1.3万亿欧元，这是十年内——截止2010年的增长。进口增长了51%，达到1.5万亿欧元。我们确实有贸易赤字，主要来自于相当大的石油和天然气购买开支。在制造产品方面，我们有大量顺差——近1900百亿欧元，增加了三倍，过去十年增加三倍。

The EU's share of world exports has remained stable at around 20% of the total over the last decade. Over the same period, the US and Japanese shares fell by six percentage points each to hit 12% and 6%, respectively.

欧盟的份额在世界出口中仍然稳定在约20%，过去十年没变。同期，美国和日本的份额下降了6个百分点，各为12%和6%。

The EU also maintains its global leadership in high-value-added products—we account for 30% of total exports—and high-tech products—where our share was 17% in 2007.

欧盟仍是全球领军者，在高价值附加产品领域领先——我们占了30%的总出口量，高科技产品也如此——我们的份额2007年是17%。

More fundamentally, it is just plain wrong to say that Europe as a whole has a problem of competitiveness or that we live beyond our means. Just look at our current account, which is, by a small amount, in surplus. In addition, the euro remains and will stay the second reserve currency in the world.

更根本的是，不能说欧洲整体有问题，竞争力有问题，或者我们寅吃卯粮。看看我们的经常账户，略有顺差。另外，欧元仍然并将保持第二大储蓄货币的全球地位。

Rest assured, then, Europe remains a strong and, dare I say it, vital partner for South East Asia.

放心，欧洲仍是强大的，我敢说，关键的合作伙伴——东南亚的伙伴。

That is good news, because the European Union and ASEAN have a great deal of work to do together.

这是好消息，因为欧盟和东盟有许多工作要共同完成。

We need a comprehensive, 21st century free trade agreement between our two regions. It should tackle the full range of barriers that obstruct flows of goods, services and investment between our regions.

我们需要广泛的、21世纪的自由贸易协议，以促进我们之间的贸易。协议应该清除所有障碍，促进货物、服务和投资的流动。

That means not only eliminating tariffs, but also: tackling regulations that block trade in goods and services, improving the protection of intellectual property rights and securing access to markets for government procurement; all within a legally binding framework.

这意味着不仅要减免关税，也意味着去监管化，不能阻碍贸易，尤其是货物和服务贸易；促进保护知识产权，确保市场准入——政府采购的市场准入；所有都在法律约束框架内做好。

You may say that that sounds like a tall order. And indeed it will take some time.

你可能说这听上去要求很高。它确实要花一些时间。

But I am happy to tell you that we are making concrete progress towards that objective:

但是我很高兴地告诉大家，我们取得了长足进展，实现了目标：

Our bilateral negotiations with Singapore are close to conclusion, we are making good progress with Malaysia.

我们的双边协商——与新加坡的协商，接近结束。我们正在取得与马来西亚的进展。

I am also happy to announce that here in Phnom Penh we decided with my Vietnamese colleague Minister Hoang to launch FTA negotiations after having concluded the scoping exercise last week.

我也很高兴宣布，在金边宣布，我们决定，和我的越南同事黄部长共同启动自由贸易协定谈判。此前结束了范围界定，上周就定了。

And I hope that we can advance discussions also with other ASEAN parners in the coming months.

我希望我们能推进讨论，和其他东盟伙伴在未来几个月展开讨论。

But I want to make very clear that as we engage in these negotiations our overarching goal of regional integration remains clear. That goal is made even more important by the programme to build an ASEAN Economic Community by 2015, which we fully support.

但是我想指明，随着我们参与这些谈判，我们的总目标，有关区域协议的总目标仍然明确。这个目标变得更为重要，因为要建立东盟经济共同体——在2015年前建成，我们完全支持。

We have momentum now. I hope we can use it to get to the critical mass that will allow us to come back to the regional process very soon.

我们势头良好。我希望我们能借此达到临界量，使我们能够回到区域进展上，为期不远。

But of course no matter what we policymakers achieve together, we will have very little impact without an active private sector.

但不论我们政策制定者共同达到什么，都不会有很大的影响力，除非有活跃的私营部门参与。

I am a liberal by political conviction. I strongly believe that the role of government in economic policymaking is to remove barriers so that business can generate growth and jobs. That is what we do in trade negotiations—we try to get governments out of the way as much as possible.

我是自由派的政治信念。我深信政府角色在经济政策制定中能移除障碍，以使商业能促进经济增长、增加就业机会。这是我们在贸易谈判中做的，我们试图使政府不挡路，尽可能放开。

And that is why today's business summit is so important.

因此，今天的商务峰会非常重要。

Of course it is a good opportunity for policymakers like me to hear your advice on what we can do better. And I look forward to hearing the recommendations you have for us.

当然，它也是一个良好机遇，使政策制定者，比如说我，能够听到你们的建议，从而使我们做得更好。我期待听到建议，你们对我们的建议。

But what are much more significant are the discussions you have with each other. Because it is you as business leaders who build our economic relationship.

但是更加重要的是讨论——这些讨论需要在你们之间进行，因为是作为商界领袖的你们建立了我们的经济关系。

The commercial relationships you create deliver the jobs and growth our countries and regions both need.

商业关系由你们建立，创造了就业和经济增长，这是我们的国家和区域都需要的。

So I hope that you understand that responsibility and take it with you in today's important discussions.

所以我希望你们理解这一责任，并带着它进行今天的重要讨论。

I, for one, look forward to a lively and stimulating debate.

4. APEC秘书处常务主任的讲话

使用提要

1. 本单元的讲话稿仍然以两种形式提供：限时视译和技巧琢磨。但是目前为止应该已经掌握了两个版本的原则，所以参考译入语只提供一个版本。
2. 限时视译每次的长短需要增加到每秒 3 个英文单词，这是实战同传必须达到的速度。另外每次选择的长度至少 40 秒，即大约 120 个单词。
3. 在使用或者参照译入语时必须注意：

   3.1. 参考译入语只是诸多可能版本之一，不是最佳版本，而且故意保留了一些不完美的地方。

   3.2. 一定不可用笔译的准确标准来衡量同传的译入语版本，因为听同传的感觉和阅读文字完全不一样。

   3.3. 避免把练习的重点放在讲解技巧的概念上，重点是熟练使用。

英译汉三词一译10大技巧

1. 缺省传译	2. 原话直译	3. 重复谓语	4. 介词转动
5. 先存后译	6. 反话正说	7. 被动变的	8. 点到为止
9. 预测先说	10. 弃卒保车		

限时视译

Keynote address at APEC Forum on Digital Economy and E-Commerce Development

(*Executive Director of the Secretariat, Muhamad Noor*)

Introduction

Distinguished guests, ladies and gentlemen,

It's a great pleasure and privilege to be here to participate in the APEC Forum on Digital Economy and E-Commerce Development here in the vibrant city of Quanzhou, China.

I would like to begin by sincerely thanking the host and organisers: China's Ministry of Commerce; The APEC E-Commerce Business Alliance; and The China International Electronic Commerce Centre.

May I also take this opportunity to acknowledge: Mr. Jiang Yaoping, Vice Minister of the Ministry of Commerce, China; Mr. Ye Shuangyu, Deputy Governor of Fujian Province; Mr. Liu Junsheng, Chairman of the APEC E-Commerce Business Alliance; and Mr. Xu Gang, Secretary of CPC, Quanzhou Municipal Committee.

This morning, I would like to open the Forum by saying a few words about APEC: to outline what APEC is doing to advance electronic commerce in the region, and to highlight how APEC is facilitating economies to move towards achieving greater prosperity in the digital age.

APEC and E-Commerce

This is APEC's core business. We are focused on liberalizing and facilitating trade and investment in the Asia-Pacific region. E-commerce plays a significant role and provides important support to advancing this agenda.

With electronic commerce, more information is made available and business transactions are also made more efficient and less costly. Importantly, entrepreneurs are now able to reach new global markets, even without establishing a physical presence.

This reminds me of the story of a craftsman in Australia who produced whips from crocodile skin. To expand his customer base beyond the tourists visiting his local community he started a website, and soon after received an order from an Inuit customer in northern Canada. It's not quite a case about selling snow to an Eskimo, but it does show the immense trade opportunities that technology creates, especially for a small business.

The same way e-commerce has transformed many of the region's small businesses; it has also redefined various industry sectors and business operations, fostering new supply networks and business models.

In fact, since the mid-1990s, we have seen a tremendous worldwide increase in the amount of trade conducted electronically. China, in particular, is leading the growth of e-commerce in the region. Recent figures show that, in China's online retail sector alone, sales are expected to more than triple to US$159.4 billion over the next five years, from US$48.8 billion in 2010.

These figures indicate the opportunities e-commerce brings to trade and the wealth it generates for economies, businesses and individuals.

APEC has long recognized the potential of e-commerce as a driver of growth for businesses. Responding to the times, in 1998, APEC Ministers developed an innovative Blueprint for Action on Electronic Commerce. It mobilized governments to create an environment in which businesses could take advantage of e-commerce.

Since then, APEC's Electronic Commerce Steering Group was formed to provide a coordinating role for APEC e-commerce activities and puts into action what was set out in the Blueprint.

Essentially, the group helps economies develop legal, regulatory and policy environments that are predictable, transparent and optimized so as to make it faster, easier and cheaper to do business. It is also working towards achieving a paperless trading environment by promoting the use of electronic documents and internet technologies when conducting cross-border trade.

Importantly these policies have resulted in actual cost savings for businesses.

APEC is continuing its work on trade facilitation and promoting electronic commerce remains a key priority area. Other priority areas include enhancing business mobility and addressing standards and customs issues. Other relevant APEC working groups are engaged in developing and implementing activities to advance each of the priority areas.

This work falls under APEC's Trade Facilitation Action Plans, which have resulted in a 5 percent reduction in business transaction costs in the region between 2002 and 2006. An additional 5.2 percent reduction, in real terms, is estimated during the 2007-2010 period under APEC's second Trade Facilitation Action Plan.

APEC enables economies to participate in the digital economy

To drive prosperity in the digital age, APEC is also keenly aware of the need to focus on technology access and education, and the development and adoption of ICTs among member economies.

That's why in the year 2000, APEC Leaders set the goals of tripling internet access throughout the region by 2005 and achieving universal access by 2010.

In 2008, APEC's Telecommunications and Information Ministers met in Bangkok and declared that the goal of tripling internet access had been met. And in 2010, APEC Ministers met in Okinawa and declared that the goal of achieving universal internet access had also been met. They went on to set the more ambitious target of guaranteeing universal access to broadband by 2015. Work to achieve this goal is already underway.

Innovation and knowledge are significant elements for economies and enterprises to grow and they are critical to APEC's progress in this area. It is therefore essential for governments and businesses to promote sound innovation policies that enable the use of electronic commerce, primarily through ICTs.

To this end, APEC has developed a Digital Prosperity Checklist which outlines specific actions economies can take to use ICTs as catalysts for economic growth and development. These actions cover enhancing ICT-related infrastructure, investment, innovation, intellectual capital, information flows, and integration.

APEC has also launched a groundbreaking initiative on data privacy that consists of a set of collaborative projects that will make cross-border flows of personal information secure and accessible, so that consumers are safe and business transactions are protected. This includes the establishment of the multilateral APEC Cross-Border Privacy Enforcement Arrangement (CPEA) that facilitates information sharing and cooperation between authorities responsible for data and consumer protection in the

APEC region.

These e-commerce issues are cross-cutting in nature and therefore are championed by different APEC working groups that cover telecommunications and human resources development. These issues are also advanced by engaging the private sector—through the APEC E-Commerce Business Alliance—to accelerate the overall development of the industry.

APEC USA 2011

This year, with the United States as host economy, APEC is focused on strengthening regional economic integration and expanding trade; promoting green growth; and advancing regulatory cooperation and convergence.

To make progress on these goals, APEC Trade Ministers have identified effective, non-discriminatory and market driven-innovation policy as one of the key "next generation" trade and investment issues on which to focus in 2011. APEC is also putting much attention on facilitating global supply chains and enhancing SME participation in global production chains.

E-commerce will, no doubt, assist economies and businesses to further realize these objectives, as trade is expanded and more products and services are bought and sold over electronic systems. In this way, APEC economies become more integrated and APEC's work on trade and investment liberalization and facilitation is further enhanced.

Conclusion

What I've shared with you is just a glimpse of the ongoing work APEC is doing to promote electronic commerce. Perhaps most importantly, APEC recognizes the importance of bringing businesses and governments together and encouraging the active participation and contribution of the private sector.

I look forward to the innovative strategies and effective policy recommendations that will arise from the discussions. They will no doubt contribute greatly towards APEC's work in electronic commerce and to advancing APEC's digital economy agenda going forward.

Thank you.

技巧琢磨

Distinguished guests, ladies and gentlemen,

It's a great pleasure and privilege to be here to participate in the APEC Forum on Digital Economy and E-Commerce Development here in the vibrant city of Quanzhou, China.

来宾们、女士们、先生们：

非常高兴和荣幸来此参加亚太经合组织数字经济和电子商业发展论坛，来到充满活力的城市泉州。

I would like to begin by sincerely thanking the host and organisers: China's Ministry of Commerce; The APEC E-Commerce Business Alliance; and The China International Electronic Commerce Centre.

我要首先衷心感谢举办和组织方：中国商务部、亚太经合组织电子商务工商联盟、中国国际电子商务中心。

May I also take this opportunity to acknowledge: Mr. Jiang Yaoping, Vice Minister of the Ministry of Commerce, China; Mr. Ye Shuangyu, Deputy Governor of Fujian Province; Mr. Liu Junsheng, Chairman of the APEC E-Commerce Business Alliance; and Mr. Xu Gang, Secretary of CPC, Quanzhou Municipal Committee.

我还要借此机会感谢：商务部副部长蒋耀平，福建副省长叶双瑜，亚太经合组织电子商务工商联盟主席刘俊生；泉州市委书记徐刚。

This morning, I would like to open the Forum by saying a few words about APEC: to outline what APEC is doing to advance electronic commerce in the region, and to highlight how APEC is facilitating economies to move towards achieving greater prosperity in the digital age.

今天早上，我在开幕式上要说几句关于亚太经合组织的话：概述我们当前推进电子商务的做法，强调我们如何促进经济体实现更大繁荣，在数字时代取得成功。

APEC and E-Commerce

This is APEC's core business. We are focused on liberalizing and facilitating trade and investment in the Asia-Pacific region. E-commerce plays a significant role and provides important support to advancing this agenda.

亚太经合组织和电子商务

这是亚太经合组织的核心业务。我们聚焦于放宽和促进投资与贸易在亚太地区的发展。电子商务发挥了重要作用，提供重要支持，推进这一议程。

With electronic commerce, more information is made available and business transactions are also made more efficient and less costly. Importantly, entrepreneurs are now able to reach new global markets, even without establishing a physical presence.

有了电子商务，更多信息的获得可以实现，商务交易效率提高、成本降低。重要的是，企业家现在能够接触新的全球市场，而不用建立实体。

This reminds me of the story of a craftsman in Australia who produced whips from crocodile skin. To expand his customer base beyond the tourists visiting his local community he started a website, and soon after received an order from an Inuit customer in northern Canada. It's not quite a case about selling snow to an Eskimo, but it does show the immense trade opportunities that technology creates, especially for a small business.

这让我想起一个故事，一位澳大利亚工匠制造鞭子，用鳄鱼皮造。为扩大客户群，不限于访问当地社区的游客。他开了一个网站，很快就收到订单，来自因纽特人，他远在加拿大北部。这并不是卖雪给爱斯基摩人，但是展示了巨大贸易机遇——技术创造的机遇，尤其是对小企业的机遇。

The same way e-commerce has transformed many of the region's small businesses; it has also redefined various industry sectors and business operations, fostering new supply networks and business models.

同样，电子商务转变了许多该地区的小企业，重新定义了各种行业领域和业务运营，培育新的供应网络和商业模式。

In fact, since the mid-1990s, we have seen a tremendous worldwide increase in the amount of trade conducted electronically. China, in particular, is leading the growth of e-commerce in the region. Recent figures show that, in China's online retail sector alone, sales are expected to more than triple to US$159.4 billion over the next five years, from US$48.8 billion in 2010.

自从上世纪 90 年代中期起，我们就看到了巨大的全球增长，有越来越多的电子贸易。中国引领增长的电子商业，在该地区领先。最近数据显示，中国的网上零售领域销售额预计翻三番以上，达 1594 亿美元，在今后五年内实现。488 亿是 2010 年的数据。

These figures indicate the opportunities e-commerce brings to trade and the wealth it generates for economies, businesses and individuals.

这些数据显示了机遇——电子商务带给贸易的机遇，所产生的财富造福于经济、商业和个人。

APEC has long recognized the potential of e-commerce as a driver of growth for businesses. Responding to the times, in 1998, APEC Ministers developed an innovative Blueprint for Action on Electronic Commerce. It mobilized governments to create an environment in which businesses could take advantage of e-commerce.

亚太经合组织早就认识到电子商务的潜力能够推动商业增长。回应时代要求，1998 年时，亚太经合组织部长制定了创新的蓝图——电子商务行动蓝图，动员政府创造环境，使各公司能够利用电子商务。

Since then, APEC's Electronic Commerce Steering Group was formed to provide a coordinating role for APEC e-commerce activities and puts into action what was set out in the Blueprint.

自那时起，我们的电子商务指导小组成立了，提供协调、推动亚太经合组织的电子商务活动，实践所制定的蓝图。

Essentially, the group helps economies develop legal, regulatory and policy environments that are predictable, transparent and optimized so as to make it faster, easier

指导小组帮助各经济体发展法律、监管和政策环境，使其可预测、透明、优化，从而更快、更简单、更便

and cheaper to do business. It is also working towards achieving a paperless trading environment by promoting the use of electronic documents and internet technologies when conducting cross-border trade.

Importantly these policies have resulted in actual cost savings for businesses.

APEC is continuing its work on trade facilitation and promoting electronic commerce remains a key priority area. Other priority areas include enhancing business mobility and addressing standards and customs issues. Other relevant APEC working groups are engaged in developing and implementing activities to advance each of the priority areas.

This work falls under APEC's Trade Facilitation Action Plans, which have resulted in a 5 percent reduction in business transaction costs in the region between 2002 and 2006. An additional 5.2 percent reduction, in real terms, is estimated during the 2007-2010 period under APEC's second Trade Facilitation Action Plan.

APEC enables economies to participate in the digital economy

To drive prosperity in the digital age, APEC is also keenly aware of the need to focus on technology access and education, and the development and adoption of ICTs among member economies.

宜，有利于商业。它还致力于实现无纸的贸易环境，方法是促进使用电子文件和互联网技术，用于跨境贸易。

重要的是，这些政策实现了实际的成本节省。

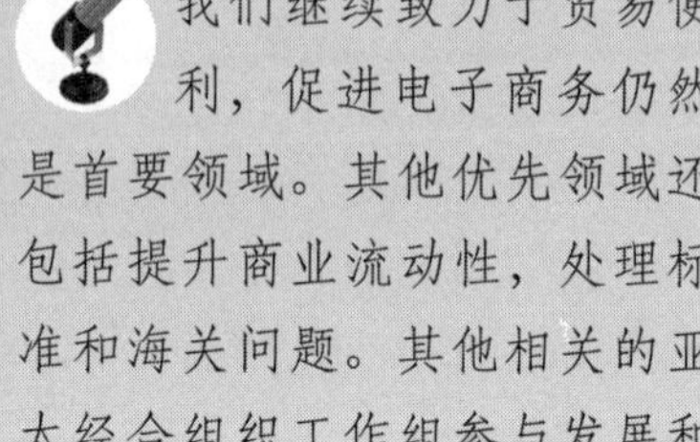

我们继续致力于贸易便利，促进电子商务仍然是首要领域。其他优先领域还包括提升商业流动性，处理标准和海关问题。其他相关的亚太经合组织工作组参与发展和实施活动，以推进所有优先领域的工作。

这项工作属于亚太经合组织的贸易便利行动计划，已经实现百分之五的下降，减少了交易成本，该地区2002年至2006年成本下降。另外还有百分之五点二的实际减少，预计是在2007年至2010年实现的，得力于亚太经合组织的第二个贸易便利行动计划。

亚太经合组织促使各经济体参与数字经济

为了驱动繁荣在数字时代的发展，亚太经合组织还很清楚需要聚焦技术获得、教育、发展和信息通信技术在各成员经济体中的使用。

That's why in the year 2000, APEC Leaders set the goals of tripling internet access throughout the region by 2005 and achieving universal access by 2010.

因此，2000年，亚太经合组织领导人设定目标，互联网接入要翻三番，在整个地区于2005年实现，普遍接入在2010年之前实现。

In 2008, APEC's Telecommunications and Information Ministers met in Bangkok and declared that the goal of tripling internet access had been met. And in 2010, APEC Ministers met in Okinawa and declared that the goal of achieving universal internet access had also been met. They went on to set the more ambitious target of guaranteeing universal access to broadband by 2015. Work to achieve this goal is already underway.

2008年，亚太经合组织通信和信息部长在曼谷开会，宣布翻三番的目标已经实现。2010年，亚太经合组织部长在冲绳开会，宣布普及互联网接入的目标也已达到。他们接着设定了更具雄心的目标，要保证普及宽带的目标在2015年之前实现。这项工作已经展开。

Innovation and knowledge are significant elements for economies and enterprises to grow and they are critical to APEC's progress in this area. It is therefore essential for governments and businesses to promote sound innovation policies that enable the use of electronic commerce, primarily through ICTs.

创新和知识是重要因素，促进经济体和企业增长。它们很重要，亚太经合组织的进步离不开它们。因此政府和企业必须推进有利的创新政策，促使电子商务发展，主要通过信息通信技术实现。

To this end, APEC has developed a Digital Prosperity Checklist which outlines specific actions economies can take to use ICTs as catalysts for economic growth and development. These actions cover enhancing ICT-related infrastructure, investment, innovation, intellectual capital, information flows, and integration.

为此，亚太经合组织开发了数字繁荣清单，概述了具体行动，各经济体能采取的行动，以信息通信技术为催化剂，促进经济增长和发展。这些活动包括提升信息通信技术相关的基础设施、投资、创新、知识资本、信息流和整合。

APEC has also launched a groundbreaking initiative on data privacy that consists of a set of collaborative projects that will make cross-border flows of personal information secure and accessible, so that consumers are safe and business transactions are protected. This includes the establishment of the multilateral APEC Cross-Border Privacy Enforcement Arrangement (CPEA) that facilitates information sharing and cooperation between authorities responsible for data and consumer protection in the APEC region.

我们还启动了开创性的动议，改善数据保密，其中有一系列协同项目，将使跨境流动的人员信息是安全的、可获得的，使消费者有安全保障，商业交易受到保护。这包括建立多边亚太经合组织跨境隐私执行安排，促进信息分享、合作，通过负责数据和消费者保护的当局在亚太经合组织地区的合作。

These e-commerce issues are cross-cutting in nature and therefore are championed by different APEC working groups that cover telecommunications and human resources development. These issues are also advanced by engaging the private sector — through the APEC E-Commerce Business Alliance — to accelerate the overall development of the industry.

这些电子商务议题具有跨领域的性质，因此其倡导者有不同亚太经合组织的工作组，包括通讯和人力资源开发。这些议题的推进要靠调动私营领域，通过我们的电子商务工商联盟来加速整个业界的发展。

APEC USA 2011

This year, with the United States as host economy, APEC is focused on strengthening regional economic integration and expanding trade; promoting green growth; and advancing regulatory cooperation and convergence.

亚太经合组织美国会议2011年

今年，美国是东道国，我们聚焦于加强区域经济整合、扩展贸易，促进绿色增长，推进监管合作和趋同。

To make progress on these goals, APEC Trade Ministers have identified effective, non-discriminatory and market driven-innovation policy as one of the key “next generation” trade and investment issues on which to focus in 2011. APEC is also putting much attention on

为取得进展，亚太经合组织贸易部长确定了有效、非歧视和市场驱动创新的政策作为其中一个主要的“下一代”贸易和投资议题，作为

facilitating global supply chains and enhancing SME participation in global production chains.

2011年的焦点。亚太经合组织也很关注促进全球供应链，提升中小企业参与全球生产链的程度。

E-commerce will, no doubt, assist economies and businesses to further realize these objectives, as trade is expanded and more products and services are bought and sold over electronic systems. In this way, APEC economies become more integrated and APEC's work on trade and investment liberalization and facilitation is further enhanced.

电子商务无疑将协助各经济体和企业进一步实现这些目标，贸易扩展后，更多产品与服务的买卖将通过电子系统完成。这样，亚太经合组织经济体越来越整合，亚太经合组织的工作，包括贸易和投资的自由化和便利化，都将进一步提升。

Conclusion

What I've shared with you is just a glimpse of the ongoing work APEC is doing to promote electronic commerce. Perhaps most importantly, APEC recognizes the importance of bringing businesses and governments together and encouraging the active participation and contribution of the private sector.

结论

我分享的只是正在进行的工作的一瞥。也许最重要的是，亚太经合组织认识到必须让企业和政府携手，鼓励积极参与和贡献，尤其是私营领域要参与。

I look forward to the innovative strategies and effective policy recommendations that will arise from the discussions. They will no doubt contribute greatly towards APEC's work in electronic commerce and to advancing APEC's digital economy agenda going forward.

Thank you.

我期待创新的战略和有效的政策建议能够提出来，通过讨论提出来。它们无疑将非常有利于亚太经合组织的工作，促进电子商务，推进亚太经合组织的数字经济议程向前发展。

谢谢。

5. 欧盟马德里宣言

使用提要

1. 国际会议同传有时会讨论文件或者提及某个文件里的某段话，此时往往需要译员能够边参照文稿、边同传。本单元的材料特意选择了一份文件稿，以达到练习这种特殊同传形式的目的。
2. 本单元的材料也是以两种形式提供：限时视译和技巧琢磨。参考译入语只提供一个版本。
3. 限时视译的速度必须按照每秒 3 个英文单词要求，这是实战同传必须达到的速度。每次选择的长度至少 40 秒，即大约 120 个单词。
4. 在使用或者参照译入语时必须注意：

   4.1. 参考译入语只是诸多可能版本之一，不是最佳版本，而且故意保留了一些不完美的地方。

   4.2. 一定不可用笔译的准确标准来衡量同传的译入语版本，因为听同传的感觉和阅读文字完全不一样。

   4.3. 避免把练习的重点放在讲解技巧的概念上，重点是熟练使用。

英译汉三词一译10大技巧

1. 缺省传译	2. 原话直译	3. 重复谓语	4. 介词转动
5. 先存后译	6. 反话正说	7. 被动变的	8. 点到为止
9. 预测先说	10. 弃卒保车		

限时视译

Declaration of Madrid within the Scope of Informal Ministerial Meeting for Tourism under the Spanish Presidency in April 2010 in Madrid under the Motto 'Towards a Socially Responsible Tourism Model'

The entry into force of the Treaty of Lisbon represents a landmark for tourism, a key economic sector of the EU, which notably contributes to the EU GDP and generates jobs and wealth in the Member States. The Lisbon Treaty acknowledges the importance of tourism outlining, for the first time, a specific competence for the European Union in this field and allowing for decisions to be taken by qualified majority (Title XXII Tourism, Art. 195). The Lisbon Treaty foresees in its article 195 a) and b) the possibility for the Union to "complement the action of the Member States in the tourism sector, in particular by promoting the competitiveness of Union undertakings in that sector". By putting in place specific measures aimed at encouraging the creation of a favourable environment for the development of undertakings in this sector and promoting cooperation between the Member States, particularly by the exchange of good practice, the tourism industry can indirectly contribute to the strategy "Europe 2020 — A European strategy for smart, sustainable and inclusive growth" and towards strengthening the concept of European citizenship. In line with the goals of the Europe 2020 Strategy and the particular objectives under the flagship initiative on "an industrial policy for the globalisation era", it is particularly important to enhance the competitiveness of the tourism sector.

The T20 Ministers' Meeting of 22-24 February 2010 in Johannesburg, South Africa, emphasised the importance of tourism and its potential contribution to the global agenda, in particular to the process of supporting economic recovery and the transformation towards a greener and more sustainable economy. The final T20 joint communiqué sent a clear message and invitation to reinforced cooperation and joint efforts in order to build a stronger, more sustainable and responsible tourism sector.

In the last few years, tourism has changed significantly due, among other reasons, to the globalization of economy, the transformation of the airline industry with the development of low-cost companies into the European market, the technological revolution linked to the Internet, the increasing importance of the individual organization of trips and the subsequent decrease of mediation in the tourist activity.

The European tourist industry faces the challenge of maintaining and strengthening its position in an increasingly competitive world, with the appearance of really powerful markets such as competitors as well as providers of new visitors.

Tourism is an industry of transverse nature, affected by many Community policies and measures in fields such as transport, environment, new information and communication technologies, rural development, consumer protection, energy or taxation, which have a direct bearing on the tourist industry, although interests of the latter are not always taken into account when taking decisions. A strong coordination of these Community policies and a holistic approach is therefore highly important.

An interaction is produced between tourist activity and the European policies with direct or indirect effect on competitiveness. The European Union must take into account these interactions and back European competitiveness in the globalized world, with the cooperation of the States and through the financial and non-financial instruments of its policies in favour of tourism.

The maintenance of competitiveness in the European tourist industry requires a strategy based on tourist excellence, aided by the creation of networks of experts and destinations to allow the creation, sharing and dissemination of knowledge, innovation, research and technological development.

The tourist industry in Europe is mainly composed by small and medium sized enterprises (SMEs), so it is essential to provide the tourist sector with a better access to instruments that can help it to improve its economic results and to strengthen its competitiveness, something that, at the same time, will allow us to increase its contribution to sustainable development, therefore favouring the creation of jobs and wealth; while boosting the active participation of companies and economic and social stakeholders.

Corporate social responsibility is essential in the tourist industry and should be therefore taken into consideration in tourism activities and practices at destination, enterprise and tourist level.

The raising of public awareness and promotion of responsible attitudes of European tourists is also essential in order to increase the demand for responsible tourist products and services in Europe.

With a view to the "Communication on the renewed EU Tourism Policy Framework", which the Commission is to present before the EU Council, the Tourism Ministers meeting in Madrid wish to invite the Commission to take into consideration the pertinence of:

1. Putting forward a consolidated framework for the EU Tourism policy, according to the provisions of the Lisbon Treaty, encouraging the creation of a favourable environment for the development of undertakings in this sector and promoting cooperation between the Member States, particularly, by the exchange of good practice. This framework should aim particularly at supporting, coordinating and supplementing the measures undertaken in the Member States through initiatives which have a European or at least multinational dimension and a high added value in comparison to purely regional or national initiatives. Therefore, any joint approach towards the coordination of the activities of the Commission and the Member States is to be based on the principle of subsidiarity.

2. Streamlining its efforts in view of mainstreaming tourism in Community policies and ensuring an adequate coordination of the various policy initiatives which may impact on tourism, ensuring also that tourism will be duly taken into consideration in the main EU financial instruments (Structural Funds, European Rural Development Fund, Framework Programme for Research etc.). In addition, the Commission might consider consolidating the current budget lines used for the support and coordination of tourism initiatives, under a coherent and comprehensive financial framework for tourism.

3. Facilitating the access to holidays to groups with impaired mobility or those who are socially and/or economically disadvantaged, promoting as the same time a better and more prolonged use of tourist infrastructures, the maintenance of tourist activity in the regions for longer periods, and a strengthening of the feeling of European citizenship.

4. Raising awareness about the importance of innovation, research and information and communication technologies for the competitiveness of the EU tourism industry, especially in the context of a globalized economic environment,

characterized by the increasing choosing capacity of well-informed clients and a vertiginous technological development.

5. Mainstreaming sustainability in the sectors related to tourism (transport, solid waste, water treatment, among others), and the creation of knowledge networks to exchange information, technology and the diffusion of best practices applicable to the tourist industry.

6. Alleviating any possible obstacles to opportunities for the growth of tourism in Europe, related to new issuing markets.

7. Reinforcing Europe´s image and visibility in the main third countries, through joint actions which may generate added value to already existing national promotional activities.

The Member States declare their willingness:

1. To take part in the implementation of the new consolidated EU tourism policy framework, to be established in light of the Lisbon Treaty, subject to the principle of subsidiarity.

2. To promote responsible and ethical tourism and, especially, social, environmental, cultural and economic sustainability of tourism.

3. To raise awareness to the importance of knowledge and innovation in tourism, the strengthening of the use of new technologies by the public and private tourism actors, the encouraging of networking and the exchange of best practices, as tools for the competitiveness of European tourism.

4. To support measures and initiatives encouraging the lengthening of the high season in tourism, thus contributing to reduce seasonality and to maintain tourist employment in off-season.

技巧琢磨

The entry into force of the Treaty of Lisbon represents a landmark for tourism, a key economic sector of the EU, which notably contributes to the EU GDP and generates jobs and wealth in the Member States. The Lisbon Treaty acknowledges the importance of tourism outlining, for the first time, a specific competence for the European Union in this field and allowing for decisions to be taken by qualified majority. The Lisbon Treaty foresees in its article 195 a) and b) the possibility for the Union to "complement the action of the Member States in the tourism sector, in particular by promoting the competitiveness of Union undertakings in that sector". By putting in place specific measures aimed at encouraging the creation of a favourable environment for the development of undertakings in this sector and promoting cooperation between the Member States, particularly by the exchange of good practice, the tourism industry can indirectly contribute to the strategy "Europe 2020—A European strategy for smart, sustainable and inclusive growth" and towards strengthening the concept of European citizenship. In line with the goals of the Europe 2020 Strategy and the particular objectives under the flagship initiative on "an industrial policy for the globalisation era", it is particularly important to enhance the competitiveness of the tourism sector.

生效的《里斯本条约》是一个里程碑，对旅游业很重要，这是重要的经济部门，欧盟不可少，所作的贡献占欧盟 GDP 很大比重，创造了就业机会和财富，惠及各成员国。《里斯本条约》承认旅游业很重要，首次概述了具体能力——欧盟在此领域的能力，使决策的制定有达标的多数。《里斯本条约》预见，在第 195（a）、（b）项中预见，欧盟有可能“补充成员国在旅游业的行动，方法是促进欧盟旅游业的竞争力。”通过实施具体措施，鼓励创造有利环境，发展旅游业，促进成员国之间的合作，尤其是通过交流良好做法，旅游业能直接贡献于战略，即“欧洲 2020：欧洲战略，实现智能、可持续和包容性质的增长”，并且有利于增强欧洲公民的概念。根据欧洲 2020 战略目标以及旗舰计划“行业政策，响应全球化”，尤其是必须提升旅游业的竞争力。

The T20 Ministers' Meeting of 22-24 February 2010 in Johannesburg, South Africa, emphasised the importance of tourism and its potential contribution to the global agenda, in particular to the process of supporting economic recovery and the transformation towards a greener and more sustainable economy. The final T20 joint communiqué sent a clear message and invitation to reinforced cooperation and joint efforts in order to build a stronger, more sustainable and responsible tourism sector.

T20部长会议，2月22至24日于2010年在南非约翰内斯堡召开，强调旅游业很重要，并有潜力为全球议程做贡献，尤其是支持经济复苏和转型，实现更加绿色和可持续的经济。T20最终的联合公报发出明确信息和邀请，要求加强合作，共同努力，以建立更强、更可持续和负责任的旅游业。

In the last few years, tourism has changed significantly due, among other reasons, to the globalization of economy, the transformation of the airline industry with the development of low-cost companies into the European market, the technological revolution linked to the Internet, the increasing importance of the individual organization of trips and the subsequent decrease of mediation in the tourist activity.

过去几年，旅游业的变化很大，原因包括经济全球化、转变的航空业、低成本公司进入欧洲市场、技术变革、互联网、越发重要的个人自己安排行程的做法以及随之减少的中介的作用。

The European tourist industry faces the challenge of maintaining and strengthening its position in an increasingly competitive world, with the appearance of really powerful markets such as competitors as well as providers of new visitors.

欧洲旅游业面临挑战，要保持和加强地位，在日益竞争激烈的世界中立足，出现了非常有力的市场，比如，既是竞争方，又是提供方——其提供新游客的市场。

Tourism is an industry of transverse nature, affected by many Community policies and measures in fields such as transport, environment, new information and communication technologies, rural development, consumer protection, energy or taxation, which have a

旅游这个行业具有横向性，受到的影响来自许多社区政策和措施，比如交通、环境、新的信息通讯技术、城市发展、消费者保护、能源

direct bearing on the tourist industry, although interests of the latter are not always taken into account when taking decisions. A strong coordination of these Community policies and a holistic approach is therefore highly important.

后者的利益经常没有被考虑到。有力协同这些社区政策和整体的做法因此极为重要。

An interaction is produced between tourist activity and the European policies with direct or indirect effect on competitiveness. The European Union must take into account these interactions and back European competitiveness in the globalized world, with the cooperation of the States and through the financial and non-financial instruments of its policies in favour of tourism.

互动的产生——在游客行为和欧洲政策之间的这种互动会直接或间接地影响竞争力。欧盟必须考虑这些互动，支持欧洲竞争力在全球化的世界中发展，成员国要合作，要通过财政和非财政工具支持旅游业。

The maintenance of competitiveness in the European tourist industry requires a strategy based on tourist excellence, aided by the creation of networks of experts and destinations to allow the creation, sharing and dissemination of knowledge, innovation, research and technological development.

保持竞争力在欧洲旅游业中不被削弱就要求战略的基础是优秀的旅游业，辅以建立专家网络、目的地网络，以创造、分享和传播知识、创新、研究和技术发展。

The tourist industry in Europe is mainly composed by small and medium sized enterprises (SMEs), so it is essential to provide the tourist sector with a better access to instruments that can help it to improve its economic results and to strengthen its competitiveness, something that, at the same time, will allow us to increase its contribution to sustainable development, therefore favouring the creation of jobs and wealth; while boosting the active participation of companies and economic and social stakeholders.

旅游业在欧洲的主要组成部分是中小企业，因此必须提供给旅游业更好的机会，获得工具，帮助改善经济效果、加强竞争力。同时，这将使我们增加贡献，有利于可持续发展，以此支持创造就业机会和财富；同时促进积极参与——公司、经济与社会的利益相关者的参与。

Corporate social responsibility is essential in the tourist industry and should be therefore taken into consideration in tourism activities and practices at destination, enterprise and tourist level.

公司社会责任必不可少，应该因此予以考虑，在旅游活动和实践中考虑，无论是在目的地、企业和游客层面都是如此。

The raising of public awareness and promotion of responsible attitudes of European tourists is also essential in order to increase the demand for responsible tourist products and services in Europe.

提高公众意识，提倡负责态度，欧洲游客的负责态度也必不可少，否则无法增加负责任的游客产品和服务在欧洲的需求。

With a view to the "Communication on the renewed EU Tourism Policy Framework", which the Commission is to present before the EU Council, the Tourism Ministers meeting in Madrid wish to invite the Commission to take into consideration the pertinence of:

考虑到"更新的欧盟旅游政策框架文件"，欧盟委员会将把文件交给欧盟理事会，旅游部长会议将在马德里召开，希望请委员会考虑相关问题：

1. Putting forward a consolidated framework for the EU Tourism policy, according to the provisions of the Lisbon Treaty, encouraging the creation of a favourable environment for the development of undertakings in this sector and promoting cooperation between the Member States, particularly, by the exchange of good practice. This framework should aim particularly at supporting, coordinating and supplementing the measures undertaken in the Member States through initiatives which have a European or at least multinational dimension and a high added value in comparison to purely regional or national initiatives. Therefore, any joint approach towards the coordination of the activities of the Commission and the Member States is to based on the principle of subsidiarity.

1. 提出一个协同的框架，用于欧盟旅游政策，根据《里斯本条约》的条款，鼓励创造有利环境，帮助发展旅游事业，推动成员国合作，尤其要交流良好做法。框架应该旨在支持、协调和补充成员国的措施，实施的举措要有全欧洲或者至少多国的维度和高附加值，而不只是地区或者国家的举措。因此，所有联合行动，协调欧委会和成员国活动的行动都必须遵循辅助性的原则。

2. Streamlining its efforts in view of mainstreaming tourism in Community policies and ensuring an adequate coordination of the various policy initiatives which may impact on tourism, ensuring also that tourism will be duly taken into consideration in the main EU financial instruments such as Structural Funds, European Rural Development Fund, Framework Programme for Research. In addition, the Commission might consider consolidating the current budget lines used for the support and coordination of tourism initiatives, under a coherent and comprehensive financial framework for tourism.

2. 精简努力，考虑让旅游主流化，社区政策中要重视，并确保足够地协调各种政策举措，确保旅游被适当考虑进主要欧盟财政工具中，比如结构基金、欧洲农村发展基金、框架项目等。另外，欧委会可能考虑巩固当前预算，支持和协调旅游计划的项目，在连贯、全面的财政框架下发展旅游。

3. Facilitating the access to holidays to groups with impaired mobility or those who are socially and/or economically disadvantaged, promoting at the same time a better and more prolonged use of tourist infrastructures, the maintenance of tourist activity in the regions for longer periods, and a strengthening of the feeling of European citizenship.

3. 协助人们获得假期，尤其是流动性受损群体和社会和/或经济上的弱势群体渡假，促进更好、更长久地使用游客基础设施、保持旅游活动持续更久，加强欧洲公民感。

4. Raising awareness about the importance of innovation, research and information and communication technologies for the competitiveness of the EU tourism industry, especially in the context of a globalized economic environment, characterized by the increasing choosing capacity of well-informed clients and a vertiginous technological development.

4. 提高意识，认识到创新、研究和信息通信技术的重要，对欧盟旅游业的竞争力很重要，尤其背景是全球化经济环境，有越来越多的选择能力，消息灵通的客户，变化迅速的技术发展。

5. Mainstreaming sustainability in the sectors related to tourism (transport, solid waste, water treatment, among others), and the

5. 主流化可持续性，在相关于旅游的领域（交通、固体废物、水处理、等），创造

information, technology and the diffusion of best practices applicable to the tourist industry.

知识网络，交流信息、技术，传播最佳做法，用于旅游业。

6. Alleviating any possible obstacles to opportunities for the growth of tourism in Europe, related to new issuing markets.

6. 减少所有可能的障碍，抓住机遇让欧洲旅游业获得增长，抓住与新发行市场相关的机遇。

7. Reinforcing Europe´s image and visibility in the main third countries, through joint actions which may generate added value to already existing national promotional activities.

7. 加强欧洲形象和可见度，在主要的第三世界国家进行，采取联合行动。这会产生附加值，帮助现有的国家宣传活动。

The Member States declare their willingness:

成员国宣布愿意：

1. To take part in the implementation of the new consolidated EU tourism policy framework, to be established in light of the Lisbon Treaty, subject to the principle of subsidiarity.

1.参加实施新的、统一的欧盟旅游政策框架，其建立将依据《里斯本条约》，遵循辅助性原则。

2. To promote responsible and ethical tourism and, especially, social, environmental, cultural and economic sustainability of tourism.

2. 倡导负责任的和符合道德的旅游，尤其是社会、环境、文化和经济可持续的旅游。

3. To raise awareness to the importance of knowledge and innovation in tourism, the strengthening of the use of new technologies by the public and private tourism actors, the encouraging of networking and the exchange of best practices, as tools for the competitiveness of European tourism.

3. 提升意识，注重知识、创新在旅游业的应用，加强使用新技术，由公共和私人旅游行动者采用，促进联络和交流的最佳做法，以提升竞争力。

4. To support measures and initiatives encouraging the lengthening of the high season in tourism, thus contributing to reduce seasonality and to maintain tourist employment in off-season.

4.支持措施和计划，激励延长旺季，以助减少季节性，稳定旅游业雇佣，尤其是在淡季的雇佣。

6. OECD秘书长的讲话

使用提要

1. 本单元的讲话稿仍然以两种形式提供：限时视译和技巧琢磨。参考译入语只提供一个版本。
2. 限时视译的速度必须达到每秒3个英文单词，这是实战同传必须达到的速度。每次选择的长度应该增加到50–60秒之间，即大约150–180个单词。
3. 在使用或者参照译入语时必须注意：

   3.1. 参考译入语只是诸多可能版本之一，不是最佳版本，而且故意保留了一些不完美的地方。

   3.2. 一定不可用笔译的准确标准来衡量同传的译入语版本，因为听同传的感觉和阅读文字完全不一样。

   3.3. 避免把练习的重点放在讲解技巧的概念上，重点是熟练使用。

英译汉三词一译10大技巧

1. 缺省传译	2. 原话直译	3. 重复谓语	4. 介词转动
5. 先存后译	6. 反话正说	7. 被动变的	8. 点到为止
9. 预测先说	10. 弃卒保车		

限时视译

The OECD and the G20—An evolving relationship

(*OECD Secretary General Angel Gurría*)

Ladies and Gentlemen,

It is a great pleasure to be here, in Ireland's leading European and international affairs policy institute, to share with you these views on the evolving relationship between the OECD and the G20.

Among its distinguished speakers, the Institute have invited many high-level global decision makers and national leaders. Thank you for the opportunity to contribute to such an important series of events.

The G20 is fast becoming the centrepiece of today's international economic, social and environmental governance architecture.

Yes, it is a very heterogeneous group. Yes, the progress achieved so far is incomplete. However, its capacity to deliver has been outstanding. At a moment when we were facing critical challenges, the G20 came up with a coordinated response to the decline in global activity and to stabilise markets. It is now focusing on the very important issue of exit strategies from the massive public interventions, and among other medium and long-term issues on how to address climate change financing.

OECD has been supporting the G20 Summit since its inception. Our substantive contribution includes work on new sources of growth; on the human and social dimension of the crisis; on innovation; open markets for trade and investment and on the exchange of information for tax purposes.

It is quite significant that leaders felt they had to call on relevant international organisations to address the worst economic crisis ever. Leaders identify key issues in the global agenda and call on us to provide advice to address them.

Through evidence-based analytical inputs, we ensure that Countries that do not participate directly at the G20 stay connected to the discussions. The OECD is strongly committed to the notion that countries such as Ireland can have, through the OECD, an additional channel by which your voice can be heard. This role will remain central to our efforts.

In Pittsburgh we reported on areas where, based on OECD work, the world has achieved important breakthroughs. Such is the case of exchange of information for tax purposes, where, since November 2008 we made more progress than in the last 10 years. We have just established the most ambitious peer review process, that includes almost 90 countries ready to measure compliance based on OECD standards.

We also worked to keep markets open to trade and investment; and we contributed to a new approach to the regulation and supervision of the financial sector through our participation in the FSB. We will also establish a peer review process to evaluate compliance with the OECD principles of corporate governance. Failure to implement them produced the massive breakdown we have experienced.

The most dramatic expression of the crisis is the level of unemployment, on which we have also worked in the context of the G20. Our mandate is to monitor labour developments and the impact of certain policies. There is a need to continue supporting workers through the stimulus packages, but in a long-term perspective it is also important to invest in skills development and re-training. Thus, the OECD was asked to contribute to the Labor Ministerial that the US will host in early 2010, building on the results of the OECD's own Employment, Labour and Social Affairs Ministerial Meeting held last September and where non-OECD countries like Brasil, South Africa and India were represented at Ministerial level.

In Pittsburgh, OECD work on these areas was welcome, and we are asked to continue working on them.But we were also asked to continue our work on energy subsidies, and the impact of their removal in demand, prices, and GHG emissions. This was a very important area where the joint work of the OECD and the IEA was the basis for an agreement among participating countries.

Our estimates on GHG reduction resulting from the removal of these subsidies (as much as 10% in 2050) were extensively quoted, including by U.S. Treasury Secretary Geithner and President Obama himself, who recently wrote to ask that we continue this work, together with the IEA.

Additionally, and based on OECD work, Leaders:

- called for the adoption and enforcement of laws against transnational bribery, such as the OECD Anti-Bribery Convention.

- agreed to continue to work on the Charter for Sustainable Economic Activity, the process initiated by Chancellor Merkel to which the OECD has contributed since the very beginning, and on the "Lecce Framework" on the need to introduce ethics, transparency integrity and propriety in economic governance.

On the way forward, the G20 is also paving the way to build a stronger, more balanced and sustainable growth process. This is one of the major achievements in Pittsburgh that will be discussed at the next G20 Finance Ministers and Central Bank Governors in Saint Andrews this week-end.

The Framework can be seen as a compact that commits countries to work together to assess the coherence of national policies and their consistency with the common objectives agreed at the G20-level. The OECD has for many decades been assessing and monitoring national policies through a peer review or mutual assessment process and we are ready to contribute to this excellent initiative.

OECD has made several very concrete proposals to the G20 on the Framework and on how we could adapt our ongoing work programs to support its implementation. One way would be through the establishment of the "Observatory for Policy Coherence", or policy assessment network, among key international organisations specialising in economic issues to provide the best possible joint input into G20 processes.

While taking into account the comparative advantage of each International Organisation, the Observatory would allow for different perspectives. It is not about duplicating efforts. It is about being complementary. The messages of the international organisations would become reciprocally reinforcing if they were better shared and more effectively coordinated.

Ladies and Gentlemen:

The crisis has accelerated the speed at which the global governance architecture has to be updated and revamped. The G20 is an important step forward in such process. The OECD is ready to contribute to its success.

Thank you very much.

技巧琢磨

Ladies and Gentlemen,

It is a great pleasure to be here, in Ireland's leading European and international affairs policy institute, to share with you these views on the evolving relationship between the OECD and the G20.

女士们、先生们，

非常高兴来到这里，来到爱尔兰领先的欧洲和国际事务政策研究所，分享看法，讨论进化的关系——经合组织与20国集团之间关系的发展。

Among its distinguished speakers, the Institute have invited many high-level global decision makers and national leaders. Thank you for the opportunity to contribute to such an important series of events.

在出色的讲话人中，研究所邀请了很多高级别的全球决策制定者和国家领导人。谢谢给我这个机会，参加如此重要的系列活动。

The G20 is fast becoming the centrepiece of today's international economic, social and environmental governance architecture.

20国集团快速成为中心，是当今国际经济、社会和环境治理架构的中心。

Yes, it is a very heterogeneous group. Yes, the progress achieved so far is incomplete. However, its capacity to deliver has been outstanding. At a moment when we were facing critical challenges, the G20 came up with a coordinated response to the decline in global activity and to stabilise markets. It is now focusing on the very important issue of exit strategies from the massive public interventions, and among other medium and long-term issues on how to address climate change financing.

是的，这是一个多样化的集团。是的，取得的进展只是局部的。但是，它的解决能力是杰出的。我们面临关键挑战时，20国集团提出协同应对下滑的全球活动，稳定市场。它现在聚焦于非常重要的议题，考虑退出战略，退出大规模公共干预，以及其他中长期议题里例如处理气候变化融资的问题。

OECD has been supporting the G20 Summit since its inception. Our substantive contribution includes work on new sources of growth; on the human and social dimension of the crisis; on innovation; open markets for trade and investment and on the exchange of information for tax purposes.

经合组织一直支持20国集团峰会，从一开始就支持。我们的实质贡献包括致力于新的增长来源、人类和社会维度、创新、开放市场、接纳贸易和投资、交换信息，有关税收的信息。

It is quite significant that leaders felt they had to call on relevant international organisations to address the worst economic crisis ever. Leaders identify key issues in the global agenda and call on us to provide advice to address them.

这点很重要，领导人们感到他们必须呼吁相关国际组织处理最糟糕的经济危机。他们确定主要议题，形成全球议程，呼吁我们提供建议，处理议题。

Through evidence-based analytical inputs, we ensure that Countries that do not participate directly at the G20 stay connected to the discussions. The OECD is strongly committed to the notion that countries such as Ireland can have, through the OECD, an additional channel by which your voice can be heard. This role will remain central to our efforts.

通过基于证据的分析输入，我们确保不直接参与20国集团的国家能够保持联系，参与讨论。经合组织强烈承诺的主张是，诸如爱尔兰这样的国家能够通过经合组织，获得另外的渠道，藉此你的声音能被听到。这种角色将仍然是我们努力的中心。

In Pittsburgh we reported on areas where, based on OECD work, the world has achieved important breakthroughs. Such is the case of exchange of information for tax purposes, where, since November 2008 we made more progress than in the last 10 years. We have just established the most ambitious peer review process, that includes almost 90 countries ready to measure compliance based on OECD standards.

在匹兹堡，我们报告了一些领域，在经合组织的努力下，世界取得了重要的突破。情况就是这样，交流信息，服务于税收目的，自2008年11月以来，我们取得了很多进展，超过了之前的10年。我们刚建立了最具雄心的同行评审过程，包括近90个国家，准备衡量合规情况，按照经合组织的标准来衡量。

We also worked to keep markets open to trade and investment; and we contributed to a new approach to the regulation and supervision of the financial sector through our participation in the FSB. We will also establish a peer review process to evaluate compliance with the OECD principles of corporate governance. Failure to implement them produced the massive breakdown we have experienced.

我们还努力保持市场开放，鼓励贸易和投资；我们做了贡献，帮助新做法监管和监督金融行业，方法是参与金融稳定委员会。我们还将建立同行评审过程来评估合规，用经合组织的公司治理原则评估。没有实施这些原则导致了大规模崩溃，我们体验过了。

The most dramatic expression of the crisis is the level of unemployment, on which we have also worked in the context of the G20. Our mandate is to monitor labour developments and the impact of certain policies. There is a need to continue supporting workers through the stimulus packages, but in a long-term perspective it is also important to invest in skills development and retraining. Thus, the OECD was asked to contribute to the Labor Ministerial that the US will host in early 2010, building on the results of the OECD's own Employment, Labour and Social Affairs Ministerial Meeting held last September and where non-OECD countries like Brasil, South Africa and India were represented at Ministerial level.

最戏剧化的表达危机的形式就是失业水平，这点我们也致力改善——在20国集团中努力。我们的任务是监测劳动力发展和部分政策的影响。需要继续支持员工，采用刺激方案，但长期来看，还有一个要点，即投资技能发展和再培训。因此，经合组织被要求参与劳动部长会议，会将由美国举办，2010年初召开。其基础是经合组织自己的雇佣、劳工和社会事务部长去年九月的会议。非经合组织国家，如巴西、南非和印度派代表出席了部长级会议。

In Pittsburgh, OECD work on these areas was welcome, and we are asked to continue working on them. But we were also asked to continue our work on energy subsidies, and the impact of their removal in demand, prices, and GHG emissions. This was a very important area where the joint work of

在匹兹堡，经合组织的工作在这些领域受到欢迎，被要求继续下去。但是我们也被要求继续做能源补助的工作、考虑取消补助对需求、价格和温室气体排放的影响。这是一个非常

the OECD and the IEA was the basis for an agreement among participating countries.

重要的领域，经合组织和国际能源署的工作奠定了基础，有利于协议在参与国家之间达成。

Our estimates on GHG reduction resulting from the removal of these subsidies (as much as 10% in 2050) were extensively quoted, including by U.S. Treasury Secretary Geithner and President Obama himself, who recently wrote to ask that we continue this work, together with the IEA.

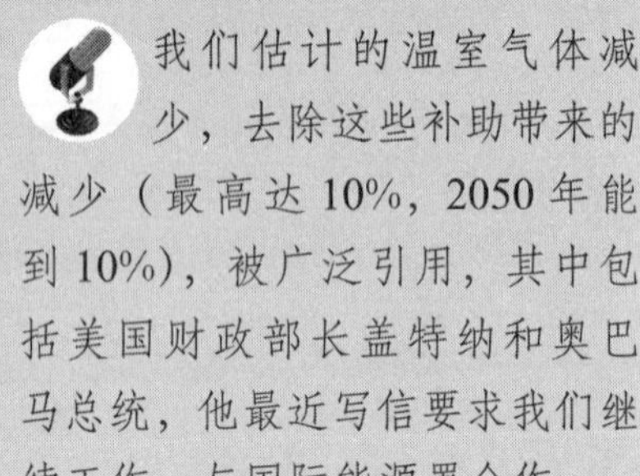

我们估计的温室气体减少，去除这些补助带来的减少（最高达 10%，2050 年能到 10%），被广泛引用，其中包括美国财政部长盖特纳和奥巴马总统，他最近写信要求我们继续工作，与国际能源署合作。

Additionally, and based on OECD work, Leaders:

- called for the adoption and enforcement of laws against transnational bribery, such as the OECD Anti-Bribery Convention.
- agreed to continue to work on the Charter for Sustainable Economic Activity, the process initiated by Chancellor Merkel to which the OECD has contributed since the very beginning, and on the "Lecce Framework" on the need to introduce ethics, transparency integrity and propriety in economic governance.

另外，基于经合组织的工作，领导们：

- 呼吁采纳和执行法律，反对跨国贿赂，如《经合组织反贿赂公约》。
- 同意继续开展《可持续经济活动宪章》的工作，进程的发起者是默克尔总理，经合组织也贡献良多，自最初就如此，而且继续"莱切框架"的工作，引进道德、透明、正直和繁荣到经济治理中。

On the way forward, the G20 is also paving the way to build a stronger, more balanced and sustainable growth process. This is one of the major achievements in Pittsburgh that will be discussed at the next G20 Finance Ministers and Central Bank Governors in Saint Andrews this week-end.

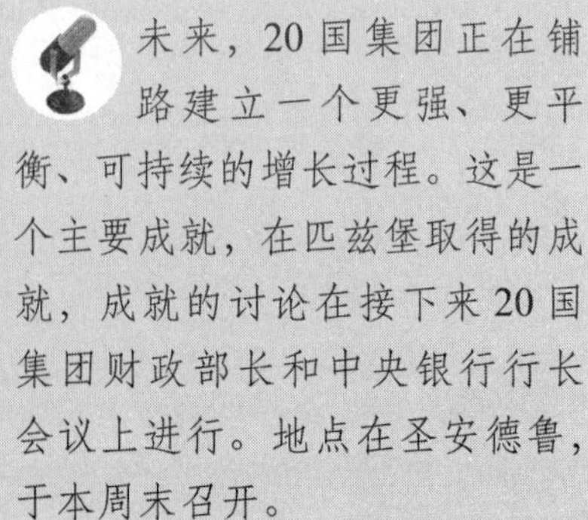

未来，20 国集团正在铺路建立一个更强、更平衡、可持续的增长过程。这是一个主要成就，在匹兹堡取得的成就，成就的讨论在接下来 20 国集团财政部长和中央银行行长会议上进行。地点在圣安德鲁，于本周末召开。

The Framework can be seen as a compact that commits countries to work together to assess the coherence of national policies and their consistency with the common objectives agreed at the G20-level. The OECD has for many decades been assessing and monitoring national policies through a peer review or mutual assessment process and we are ready to contribute to this excellent initiative.

框架可被视作一个契约，使各国合作评估国家政策是否连贯，是否符合共同的、20国集团的目标。经合组织几十年来都在评估和监测国家政策，通过同行评审或者相互评估过程进行，我们愿意做贡献，推进这个卓越的计划。

OECD has made several very concrete proposals to the G20 on the Framework and on how we could adapt our ongoing work programs to support its implementation. One way would be through the establishment of the "Observatory for Policy Coherence", or policy assessment network, among key international organisations specialising in economic issues to provide the best possible joint input into G20 processes.

经合组织做了几个非常具体的提议，向20国集团提议有关框架以及如何调整正在进行的工作项目以支持框架实施。一个方法是建立“政策连贯性观察站”，或政策评估网络，包括主要国际组织，专长于经济问题的组织，由他们提供最佳联合输入给20国集团的进程。

While taking into account the comparative advantage of each International Organisation, the Observatory would allow for different perspectives. It is not about duplicating efforts. It is about being complementary. The messages of the international organisations would become reciprocally reinforcing if they were better shared and more effectively coordinated.

考虑到比较优势，国际组织各不相同，观察站将允许不同的视角，不是重复工作，而是作为补充。国际组织的信息也将相互得到加强，但是需要更好地分享，更有效地协调。

Ladies and Gentlemen:

The crisis has accelerated the speed at which the global governance architecture has to be updated and revamped. The G20 is an important step forward in such process. The OECD is ready to contribute to its success.

Thank you very much.

女士们、先生们：

危机加速了全球治理架构升级和修改的需要。20国集团是重要的一步。经合组织愿意为其成功做出贡献。

谢谢。

7. 欧佩克秘书长的讲话

使用提要

1. 本单元的讲话稿仍然以两种形式提供：限时视译和技巧琢磨。
2. 限时视译的速度必须达到每秒3个英文单词，每次选择的长度应该增加到50-60秒之间，即大约150-180个单词。
3. 在使用或者参照译入语时必须注意：

   3.1. 参考译入语只是诸多可能版本之一，不是最佳版本，而且故意保留了一些不完美的地方。

   3.2. 一定不可用笔译的准确标准来衡量同传的译入语版本，因为听同传的感觉和阅读文字完全不一样。

   3.3. 避免把练习的重点放在讲解技巧的概念上，重点是熟练使用。

英译汉三词一译10大技巧

1. 缺省传译	2. 原话直译	3. 重复谓语	4. 介词转动
5. 先存后译	6. 反话正说	7. 被动变的	8. 点到为止
9. 预测先说	10. 弃卒保车		

限时视译

Asian Energy Outlook up to 2030

(*OPEC Secretary General Abdalla Salem el-Badri*)

Excellencies, Ladies and Gentlemen,

I would like to begin by thanking His Excellency Sheikh Ahmad Al-Abdullah Al-Ahmad Al-Sabah for the invitation to participate in this Roundtable. It gives me great pleasure to be in Kuwait, a founding Member of OPEC.

The first quarter of 2011 has seen a number of significant events that none could have predicted at the turn of the year.

In the Asian region, there was Japan's huge earthquake, devastating tsunami and subsequent nuclear crisis. Our sympathies are with all those affected by these catastrophic events.

And in North Africa and the Middle East, unrest has been witnessed in a number of countries. Our thoughts and hearts are with all those civilians who have suffered tremendously and whose daily lives have been adversely impacted. Where unrest remains, it is hoped that peaceful solutions can be found.

These events, as well as the continued uncertainties surrounding the global economy, have obviously had an impact on oil and energy markets. However, oil markets, which are global in nature, have rapidly adjusted, both in terms of volume and quality. Consequently, and as OPEC has indicated many times, there is no shortage of oil anywhere in the world, even with the partial absence of production from one of OPEC's Member Countries. Moreover, stock levels remain high; OPEC's spare capacity is around 4.5 million barrels a day, even after the recent disruption; the refining system has adequate flexibility; and the Organization's current production is at the level it was in December.

Nonetheless, we have all seen prices increasing in the first quarter and speculator activity on the Nymex has surged to record highs. For example, by mid-March, open interest for the Nymex WTI exceeded the unprecedented level of 1.5 million futures contracts, which is 18 times higher than the daily traded physical crude. Such an increase has been the result of concerns on supply further deteriorating beyond the current situation. A risk premium of about 15 to 20 dollars is currently embedded in the price.

It is important the market focuses on its balanced supply and demand fundamentals. A curb in speculative activities is needed. None of us want a return to the price levels we witnessed in mid-2008.

The rise in prices has been even more pronounced at the consumer end, where the effect of consuming country taxation is greatly felt. While OPEC has played its role by ensuring the market remains well supplied in crude, it would be helpful at this point in time if consuming countries that have a high level of taxation on oil products consider revising down these levels, at least temporarily, to alleviate the impact on end-consumers.

These are exceptional circumstances that need exceptional remedies.

Looking to the longer term and the theme of this session—'Asian Energy Outlook up to 2030'—what is clear is that the Asian region has become, and will increasingly become, ever more important in terms of global economic growth and energy demand. This is highlighted in last November's publication of OPEC's annual World Oil Outlook.

First, in terms of demographics: Asia is home to two-thirds of the world's population, a population that is young, growing quickly and increasingly located in large urban areas.

In terms of the economy, Asia's role and its global weight is rapidly expanding: today, it contributes 36% of the world's gross domestic product and this share is expected to reach 49% by 2030. Asia will economically be the fastest growing region over the next 20 years.

This economic strength can also be viewed in the region's recovery from the global economic crisis. Emerging economies, with China and India to the fore, are now back to strong growth rates. This is in contrast to many OECD countries that are juggling the need for additional monetary and fiscal policies to support fragile growth and the necessity for fiscal consolidation. This is particularly evident in the sovereign debt situations of a number of Euro-zone countries.

This expected economic growth also translates into Asia's expanding importance for energy demand, in general, and oil demand, in particular. In fact, the hub for oil demand has been progressively shifting towards Asia in recent years. For example, over the last five years, OECD oil demand contracted by around 3.8 million barrels a day. While Asia, including the Middle East, actually saw an increase of almost 4.8 million barrels a day over the same period.

Looking ahead, developing countries are set to account for most of the long-term oil demand increase, with consumption rising 22 million barrels a day over the period

2009-to-2030 to reach almost 57 million barrels a day. And around 75% of the net growth in oil demand in this period is in developing Asian economies.

It is clear that transportation will remain the main source of the region's oil demand growth. With strong economic expansion, improvements in living standards and greater disposable incomes, a significant increase in vehicle volumes for Asia's developing countries is expected. Today, 22% of world passenger cars are in Asia; this figure is projected to reach 39% in 2030. This represents phenomenal growth.

It should be noted, however, that per capita oil use in developing countries will remain far below that of the developed world by 2030. For example, oil use per person in North America will still be more than ten times that in South Asia.

Moreover, energy poverty will remain a very real concern for many billions of people, the majority of whom are to be found in Asia.

Of course, the region's growing energy use can be expected to result in higher levels of greenhouse gas emissions. It is important, however, to put this in context.

This is specifically in terms of sustainable development, with its intertwined and mutually supportive pillars of economic development, social progress and the protection of the environment. And in regards to priorities and responsibilities, with the United Nations Framework Convention on Climate Change stating that economic and social development and poverty eradication are the first and overriding priorities of developing country Parties. Developed countries should take the lead in combating climate change and the subsequent adverse effects.

Nonetheless, it should be stressed that many Asian countries are already playing a role in reducing their economy's carbon intensity.

For example, China's recent five-year plan calls for a drastic reduction in both energy consumption and CO2 emission per unit of GDP, by 16 and 17% respectively, by the end of 2015. And many countries in the region are also seeing a significant expansion in renewables, albeit from a low base.

There has also been much talk of nuclear in recent years, with a number of countries in the region looking to build nuclear plants. Events at the Fukushima nuclear complex in Japan, however, have led to many questions being asked about nuclear power, particularly in terms of safety, waste and decommissioning.

From an oil market perspective, for fast-growing Asian economies it is important that there is adequate supply to meet the growing demand. This is clear, both in terms of production and available resources.

While suppliers continue to face significant challenges, such as the impact of the global financial and economic crisis, market volatility and the role of speculation, and an often unclear demand picture as a result of a number of consuming countries policies, investments to increase capacity are being made.

In the medium-term to 2015, OPEC Member Countries are expected to invest an estimated $290 billion in upstream projects, with $120 billion in Iraq alone. We remain committed to future investment plans to boost our capacity.

Resources are also plentiful. The Middle East alone has an abundant natural resource endowment: over 750 billion barrels in proven crude oil reserves and almost 76 trillion cubic metres in proven gas reserves, which is around 56% and 40% of global totals, respectively.

What all this underlines is the ever-expanding interdependence between the Middle East and Asian regions. This is not only in terms of oil trade, which continues to grow, but also from a broader economic perspective. For example, between 2000 and 2009, exports to the Middle East from Asia and the Far East increased by around 300%, compared to an increase of about 120% in terms of total world exports from Asia and the Far East. Exports from the Middle East to Asia and the Far East also increased around 180%, compared to a global figure of about 145%.

In looking at Asia's future energy outlook, it is clear that the relationship between this region and the Middle East is an extremely important one and one which will continue to grow. There is much that each can offer the other.

In general, the growing interdependence between us is all the more clear today given that many regions and countries are facing an array of challenges, such as those originating from economic and financial uncertainties, natural disasters and domestic social unrest.

With this in mind, our goal must be one of stability, with a clear and consistent environment that enables the industry to continue to develop, produce, transport, refine and deliver energy in an efficient and economic manner. This will benefit producers and consumers, as well as present and future generations, and hopefully deliver a better standard of living for all peoples around the world, as well as a greater hope that tomorrow will be better than today.

Thank you for your attention.

技巧琢磨

Excellencies, Ladies and Gentlemen,

I would like to begin by thanking His Excellency Sheikh Ahmad Al-Abdullah Al-Ahmad Al-Sabah for the invitation to participate in this Roundtable. It gives me great pleasure to be in Kuwait, a founding Member of OPEC.

各位阁下，女士们，先生们：

我想首先感谢谢赫·艾哈迈德·阿尔-阿卜杜拉·阿尔-艾哈迈德·阿尔-萨巴赫阁下邀请我们参加此次圆桌会议。我很高兴来到科威特，这个欧佩克的创始成员国。

The first quarter of 2011 has seen a number of significant events that none could have predicted at the turn of the year.

2011年第一季度有几个突出事件，都是无法预计的。

In the Asian region, there was Japan's huge earthquake, devastating tsunami and subsequent nuclear crisis. Our sympathies are with all those affected by these catastrophic events.

在亚洲，有日本大地震，破坏性的海啸和随后的核危机。我们同情所有遭受这些灾难性事件的人们。

And in North Africa and the Middle East, unrest has been witnessed in a number of countries. Our thoughts and hearts are with all those civilians who have suffered tremendously and whose daily lives have been adversely impacted. Where unrest remains, it is hoped that peaceful solutions can be found.

在北美和中东，动荡冲击着几个国家。我们关注和担忧所有受苦的人们，他们的日常生活受到严重影响。在动荡仍存在的地方，希望能有和平解决方案。

These events, as well as the continued uncertainties surrounding the global economy, have obviously had an impact on oil and energy markets. However, oil markets, which are global in nature, have rapidly adjusted, both in terms of volume and quality. Consequently, and as OPEC has indicated many

这些事件，以及持续的不确定性围困着全球经济，明显影响了石油和能源市场。但是，石油市场是全球性的，它快速调整了数量和质量。因此，就像欧佩克多次指出的，不缺石

times, there is no shortage of oil anywhere in the world, even with the partial absence of production from one of OPEC's Member Countries. Moreover, stock levels remain high; OPEC's spare capacity is around 4.5 million barrels a day, even after the recent disruption; the refining system has adequate flexibility; and the Organization's current production is at the level it was in December.

油，哪里都不缺，即使有部分生产缺失，一个欧佩克成员减产不会造成短缺。此外，储存水平仍然很高；欧佩克的后备储量约为450万桶一天，即使在最近的干扰后仍然如此；炼油系统有足够的灵活性；欧佩克的现有生产相当于12月的水平。

Nonetheless, we have all seen prices increasing in the first quarter and speculator activity on the Nymex has surged to record highs. For example, by mid-March, open interest for the Nymex WTI exceeded the unprecedented level of 1.5 million futures contracts, which is 18 times higher than the daily traded physical crude. Such an increase has been the result of concerns on supply further deteriorating beyond the current situation. A risk premium of about 15 to 20 dollars is currently embedded in the price.

尽管如此，我们看到价格上涨，第一季度看涨，投机活动在纽约商业交易所达到历史新高。比如，到三月中旬，未平仓量合约在纽约商业交易所超过了前所未有的150万期货合约,18倍于日常交易的实物原油。这个增量的原因是担心供应进一步恶化。风险溢价约15到20美元现在已包含在价格中。

It is important the market focuses on its balanced supply and demand fundamentals. A curb in speculative activities is needed. None of us want a return to the price levels we witnessed in mid-2008.

市场确实需要关注平衡供需的基本原则。抑制投机活动很有必要。我们都不希望回到价格水平2008年中期的状况。

The rise in prices has been even more pronounced at the consumer end, where the effect of consuming country taxation is greatly felt. While OPEC has played its role by ensuring the market remains well supplied in crude, it would be helpful at this point in time if consuming countries that have a high level of taxation on oil products consider revising

价格上涨更显著地影响了消费者这一端，消费国税收的影响感觉很明显。欧佩克扮演了它的角色，确保市场保持供应充足原油，此时如果消费国已在较高水平征收石油产品税时能考虑降低税收水平，至少是暂时

down these levels, at least temporarily, to alleviate the impact on end-consumers.

These are exceptional circumstances that need exceptional remedies.

Looking to the longer term and the theme of this session—'Asian Energy Outlook up to 2030'—what is clear is that the Asian region has become, and will increasingly become, ever more important in terms of global economic growth and energy demand. This is highlighted in last November's publication of OPEC's annual World Oil Outlook.

First, in terms of demographics: Asia is home to two-thirds of the world's population, a population that is young, growing quickly and increasingly located in large urban areas.

In terms of the economy, Asia's role and its global weight is rapidly expanding: today, it contributes 36% of the world's gross domestic product and this share is expected to reach 49% by 2030. Asia will economically be the fastest growing region over the next 20 years.

This economic strength can also be viewed in the region's recovery from the global economic crisis. Emerging economies, with China and India to the fore, are now back to strong growth rates. This is in contrast to many OECD countries that are juggling the need for additional monetary and

减税，也能缓解对终端消费者的影响。

这些特殊情况需要特殊对策。

看看长期情况和会议主题：“亚洲能源至2030年的展望”。很显然，亚洲地区已成为并将越来越成为重要地区，全球经济增长和能源需求离不开亚洲。这体现在去年11月出版的欧佩克年度《世界石油展望》中。

首先，人口分布：亚洲拥有三分之二的世界人口，人口很年轻，增长迅速，而且越来越多地居住在大城市。

就经济而言，亚洲的角色及其全球份量快速扩展。今天，亚洲贡献了36%的GDP，这个份额预计会达到49%，在2030年达到。亚洲将在经济上成为增长最快的区域，今后20年都是如此。

经济优势也体现在该地区的复苏、摆脱经济危机上。新兴经济体，以中国和印度为首，恢复了强劲的增长。与此相反，很多经合组织国家一方面需要额外货币和财政政策支

fiscal policies to support fragile growth and the necessity for fiscal consolidation. This is particularly evident in the sovereign debt situations of a number of Euro-zone countries.

持脆弱的增长，另一方面需要财政巩固。尤为明显的是在主权债务危机中，几个欧元区国家都有这样的问题。

This expected economic growth also translates into Asia's expanding importance for energy demand, in general, and oil demand, in particular. In fact, the hub for oil demand has been progressively shifting towards Asia in recent years. For example, over the last five years, OECD oil demand contracted by around 3.8 million barrels a day. While Asia, including the Middle East, actually saw an increase of almost 4.8 million barrels a day over the same period.

预期的经济增长也成为亚洲不断扩大的重要性。能源需求，尤其是石油需求如此。其实，石油需求枢纽不断转移到亚洲，近年来一直如此。比如，过去五年中，欧佩克石油需求收缩达380万桶一天。而亚洲，包括中东，却出现了增长，约480万桶一天。

Looking ahead, developing countries are set to account for most of the long-term oil demand increase, with consumption rising 22 million barrels a day over the period 2009-to-2030 to reach almost 57 million barrels a day. And around 75% of the net growth in oil demand in this period is in developing Asian economies.

向前展望，发展中国家会占大部分的长期石油需求增长，消费量上涨2200万桶一天，在09年到30年期间不断上涨，达到5700万桶一天。约75%的净增长在这期间将来自亚洲经济体。

It is clear that transportation will remain the main source of the region's oil demand growth. With strong economic expansion, improvements in living standards and greater disposable incomes, a significant increase in vehicle volumes for Asia's developing countries is expected. Today, 22% of world passenger cars are in Asia; this figure is projected to reach 39% in 2030. This represents phenomenal growth.

显然，运输将仍是主要来源，导致该地区的石油需求增长。由于强劲的经济扩展改善了生活条件，增加了可支配收入，显著增长的汽车数量在亚洲发展中国家是预料之内的。今天，22%的世界乘用车都在亚洲；这个数字据推算将达到39%，在2030年达到。这将是很大的增长。

It should be noted, however, that per capita oil use in developing countries will remain far below that of the developed world by 2030. For example, oil use per person in North America will still be more than ten times that in South Asia.

值得注意的是，人均石油使用量在发展中国家将保持远低于发达国家的水平，到 2030 年都是如此。比如，人均石油用量在北美仍将很大，十倍于南亚水平。

Moreover, energy poverty will remain a very real concern for many billions of people, the majority of whom are to be found in Asia.

此外，能源贫困仍将是重要担忧，影响数十亿人口，其中大部分是亚洲人口。

Of course, the region's growing energy use can be expected to result in higher levels of greenhouse gas emissions. It is important, however, to put this in context.

当然，该区域不断增长的能源使用预计会带来更高的温室气体排放。但这必须分析对待。

This is specifically in terms of sustainable development, with its intertwined and mutually supportive pillars of economic development, social progress and the protection of the environment. And in regards to priorities and responsibilities, with the United Nations Framework Convention on Climate Change stating that economic and social development and poverty eradication are the first and overriding priorities of developing country Parties. Developed countries should take the lead in combating climate change and the subsequent adverse effects.

尤其是在可持续发展方面，其中紧密联系并互相支持的支柱支持经济发展、社会进步和保护环境。在优先要务和责任方面，《联合国气候变化框架公约》申明，经济和社会发展以及脱贫优先，是发展中国家政党的重心。发达国家应率先应对气候变化和随后的负面影响。

Nonetheless, it should be stressed that many Asian countries are already playing a role in reducing their economy's carbon intensity.

然而，要强调的是，很多亚洲国家已经扮演了关键角色以降低其经济的碳密度。

For example, China's recent five-year plan calls for a drastic reduction in both energy consumption and CO_2 emission per unit of GDP, by 16 and 17% respectively, by the end of 2015. And many countries in the region are also seeing a significant expansion in renewables, albeit from a low base.

比如，中国最近的五年计划呼吁显著降低能源消耗和二氧化碳排量在每单位GDP中的份额，16%和17%分别是2015年底的目标。很多国家在该地区也看到显著扩展的可再生能源，不过起点较低。

There has also been much talk of nuclear in recent years, with a number of countries in the region looking to build nuclear plants. Events at the Fukushima nuclear complex in Japan, however, have led to many questions being asked about nuclear power, particularly in terms of safety, waste and decommissioning.

人们经常谈及核问题，近年来，几个亚洲国家试图建核电站。福岛事件在日本引发了很多疑问，讨论核能，尤其是安全、废料和电站报废问题。

From an oil market perspective, for fast-growing Asian economies it is important that there is adequate supply to meet the growing demand. This is clear, both in terms of production and available resources.

从石油市场的角度，对于快速增长的亚洲经济体来说，重点是要有充足供应，以满足增长的需求。这很明确，在生产和可获资源上都是如此。

While suppliers continue to face significant challenges, such as the impact of the global financial and economic crisis, market volatility and the role of speculation, and an often unclear demand picture as a result of a number of consuming countries policies, investments to increase capacity are being made.

供应方持续面临严峻挑战，比如全球金融经济危机的影响，市场波动和投机的作用，加上通常不明确的需求情况，原因是一些消费国的政策，投资增加产量的做法正在进行中。

In the medium-term to 2015, OPEC Member Countries are expected to invest an estimated $290 billion in upstream projects, with $120 billion in Iraq alone. We remain committed to future investment plans to boost our capacity.

中期，即到2015年，欧佩克成员国预期投资约2900亿美元到上游项目中，其中1200亿美元是在伊拉克的投资。我们仍然致力于未来投资计划以提高产能。

Resources are also plentiful. The Middle East alone has an abundant natural resource endowment: over 750 billion barrels in proven crude oil reserves and almost 76 trillion cubic metres in proven gas reserves, which is around 56% and 40% of global totals, respectively.

资源也是充足的。中东就有充裕的自然资源:7500亿多桶探明原油储备和近76万亿立方米探明天然气储备，约占56%和40%的全球总量。

What all this underlines is the ever-expanding interdependence between the Middle East and Asian regions. This is not only in terms of oil trade, which continues to grow, but also from a broader economic perspective. For example, between 2000 and 2009, exports to the Middle East from Asia and the Far East increased by around 300%, compared to an increase of about 120% in terms of total world exports from Asia and the Far East. Exports from the Middle East to Asia and the Far East also increased around 180%, compared to a global figure of about 145%.

这些说明的是不断扩大的相互依赖，中东和亚洲地区谁也少不了谁。这不仅是石油贸易方面，石油贸易持续增长，但也体现在更广的经济角度上。比如，在00到09年之间，出口到中东——光是亚洲和远东的出口量就增长了300%，与此相比，增长120%是整体世界出口中来自亚洲和远东的数据。中东到亚洲和远东的出口也增加了180%，与此相比，全球数据约为145%。

In looking at Asia's future energy outlook, it is clear that the relationship between this region and the Middle East is an extremely important one and one which will continue to grow. There is much that each can offer the other.

看待亚洲未来能源展望时，很清楚，该地区和中东的关系是及其重要的，并将继续发展。有很多彼此可以相互提供的。

In general, the growing interdependence between us is all the more clear today given that many regions and countries are facing an array of challenges, such as those originating from economic and financial uncertainties, natural disasters and domestic social unrest.

总体上，越来越大的相互依赖性更明确了，因为很多地区和国家都面临一系列挑战，比如经济和金融的不确定性、自然灾害和国内社会动荡。

With this in mind, our goal must be one of stability, with a clear and consistent environment that enables the industry to continue to develop, produce, transport, refine and deliver energy in an efficient and economic manner. This will benefit producers and consumers, as well as present and future generations, and hopefully deliver a better standard of living for all peoples around the world, as well as a greater hope that tomorrow will be better than today.

Thank you for your attention..

考虑到这些，我们的目标必须是稳定的，要有清楚和一致的环境，使工业持续发展、生产、运输、精炼、交付能源，以高效、经济的方式完成。这将惠及生产者和消费者，以及当今的一代和后人，希望这能改善生活水平，惠及所有人，无论哪个国家；更希望明天将比今天更美好。

谢谢。

8. IMF总裁拉加德的讲话

使用提要

1. 本单元的讲话稿仍然以两种形式提供：限时视译和技巧琢磨。
2. 限时视译的速度必须达到每秒 3 个英文单词，每次选择的长度应该增加到 50–60 秒之间，即大约 150–180 个单词。
3. 在使用或者参照译入语时必须注意：

    3.1. 参考译入语只是诸多可能版本之一，不是最佳版本，而且故意保留了一些不完美的地方。

    3.2. 一定不可用笔译的准确标准来衡量同传的译入语版本，因为听同传的感觉和阅读文字完全不一样。

    3.3. 避免把练习的重点放在讲解技巧的概念上，重点是熟练使用。

英译汉三词一译10大技巧

1. 缺省传译	2. 原话直译	3. 重复谓语	4. 介词转动
5. 先存后译	6. 反话正说	7. 被动变的	8. 点到为止
9. 预测先说	10. 弃卒保车		

限时视译

Speech to China Development Forum 2012 Opening Ceremony

Christine Lagarde

Good morning.

It is an absolute pleasure to be back in Beijing and so soon after my excellent visit last November. My desire to be here reflects just how important China has become for the global economy.

It is a great privilege to be among such esteemed company. I would also like to thank Li Wei and his colleagues at the Development Research Center of the State Council for inviting me here today.

"China & the World: Macroeconomic Stabilization and Economic Restructuring." At this juncture, I cannot think of a better theme for this year's forum.

The specific economic challenges that countries face today naturally differ, with positive signs emerging in some corners of the globe and severe stresses still prominent in others. Yet, there are common goals that unite us all—the quest for growth and stability—lasting growth, shared growth, growth that delivers jobs and a better livelihood for all.

This event provides an excellent opportunity to reflect on the remarkable role that China is playing, and can continue to play, in pursuing these global goals.

I am very much looking forward to hearing Vice Premier Li Keqiang speak, as I'm sure you all are too. So, let me reflect briefly on two things: first, the state of the global economy; and second, China's leading role in securing economic stability and prosperity.

Global Economic Challenges

The past few years have been extremely difficult for many parts of the world. And, even just a few months ago, the situation was decidedly gloomy. Indicators for the last quarter of 2011—namely for Europe and the United States—did not provide much reassurance.

Yet, today, we are seeing signs of stabilization; signs that policy actions are paying off. Financial-market conditions are more comfortable and recent economic indicators are beginning to look a little more upbeat, including in the United States.

Important decisions and policy actions, particularly by the European Central Bank and some European countries, have helped. I have said for some time that we can avoid the worst if all partners play their part.

Moving forward with renewed support for Greece — from both the IMF and European partners — is an important milestone in this regard. The measures are ambitious and it will be important to focus on implementation and monitoring, but we have made an important step forward.

On the back of these collective efforts, the world economy has stepped back from the brink and we have cause to be more optimistic.

Still, optimism must not lull us into a false sense of security. There are still major economic and financial vulnerabilities we must confront. I'll mention three.

- First, financial systems are still fragile and high public and private debt persists in many advanced economies — euro area public sector and bank rollover needs total about 23 percent of GDP during 2012. Renewed pressure in either area could compound the other, leading to much larger, and more protracted, contractions in credit and output.

- Second, the rising price of oil is becoming a threat to global growth.

- And, third, there is a growing risk that activity in emerging economies will slow over the medium term.

And we must not forget that there are still too many people, in too many countries, who are enduring the hardship of unemployment.

So, the global economy may be on a path to recovery, but there is not a great deal of room for maneuver and no room for policy mistakes.

It is often said that a reputation is "gained in inches and lost in miles". The same could be said of economic progress. All countries must persevere with their policy efforts if the progress of yesterday is to translate into the promise of a brighter tomorrow.

So, what are the main challenges?

- The advanced economies need to capitalize on the newly gained breathing space and push forward with policies that will enable them to emerge from the crisis. This means continued macroeconomic support and a balanced fiscal approach, together with financial sector reforms and structural and institutional reforms to repair the damage done by the crisis and to improve competitiveness.
- Emerging market economies need to calibrate macroeconomic policies—both to guard against further fallout from the advanced economies as well as to keep overheating pressures in check. And, by continuing to invest in reforms—such as increasing social transfers or lowering consumption taxes—they can, over time, translate higher growth into better living standards for all.

China's Leadership

This brings me to my second point—China's global leadership.

For many years now, China's economic successes have captured the world's attention. We have looked on in awe as, year after year, China has posted spectacular growth and, in the space of three decades, created 370 million jobs and lifted half a billion people out of poverty.

When the global crisis hit, China again showed leadership and adept policy skills. Indeed, the global economic situation might have been even more calamitous had it not been for the impetus that China provided to growth and stability.

China's leadership role in global institutions has mirrored these economic successes. As one of the IMF's largest shareholders and as an influential member of the G-20, China has been instrumental in helping to make the global economic system less prone to damaging crises.

Yet, lingering weaknesses in the global outlook reinforce the importance of China continuing to forge ahead—by maintaining a prominent role in global policy discussions and by sustaining its efforts to accelerate the transformation of the Chinese economy.

So, as I see it, the priorities for China are now threefold:

- First, to support growth. On this score, China is in the enviable position of having the space to provide some modest fiscal support for its economy as outlined at the recent National People's Congress.

- Second, to continue shifting the drivers of economic growth away from investment and exports, and toward domestic consumption.
- Third, to improve household livelihoods so that China's citizens may all share in the dividends of high and sustained growth.

I am encouraged that the government has embraced these goals, reflected in the comprehensive policy agenda in the recent 12th Five Year Plan.

Conclusion

Finally: If I had one piece of advice for policymakers around the world, I might borrow the words of Confucius:

"In all things, success depends on previous preparation."

We have seen China's previous preparation bear the fruits of today's success. And we are beginning to see the small successes from recent action in Europe.

But today's risks are still very much global. We are all interconnected and we are all affected by each other's policy actions. We need to prepare for success together. If we stand together, the whole will be more than the sum of the parts.

And, in this, China is a leader of the global economy—leading by example, leading by responsible economic policy, leading by engagement.

Thank you.

技巧琢磨

Good morning.

It is an absolute pleasure to be back in Beijing and so soon after my excellent visit last November. My desire to be here reflects just how important China has become for the global economy.

早上好。

我非常很高兴回到北京，不久前我刚来过，也就是11月份。我希望来，这就反应出中国很重要，影响到全球经济。

It is a great privilege to be among such esteemed company. I would also like to thank Li Wei and his colleagues at the Development Research Center of the State Council for inviting me here today.

非常荣幸加入到备受尊重的各位之中。我要感谢李伟和他的同事们，国务院发展研究中心的同事们，邀请我参加今天的活动。

"China & the World: Macroeconomic Stabilization and Economic Restructuring." At this juncture, I cannot think of a better theme for this year's forum.

“中国与世界：宏观经济稳定与经济重组”。此时，我想最好的主题对今年的论坛来说不过于此。

The specific economic challenges that countries face today naturally differ, with positive signs emerging in some corners of the globe and severe stresses still prominent in others. Yet, there are common goals that unite us all—the quest for growth and stability—lasting growth, shared growth, growth that delivers jobs and a better livelihood for all.

具体的经济挑战，各国自然不同。积极迹象出现在一些地方，严峻压力仍然主导其它地方。但是，有个共同目标将我们团结在一起：寻求增长和稳定、延长增长、分享增长、带来就业、改善生活，惠及所有人。

This event provides an excellent opportunity to reflect on the remarkable role that China is playing, and can continue to play, in pursuing these global goals.

这次活动提供了极佳的机会来反思中国的重要作用，中国能继续发挥作用，追求这些全球目标。

I am very much looking forward to hearing Vice Premier Li Keqiang speak, as I'm sure you all are too. So, let me reflect briefly on two things: first, the state of the global economy; and second, China's leading role in securing economic stability and prosperity.

我非常期待听取副总理李克强的演讲，我相信大家也是。请允许我简要说两点：一，全球经济的现状；二，中国的领导作用，在保证经济稳定和繁荣中的作用。

Global Economic Challenges

The past few years have been extremely difficult for many parts of the world. And, even just a few months ago, the situation was decidedly gloomy. Indicators for the last quarter of 2011 — namely for Europe and the United States — did not provide much reassurance.

全球经济挑战

过去几年非常艰难，许多地方都如此。仅仅几个月前，情况还是很黯淡。根据数据，2011年第四季度，欧洲和美国的情况都不能让人放心。

Yet, today, we are seeing signs of stabilization; signs that policy actions are paying off. Financial-market conditions are more comfortable and recent economic indicators are beginning to look a little more upbeat, including in the United States.

但是，今天，我们看到稳定的迹象，表明政策行动产生效果了。金融市场的情况比较好了，近期经济指标开始有些上扬，其中包括美国的指标。

Important decisions and policy actions, particularly by the European Central Bank and some European countries, have helped. I have said for some time that we can avoid the worst if all partners play their part.

重要的决策和政策行动，尤其是欧洲央行和一些欧洲国家的行动产生了效果。我说过多次，我们能够避免最坏情形，但必须所有伙伴都发挥作用。

Moving forward with renewed support for Greece — from both the IMF and European partners — is an important milestone in this regard. The measures are ambitious and it will be important to focus on implementation and monitoring, but we have made an important step forward.

采取措施，更多地支持希腊，国际货币基金组织和欧洲伙伴都要支持，这是一个重要里程碑。这些措施雄心勃勃，然而必须聚焦实施和监测，但是我们已经取得了重要进展。

On the back of these collective efforts, the world economy has stepped back from the brink and we have cause to be more optimistic.

这些集体努力之后，世界经济回转，我们有理由更乐观。

Still, optimism must not lull us into a false sense of security. There are still major economic and financial vulnerabilities we must confront. I'll mention three.

但是，乐观不能让我们落入虚假的安全感。仍有重大的经济和金融脆弱性，我们必须应对。我提三点。

• First, financial systems are still fragile and high public and private debt persists in many advanced economies—euro area public sector and bank rollover needs total about 23 percent of GDP during 2012. Renewed pressure in either area could compound the other, leading to much larger, and more protracted, contractions in credit and output.

• 一，金融系统依然脆弱，公共和私人债务居高不下，许多发达经济体中都这样。欧元区公共领域和银行滚动债务需要大约百分之23的GDP，这是2012年的情况。新压力在哪个领域都可能导致另外一个领域恶化，导致更大、更长时间的收缩，信贷和输出都会收缩。

• Second, the rising price of oil is becoming a threat to global growth.

• 二，上升的油价成为威胁，不利于全球增长。

• And, third, there is a growing risk that activity in emerging economies will slow over the medium term.

• 三，还有一个越来越大的风险，即新兴经济体的活动将放慢，中期不看好。

And we must not forget that there are still too many people, in too many countries, who are enduring the hardship of unemployment.

我们不能忘记仍有很多人，在很多国家，正经受严峻的失业。

So, the global economy may be on a path to recovery, but there is not a great deal of room for maneuver and no room for policy mistakes.

因此，全球经济可能在复苏，但是没有太多的回旋空间，不能犯政策错误。

It is often said that a reputation is "gained in inches and lost in miles". The same could be said of economic progress. All countries must persevere with their policy efforts if the progress of yesterday is to translate into the promise of a brighter tomorrow.

通常说名声“获得仅为英寸，失去却是英里”。同样，可以说经济进步也如此。每个国家都必须坚持他们的政策努力，如果昨天的进步要变成承诺，实现光明未来，就要这样做。

So, what are the main challenges?

那么，主要挑战是哪些？

• The advanced economies need to capitalize on the newly gained breathing space and push forward with policies that will enable them to emerge from the crisis. This means continued macroeconomic support and a balanced fiscal approach, together with financial sector reforms and structural and institutional reforms to repair the damage done by the crisis and to improve competitiveness.

• 发达经济体需要运用新近获得的喘气空间，推进政策，浮出危机。这意味着继续宏观经济支持和平衡的财务做法，再加上金融领域改革和结构与机构改革，以修复损害，改善竞争力。

• Emerging market economies need to calibrate macroeconomic policies — both to guard against further fallout from the advanced economies as well as to keep overheating pressures in check. And, by continuing to invest in reforms — such as increasing social transfers or lowering consumption taxes — they can, over time, translate higher growth into better living standards for all.

• 新兴市场经济体需要调整宏观经济政策，既防范进一步受波及，免受发达经济体影响，又要保持过热的压力不失控，继续投资于改革，比如增加社会转移或削减消费税。一段时间后就能把更高的增长转变为更好的生活标准，惠及所有人。

China's Leadership

中国的领导力

This brings me to my second point — China's global leadership.

这就涉及到我的第二点：中国的全球领导力。

For many years now, China's economic successes have captured the world's attention. We have looked on in awe as, year after year, China has posted

多年来，中国的经济成功获得了全世界的关注。我们看中国，怀着敬畏。年复一年，中国展示了惊人的增长。三十年

spectacular growth and, in the space of three decades, created 370 million jobs and lifted half a billion people out of poverty.

内，创造了3亿7千万个工作岗位，5亿人脱贫。

When the global crisis hit, China again showed leadership and adept policy skills. Indeed, the global economic situation might have been even more calamitous had it not been for the impetus that China provided to growth and stability.

全球经济危机时，中国再次显示了领导力和娴熟的政治技巧。全球经济情况本来可能会更加糟糕，还好有了中国的动力，刺激了增长和稳定。

China's leadership role in global institutions has mirrored these economic successes. As one of the IMF's largest shareholders and as an influential member of the G-20, China has been instrumental in helping to make the global economic system less prone to damaging crises.

中国的领导作用在全球性机构中反映了这些经济成功，是国际货币基金组织最大的股东之一，也是有影响力的G20成员。中国有助于使全球经济系统不易发生破坏性危机。

Yet, lingering weaknesses in the global outlook reinforce the importance of China continuing to forge ahead—by maintaining a prominent role in global policy discussions and by sustaining its efforts to accelerate the transformation of the Chinese economy.

但是，全球经济展望中不断出现的弱点加强了中国继续进取的重要性，中国要保持重要角色，参与全球政策讨论，持续努力，加速转变中国经济。

So, as I see it, the priorities for China are now threefold:

在我看来，中国的优先事项有三个：

• First, to support growth. On this score, China is in the enviable position of having the space to provide some modest fiscal support for its economy as outlined at the recent National People's Congress.

• 一，支持增长。这方面，中国令人称羡，有空间提供一些温和的财政支持，提纲在最近的全国人大上也提出了。

• Second, to continue shifting the drivers of economic growth away from investment and exports, and toward domestic consumption.

• 二，继续转变驱动力，减少对投资和出口的依赖而转向国内消费。

• Third, to improve household livelihoods so that China's citizens may all share in the dividends of high and sustained growth.

I am encouraged that the government has embraced these goals, reflected in the comprehensive policy agenda in the recent 12th Five Year Plan.

Conclusion

Finally: If I had one piece of advice for policymakers around the world, I might borrow the words of Confucius:

"In all things, success depends on previous preparation."

We have seen China's previous preparation bear the fruits of today's success. And we are beginning to see the small successes from recent action in Europe.

But today's risks are still very much global. We are all interconnected and we are all affected by each other's policy actions. We need to prepare for success together. If we stand together, the whole will be more than the sum of the parts.

And, in this, China is a leader of the global economy—leading by example, leading by responsible economic policy, leading by engagement.

Thank you.

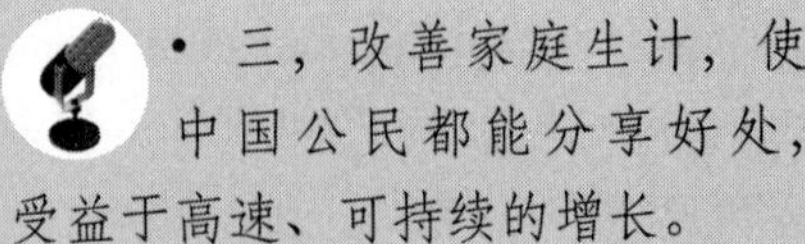

• 三，改善家庭生计，使中国公民都能分享好处，受益于高速、可持续的增长。

我备受鼓舞，因为中国政府采纳了这些目标，这反映在广泛的政策议程中，近期的“十二五规划”就是例证。

结论

最后，如果我要提一个建议给决策者，我会借用孔子的一句话：

“凡事预则立，不预则废。”

我们看到中国此前的准备孕育了今天的成功。我们也开始看到小成功在近期欧洲行动中的例子。

但是今天的风险仍然非常国际化。我们都互相联系，都受彼此政策行动的影响。我们要准备好共赢。如果我们站在一起，整体将大于部分的总和。

中国是领导者，引领全球经济，以身作则、以负责的经济政策、通过参与起到领导作用。

谢谢。

9. 国际奥委会主席罗格的讲话

使用提要

1. 本单元的讲话稿仍然以两种形式提供：限时视译和技巧琢磨。
2. 限时视译的速度必须达到每秒 3 个英文单词，每次选择的长度应该增加到 60-70 秒之间，即大约 180-210 个单词。
3. 在使用或者参照译入语时必须注意：

   3.1. 参考译入语只是诸多可能版本之一，不是最佳版本，而且故意保留了一些不完美的地方。

   3.2. 一定不可用笔译的准确标准来衡量同传的译入语版本，因为听同传的感觉和阅读文字完全不一样。

   3.3. 避免把练习的重点放在讲解技巧的概念上，重点是熟练使用。

英译汉三词一译10大技巧

1. 缺省传译	2. 原话直译	3. 重复谓语	4. 介词转动
5. 先存后译	6. 反话正说	7. 被动变的	8. 点到为止
9. 预测先说	10. 弃卒保车		

限时视译

Speech to World Conference on Doping in Sport

(*IOC President Jacques Rogge*)

Minister,

Distinguished Authorities, my fellow delegates, honoured guests:

Before I begin my formal remarks, I would like to thank the World Anti-Doping Agency, the Government of Spain, the Ministry of Education and Science, and the Spanish Sports Council for organising this important conference.

Minister, I thank you and your colleagues for your support. For your tough antidoping legislation passed in the last year. And for your ongoing attention to the Operation Puerto case, which I am confident will be resolved soon. We respect the separation of power and the independence of the justice and do hope that Spanish justice will take a decision in the Puerto case as a matter of priority. I hope that the sports organisations will then soon be authorised to use the information contained in the Puerto Report to take the necessary disciplinary sanctions against the guilty athletes.

It is a great pleasure to be with you today…

To reflect on the importance of our anti-doping efforts. To review the successes we have achieved so far. To explore the challenges and opportunities that lie ahead. And to reaffirm our joint commitment to eliminate doping in sport.

The importance of our efforts

Doping is one of the most serious threats the Olympic Movement has ever seen. It undermines all we stand for. It endangers the health of athletes. It undermines the credibility of results. It risks drying out the recruitment of sport, as, one day, parents might refuse to send their children to sports clubs.

The fight against doping involves however much more than elite sport alone. It is not only about testing and sanctioning well-known athletes, it is about the health and future of our population. It is therefore a public health problem. Recent studies indicate the same dynamics that exist in professional sports are emerging in high school and university sport programmes around the world. These studies indicate that hundreds of thousands of teenagers and even pre-teenagers are in danger.

Doping also affects the general sporting public — namely the millions of so called "weekend athletes," runners and fitness club members who want to incorporate sport and exercise into their lives for the purpose of maintaining or improving their health, boosting their muscle mass or bolstering their body image. A European Union report estimates that the incidence of doping among recreational athletes in the European Union has risen during the past two decades from approximately 5% to more than 20%. And let us not forget about the enormous amounts of anabolic steroids and Ecstasy pills that are seized by the authorities in many countries. They are sold to much more people than athletes alone.

As an advocate for sport and athletes around the world, the International Olympic Committee is unwavering in its commitment to combat doping in sport. This fight is our number one priority.

Successes

The IOC has been a leader in the fight against doping for more than 40 years. We established a Medical Commission in 1967. We developed the first list of prohibited drugs and worked out methods for their detection. We also established a system of sanctions. We accredited drug-testing laboratories. All these measures were adopted by the Olympic Movement. We established the Court of Arbitration for Sport, introduced out-of-competition testing and funded early research into doping trends and detection methods. And we also funded the WADA budget for the first two years.

After the Festina scandal and the Tour de France in 1998, we realised more was needed. In 1999, we organised a World Conference on Doping in Lausanne toharmonise anti-doping rules across the world of sport, and we called for the support of governments. This led to the creation of WADA.Today, the IOC continues to be a leader in the fight against doping. In response to the seriousness of the threat, we have championed a policy of zero tolerance.

We enforce this policy through a comprehensive programme of testing during each edition of the Olympic Games. Next year in Beijing, we plan to conduct 4,500 in- and out-of-competition tests. This is roughly 25 per cent more than were carried out during the 2004 Games in Athens. And 90 per cent more than the number of tests carried out in Sydney in 2000.

We have also recently proposed a series of measures to strengthen our zero tolerance policy. These measures include the denial of participation in the next Olympic Games for athletes and their entourage who have been sanctioned for more than six months. We will impose automatic suspensions after a positive A sample, we will impose stronger financial penalties for National Olympic Committees and athletes and implement stricter interpretations related to Therapeutic Use Exemptions.

Our effort to eliminate doping among athletes during the 16 days of the Olympic Games is of course a necessary component of an effective, international antidoping agenda. But it is by no means sufficient. We rely on other stakeholders within the Olympic Movement to help. The Olympic Movement adopted the WADA code by the Opening of the Athens Games in July 2004. A number of International Federations and National Olympic Committees still need to implement some aspects of the WADA Code to be fully compliant. I urge the International Federations and National Olympic Committees to accelerate their efforts to achieve full compliance with WADA's guidelines by 1 January 2009.

Opportunities and Challenges

The impact of doping, of course, extends far beyond the boundaries of the Olympic Movement. No one is unaffected. For this reason, we must work harder to establish a unified voice for fair play. Collaboration among the sports community and governments is necessary if we are to make a lasting difference.

It is through our combined efforts that we will educate young people to make the right decisions. The value of the governments' support was made clear in 2006. That year, the Spanish Civil Guard launched the Operation Puerto investigation. The same year the IOC asked for the support of the Italian authorities to pursue those involved in a complex doping operation during the Turin Games. Recently, the operation "Raw Deal", conducted by the US authorities and with the collaboration of many governments, unveiled a huge doping network.

While government responsibility has received much press lately, the truth is that many governments have always been important players in the anti-doping movement. Many governments have passed anti-doping legislation. In 1989, the Council of Europe was a key player, along with the IOC, in preparing the International Charter Against Doping in Sport. This paved the way for the Copenhagen Declaration and the UNESCO International Convention against Doping in Sport.

As we meet now to open the next chapter in our unified fight against doping, I respectfully urge all governments to assume their full responsibility by ratifying the UNESCO Convention. I hope that the governments will accelerate the ratification process. Just as we must finalise the compliance of some International Federations and National Olympic Committees by 1 January 2009.

WADA will only have a full credibility when the governments and the Olympic Movement are compliant. Both partners of WADA, the governments and the sports movement, have to do a lot and have to do it fast.

Further challenges remain.

Spectators and public opinion are unfortunately still too complacent. This makes our task difficult. This means we must be even more active in promoting education through sport. We are challenged by new forms of unfair practices and the prospect of gene doping. We must work with researchers, laboratories and the pharmaceutical industry for better science.

Much of WADA's success over the past eight years is due to the great efforts of its outgoing Chairman, Richard Pound. On behalf of the Olympic Movement I would like to extend my warmest thanks to Richard Pound for all the good work he has done.

Joint Committment

Over the next few days, we will discuss the new anti-doping code. Representatives from the Olympic Movement will offer suggestions to improve the draft. We will also elect a new Chairman of WADA from the government sector. The Olympic Movement will support WADA wholeheartedly.

We remain committed to our course of zero tolerance. And we look forward to working with all of you to create an environment of clean sport for generations to come.

The third World Conference on Doping in Sport, marks a milestone in our fight against doping. It will shape the next phase of our fight. As we move forward, let us build on our past success to promote cleaner sports. Let us tackle the challenges and opportunities we face with conviction and a unified voice. Above all, let us never lose sight of why we are here . . . To give athletes at all levels the fair chance they deserve. To create an environment that allows champions to shine as role models for children, parents and fans alike. To preserve the integrity — and the very future — of sport.

Thank you.

技巧琢磨

Minister, Distinguished Authorities, my fellow delegates, honoured guests:

Before I begin my formal remarks, I would like to thank the World Anti-Doping Agency, the Government of Spain, the Ministry of Education and Science, and the Spanish Sports Council for organising this important conference.

Minister, I thank you and your colleagues for your support. For your tough anti-doping legislation passed in the last year. And for your ongoing attention to the Operation Puerto case, which I am confident will be resolved soon. We respect the separation of power and the independence of the justice and do hope that Spanish justice will take a decision in the Puerto case as a matter of priority. I hope that the sports organisations will then soon be authorised to use the information contained in the Puerto Report to take the necessary disciplinary sanctions against the guilty athletes.

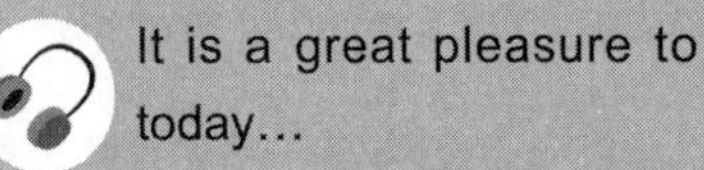

It is a great pleasure to be with you today...

To reflect on the importance of our anti-doping efforts. To review the successes we have achieved so far. To explore the challenges and opportunities that lie ahead. And to reaffirm our joint commitment to eliminate doping in sport.

部长，尊敬的当局，各位代表，嘉宾们：

开始正式演讲之前，我要感谢世界反兴奋剂机构、西班牙政府、教育与科学部、西班牙体育理事会，感谢你们组织了这个重要的会议。

部长，感谢您和同事的支持。感谢严格的反兴奋剂立法去年通过。感谢您持续关注波多黎各行动，我相信问题将会解决，不需多久。我们尊重权力分开和独立司法，希望西班牙司法体系将做出决定，把波多黎各案件作为优先要务。我希望体育组织将很快被授权使用信息，包含在波多黎各报告中的信息，以采取所需的处分，制裁违禁运动员。

非常高兴今天与大家在一起……

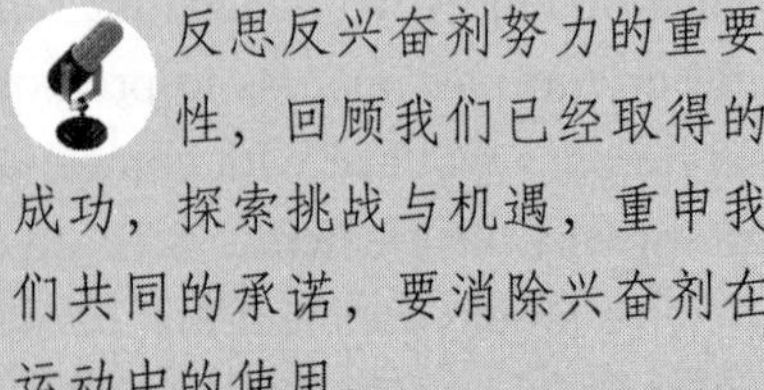

反思反兴奋剂努力的重要性，回顾我们已经取得的成功，探索挑战与机遇，重申我们共同的承诺，要消除兴奋剂在运动中的使用。

The importance of our efforts

Doping is one of the most serious threats the Olympic Movement has ever seen. It undermines all we stand for. It endangers the health of athletes. It undermines the credibility of results. It risks drying out the recruitment of sport, as, one day, parents might refuse to send their children to sports clubs.

我们努力的重要性

兴奋剂是其中一个最严重的威胁，危及奥林匹克运动。它破坏我们所有的主张，危及运动员健康，破坏成绩的可信度。它危及运动员的招募，因为，有一天，父母会拒绝送他们的孩子去体育俱乐部。

The fight against doping involves however much more than elite sport alone. It is not only about testing and sanctioning well-known athletes, it is about the health and future of our population. It is therefore a public health problem. Recent studies indicate the same dynamics that exist in professional sports are emerging in high school and university sport programmes around the world. These studies indicate that hundreds of thousands of teenagers and even pre-teenagers are in danger.

反兴奋剂涉及到的不仅是精英体育。不只是检测和制裁知名运动员，而是关乎健康与未来。因此，这是一个公共健康问题。最近的研究表明，存在于专业体育中的动因正在出现于中学和大学体育项目中，遍布世界。这些研究指出，成千上万的青少年，甚至儿童处于危险中。

Doping also affects the general sporting public — namely the millions of so called "weekend athletes," runners and fitness club members who want to incorporate sport and exercise into their lives for the purpose of maintaining or improving their health, boosting their muscle mass or bolstering their body image. A European Union report estimates that the incidence of doping among recreational athletes in the European Union has risen during the past two decades from approximately 5% to more than 20%. And let us not forget about the enormous amounts of anabolic steroids and Ecstasy pills that are seized by the authorities in many countries. They are sold to much more people than athletes alone.

兴奋剂还影响一般的公众体育，也就是数百万所谓的“周末运动员”。跑步者、健身俱乐部会员，想参与体育和锻炼，在生活中维持和改善健康，增强肌肉质量或改善体型。欧盟一份报告估计，兴奋剂在娱乐性运动员中的数据上升，过去二十年从约 5% 上升到了 20% 以上。我们别忘了大量合成类固醇和摇头丸的缴获，很多国家的当局都有缴获。这些药品被出售给很多人，不仅限于运动员。

As an advocate for sport and athletes around the world, the International Olympic Committee is unwavering in its commitment to combat doping in sport. This fight is our number one priority.

作为倡导体育和运动员的机构，国际奥林匹克委员会坚定地承诺反对兴奋剂。这个斗争是我们的第一要务。

Successes

The IOC has been a leader in the fight against doping for more than 40 years. We established a Medical Commission in 1967. We developed the first list of prohibited drugs and worked out methods for their detection. We also established a system of sanctions. We accredited drug-testing laboratories. All these measures were adopted by the Olympic Movement. We established the Court of Arbitration for Sport, introduced out-of-competition testing and funded early research into doping trends and detection methods. And we also funded the WADA budget for the first two years.

成功

国际奥委会是领军者，领导反对兴奋剂的斗争，逾40年之久。我们建立了医务委员会，那是1967年。我们制订了第一份清单，列出了禁用药物，并找出方法检测它们。我们还建立了制裁体制。我们认证检测实验室。所有这些措施的采纳都是奥林匹克运动的决定。我们建立了国际体育仲裁院，引进了赛外兴奋剂检查，资助了早期研究兴奋剂趋势和检测方法的活动。我们还资助了世界反兴奋剂机构的预算，资助了两年。

After the Festina scandal and the Tour de France in 1998, we realised more was needed. In 1999, we organised a World Conference on Doping in Lausanne to harmonise antidoping rules across the world of sport, and we called for the support of governments. This led to the creation of WADA. Today,the IOC continues to be a leader in the fight against doping. In response to the seriousness of the threat, we have championed a policy of zero tolerance.

之前发生了费斯迪纳丑闻和环法自行车赛，那是1998年，我们意识到需要做得更多。1999年，我们组织了一次世界兴奋剂会议，在洛桑协调反兴奋剂规则以适用于全世界。我们呼吁政府支持，由此建立了世界反兴奋剂机构。今天，国际奥委会继续领导反兴奋剂斗争。为了应对严峻威胁，我们倡导的政策是零容忍。

We enforce this policy through a comprehensive programme of testing during each edition of the Olympic Games. Next year in Beijing, we plan to conduct 4,500 in- and out-of-competition tests. This is roughly 25 per cent more than were carried out during the 2004 Games in Athens. And 90 per cent more than the number of tests carried out in Sydney in 2000.

我们实施这一政策，方法是广泛的检测项目，每届奥运会都如此。明年在北京，我们计划实施4500个赛中和赛外检测。这大约多了25%，超过2004年雅典奥运会。以90%的幅度超过2000年悉尼奥运会。

We have also recently proposed a series of measures to strengthen our zero tolerance policy. These measures include the denial of participation in the next Olympic Games for athletes and their entourage who have been sanctioned for more than six months. We will impose automatic suspensions after a positive A sample, we will impose stronger financial penalties for National Olympic Committees and athletes and implement stricter interpretations related to Therapeutic Use Exemptions.

我们最近还提议了一系列措施加强我们的零容忍政策。这些措施包括不准参加下一届奥运会——运动员和他们的随从如果受罚超过六个月就不能参加。我们将强制自动禁赛，如果是阳性A样品就禁赛。我们将实施更有力的财政处罚，处罚国家奥委会和运动员，实施更严格的解释，严格使用《治疗用药豁免》。

Our effort to eliminate doping among athletes during the 16 days of the Olympic Games is of course a necessary component of an effective, international anti-doping agenda. But it is by no means sufficient. We rely on other stakeholders within the Olympic Movement to help. The Olympic Movement adopted the WADA code by the Opening of the Athens Games in July 2004. A number of International Federations and National Olympic Committees still need to implement some aspects of the WADA Code to be fully compliant. I urge the International Federations and National Olympic Committees to accelerate

我们努力消除兴奋剂，在16天的奥运会期间，这是必要的，有利于有效地开展国际反兴奋剂运动。但是这还不够。我们依赖利益相关者，在奥林匹克运动内的利益相关者帮助我们。奥林匹克运动采纳了世界反兴奋剂机构的准则，之后雅典奥运会开幕，那是2004年7月。几个国际联合会和国家奥委会仍然需要实施一些世界反兴奋剂机构的准则，以全面合规。我敦促

their efforts to achieve full compliance with WADA's guidelines by 1 January 2009.

国际联合会和国家奥委会加速努力，实现全面合规，遵守世界反兴奋剂机构的指导方针，以2009年1月1日为限期。

Opportunities and Challenges

The impact of doping, of course, extends far beyond the boundaries of the Olympic Movement. No one is unaffected. For this reason, we must work harder to establish a unified voice for fair play. Collaboration among the sports community and governments is necessary if we are to make a lasting difference.

机遇与挑战

兴奋剂的影响，延伸到奥林匹克运动之外。所有人都受影响。因此，我们必须更努力，建立统一的声音，呼吁公平竞争。合作，体育社区和政府的合作是必须的，要实现更久的改变就要合作。

It is through our combined efforts that we will educate young people to make the right decisions. The value of the governments' support was made clear in 2006. That year, the Spanish Civil Guard launched the Operation Puerto investigation. The same year the IOC asked for the support of the Italian authorities to pursue those involved in a complex doping operation during the Turin Games. Recently, the operation "Raw Deal", conducted by the US authorities and with the collaboration of many governments, unveiled a huge doping network.

通过我们的共同努力，我们将教育年轻人做出正确的决定。政府支持的价值的明确是在2006年。当时，西班牙国民警卫队启动了波多黎各行动调查。同年，国际奥委会寻求意大利当局的支持，追究那些涉及复杂的兴奋剂运作的人，在都灵运动会期间行动。最近，"不公平待遇"行动的实施是美国当局，协作方是多国政府。他们发现了一个巨大的兴奋剂网络。

While government responsibility has received much press lately, the truth is that many governments have always been important players in the anti-doping movement. Many governments have passed anti-doping legislation. In 1989, the Council of Europe was a key player, along with the IOC, in preparing the International Charter Against Doping in

尽管政府的责任多有报导，真相是：许多政府一直是重要参与者，一直在反兴奋剂。许多政府已经通过了反兴奋剂立法。1989年，欧洲理事会是一个主要参与者，与国际奥委会一起，准备国际宪章反兴奋

Sport. This paved the way for the Copenhagen Declaration and the UNESCO International Convention against Doping in Sport.

剂。这铺平了道路，有利于哥本哈根宣言和联合国科教文组织的《国际反兴奋剂公约》。

As we meet now to open the next chapter in our unified fight against doping, I respectfully urge all governments to assume their full responsibility by ratifying the UNESCO Convention. I hope that the governments will accelerate the ratification process. Just as we must finalise the compliance of some International Federations and National Olympic Committees by 1 January 2009.

我们的会议开启了新篇章，团结起来共同开展反兴奋剂斗争，我敬请所有政府担负起他们的全面责任，批准联合国科教文组织的《公约》。我希望各国政府加速批准过程。我们必须完成合规，一些国际联合会和国家奥委会尚需合规，限期为2009年1月1日。

WADA will only have a full credibility when the governments and the Olympic Movement are compliant. Both partners of WADA, the governments and the sports movement, have to do a lot and have to do it fast.

世界反兴奋剂机构要有完全的可信度，那么政府和奥林匹克运动就必须合规。两个伙伴，即政府和体育运动，必须做很多事，必须做得很快。

Further challenges remain.

未来挑战仍然存在。

Spectators and public opinion are unfortunately still too complacent. This makes our task difficult. This means we must be even more active in promoting education through sport. We are challenged by new forms of unfair practices and the prospect of gene doping. We must work with researchers, laboratories and the pharmaceutical industry for better science.

观众和公众的看法，很不幸，仍然太掉以轻心。这使我们的任务很艰难。这意味着我们必须更加活跃，促进运动中教育的发展。我们的挑战来自新形式的不公平做法和未来的基因兴奋剂。我们必须联合研究人员、实验室和制药业，以获得更好的科学知识。

Much of WADA's success over the past eight years is due to the great efforts of its outgoing Chairman, Richard Pound. On behalf of the Olympic Movement I would like to

许多世界反兴奋剂机构的成功，在过去八年中，都离不开即将离任的主席理查德·庞德的巨大努力。我代表奥林匹

extend my warmest thanks to Richard Pound for all the good work he has done.

Joint Commitment

Over the next few days, we will discuss the new anti-doping code. Representatives from the Olympic Movement will offer suggestions to improve the draft. We will also elect a new Chairman of WADA from the government sector. The Olympic Movement will support WADA wholeheartedly.

We remain committed to our course of zero tolerance. And we look forward to working with all of you to create an environment of clean sport for generations to come.

The third World Conference on Doping in Sport, marks a milestone in our fight against doping. It will shape the next phase of our fight. As we move forward, let us build on our past success to promote cleaner sports. Let us tackle the challenges and opportunities we face with conviction and a unified voice. Above all, let us never lose sight of why we are here... To give athletes at all levels the fair chance they deserve. To create an environment that allows champions to shine as role models for children, parents and fans alike. To preserve the integrity — and the very future — of sport.

Thank you.

克运动，感谢理查德· 庞德的杰出工作。

共同承诺

未来几天，我们将讨论新的反兴奋剂准则。来自奥林匹克运动的代表们将提出建议，改善草案。我们将选举新的世界反兴奋剂机构主席，从政府领域选举。奥林匹克运动将支持世界反兴奋剂机构，不遗余力。

我们仍然致力于零容忍。我们期待合作，创造环境，发展清白的体育，造福后代。

第三次世界反兴奋剂大会是个里程碑。它将影响新阶段的斗争。前进中，让我们发扬过去成功的传统，促进更清白的体育。让我们应对挑战和机遇，坚定不移，同仇敌忾。尤其是，我们永远不要忘记为何我们在这里……就是要为运动员——无论其水平——提供公平的机会，就是要创造环境，使冠军焕发光芒，成为榜样、无论是儿童、父母还是爱好者；就是要保持正直和未来，体育的未来。

谢谢。

10.世界银行行长佐利克的讲话

使用提要

1. 本单元的讲话稿仍然以两种形式提供：限时视译和技巧琢磨。
2. 限时视译的速度必须达到每秒 3 个英文单词，每次选择的长度应该增加到 60–70 秒之间，即大约 180–210 个单词。
3. 在使用或者参照译入语时必须注意：

   3.1. 参考译入语只是诸多可能版本之一，不是最佳版本，而且故意保留了一些不完美的地方。

   3.2. 一定不可用笔译的准确标准来衡量同传的译入语版本，因为听同传的感觉和阅读文字完全不一样。

   3.3. 避免把练习的重点放在讲解技巧的概念上，重点是熟练使用。

英译汉三词一译10大技巧

1. 缺省传译	2. 原话直译	3. 重复谓语	4. 介词转动
5. 先存后译	6. 反话正说	7. 被动变的	8. 点到为止
9. 预测先说	10. 弃卒保车		

限时视译

Remarks for the High-Level China-Africa Experience-Sharing Program on Special Economic Zones and Infrastructure Development

(*President of the World Bank, Robert B. Zoellick*)

It is my pleasure to participate in the opening of this year's High Level China-Africa Experience-Sharing Program, now in its third year. I would like to thank our Chinese partners, the Ministry of Finance, Ministry of Commerce, and Leading Group on Poverty Alleviation.

China's cooperation with Africa is by no means new. Trade between China and Africa goes back hundreds of years, and modern China has been cooperating with Africa since the early days of the People's Republic.

What is new, however, is the level and significance of China's partnership with Africa. Two-way trade between China and Africa has grown at more than 40 percent a year since the beginning of the decade, reaching nearly US$107 billion in 2008.

Chinese foreign direct investment in Africa is also growing rapidly, topping US$5.4 billion in 2008, and more than 1,500 Chinese companies have invested in Africa.

China has been particularly significant as a source of financing for investment in African infrastructure. A World Bank report estimates that China's investment in infrastructure in Africa over the period 2001-2006 was roughly comparable to that financed by all OECD countries combined over the same period.

This growing role of China in Africa is part of a broader shift to a new multipolar economy, in which the developing world represents an increasingly important source of global demand. We see a similar trend in the global development landscape, with China and other developing countries assuming important roles alongside traditional development partners. These new partners are contributing not only aid, but more importantly are becoming major trading partners and sources of investment and know-how.

This is particularly true in the case of China's engagement with Africa. African countries want to learn about China's development experience, particularly about overcoming poverty and sustaining economic growth.

The two themes for this year's program—special economic zones and infrastructure development—are particularly important.

Let's look first at special economic zones.

A key to China's economic success has been the development of a competitive manufacturing sector. How did China move in three decades from being a poor agrarian economy to become one of the world's largest manufacturing centers? Special Economic Zones played a key role—as a test-bed for economic reforms, for attracting foreign direct investment, for catalyzing development of industrial clusters, and for attracting new technologies and adopting new management practices. Even though their importance has diminished over time, a recent World Bank study estimates that as of 2007, SEZs still accounted for about 22% of national GDP, about 46% of FDI, and about 60% of exports—and generated in excess of 30 million jobs.

African countries want to learn from such success, and China is ready to help.

The Chinese government is supporting the establishment of industrial zones in several countries in Africa, with the hope that the success of China's special economic zones can be replicated. This is a welcome initiative to expand Chinese investment in Africa beyond the minerals, energy, and infrastructure sectors into activities that offer greater opportunities for creating jobs and transferring know-how.

The World Bank Group is exploring with the Chinese government and with several African governments, ways in which we can work together to ensure win-win-win outcomes.

We believe there are a number of things that the Bank can bring to the table:

First, we can help develop the necessary legal, regulatory, and institutional framework for the zones to offer a world-class business environment, attractive not only to Chinese firms, but also to other foreign investors, and equally importantly, to domestic firms as well.

Second, we can support measures to ensure linkages to the local economy by creating a level playing field for both foreign and local firms and through interventions to provide opportunities for local supply chain, skills, and technology enhancement.

Third, we can support complementary infrastructure, as well as the establishment of efficient trade facilitation and logistics procedures and infrastructure.

Fourth, we can help governments to integrate the zone development plans into broader master plans at city or regional level in order to promote more efficient and integrated mixed-use of land and to avoid the risk of the zones becoming enclaves.

Fifth, through the IFC and MIGA, we can offer financing and insurance to the zone development companies and can support them in undertaking feasibility studies and in developing phased development plans of international standards.

Finally, and most relevant to this program, we can help to facilitate mutual learning and sharing of knowledge.

One aspect will be to work with relevant Chinese partners to ensure that African policymakers and practitioners get access not only to the strong expertise in zone construction that is offered by the Chinese zone development companies, but also to other aspects of China's successful SEZ experience, including such areas as development, management, promotion, and marketing of zones. Another aspect will be to share—both with our African and Chinese partners—lessons from SEZ experience in other countries.

Let me now turn briefly to infrastructure.

Africa lags on infrastructure development, with major deficits in transport, roads, water, telecoms, and energy.

China's experience can be instructive for African countries. It also suffered from infrastructure deficits at the beginning of its development process but succeeded in putting in place world-class infrastructure—covering both urban and rural areas. Africa may also draw from China's attention to rural infrastructure as a way to improving productivity and overcoming poverty.

Let me return to an earlier theme—the changing global economic and development landscape—and to look at this from the perspective of sharing knowledge.

Development is no longer a North-South transfer. It is South-South, even South-North, with lessons for all with open minds.

It is Africa learning from China on SEZs and infrastructure; it is China learning from Africa about effective community-driven development approaches; it is the United States learning from China about high-speed railways; and so on.

Nor is development any longer about simplistic panaceas, theory untested by realities, or one-size-fits-all structures. Rather, development is about a humble pragmatism, learning from experience, and applying sound principles while adapting to local needs.

This logic was recognized by Deng Xiaoping when, in 1985, he told Ghana's President Jerry Rawlings: "Please don't try to copy our model. If there is any experience on our part, it is to formulate policies in light of one's own national conditions." This was wise advice. There is indeed a lot that African countries can learn from China's experience. The key, however, is to adapt that experience to Africa's own needs, circumstances and conditions. This is precisely the type of understanding and adaptation that the World Bank Group aims to support though this and other China-Africa experience-sharing programs.

In closing, I want to again thank our Chinese partners: the Ministry of Finance, the Ministry of Commerce, and the Leading Group on Poverty Alleviation. It is exciting to see representatives from so many African countries here in China to share experiences. We look forward to learning from all of you.

I wish you a successful program. Thank you.

技巧琢磨

It is my pleasure to participate in the opening of this year's High Level China-Africa Experience-Sharing Program, now in its third year. I would like to thank our Chinese partners, the Ministry of Finance, Ministry of Commerce, and Leading Group on Poverty Alleviation.	我非常高兴参加开幕式，参加今年的高层次中非经验分享项目开幕式，今年是第三届。我要感谢我们的中国伙伴：财政部、商务部和扶贫领导小组。
China's cooperation with Africa is by no means new. Trade between China and Africa goes back hundreds of years, and modern China has been cooperating with Africa since the early days of the People's Republic.	中国与非洲的合作不是新事。中非贸易可以追溯到几百年前，现代中国与非洲的合作，始于很早，中华人民共和国建立之初就开始了。

What is new, however, is the level and significance of China's partnership with Africa. Two-way trade between China and Africa has grown at more than 40 percent a year since the beginning of the decade, reaching nearly US$107 billion in 2008.

新的是水平和意义，中非伙伴关系有了很大发展。双向贸易在中非之间的增长速度超过40%，每年如此，持续了十年，达到近1070亿美元，这是2008年的数据。

Chinese foreign direct investment in Africa is also growing rapidly, topping US$5.4 billion in 2008, and more than 1,500 Chinese companies have invested in Africa.

中国的外商直接投资在非洲也增长很快，2008年达到54亿英镑，1500多家中国公司投资非洲。

China has been particularly significant as a source of financing for investment in African infrastructure. A World Bank report estimates that China's investment in infrastructure in Africa over the period 2001-2006 was roughly comparable to that financed by all OECD countries combined over the same period.

中国有相当多的金融资源，可以投资非洲基础设施。世界银行的一份报告估计，中国对非洲基础设施的投资，在2001至2006年期间，大致相当于所有经合组织国家同期所有投资。

This growing role of China in Africa is part of a broader shift to a new multipolar economy, in which the developing world represents an increasingly important source of global demand. We see a similar trend in the global development landscape, with China and other developing countries assuming important roles alongside traditional development partners. These new partners are contributing not only aid, but more importantly are becoming major trading partners and sources of investment and know-how.

中国日益重要的作用在非洲构成了更广泛的转移，向新的多极经济的转移，发展中国家将日益重要，供应全球需求。我们看到了相似的趋势在全球发展中再现，中国和其他发展中国家发挥重要作用，不仅是传统的发展伙伴。这些新伙伴的贡献不只是援助，更重要的是成为主要贸易伙伴，提供投资和专有知识。

This is particularly true in the case of China's engagement with Africa. African countries want to learn about China's development experience, particularly about overcoming poverty and sustaining economic growth.

这尤其体现在中非交流中。非洲国家想学习中国的发展经验，尤其是如何战胜贫困、持续发展经济。

The two themes for this year's program—special economic zones and infrastructure development—are particularly important.

两个今年项目的主题是经济特区和基础设施发展，这两点尤为重要。

Let's look first at special economic zones.

首先看经济特区。

A key to China's economic success has been the development of a competitive manufacturing sector. How did China move in three decades from being a poor agrarian economy to become one of the world's largest manufacturing centers? Special Economic Zones played a key role—as a test-bed for economic reforms, for attracting foreign direct investment, for catalyzing development of industrial clusters, and for attracting new technologies and adopting new management practices. Even though their importance has diminished over time, a recent World Bank study estimates that as of 2007, SEZs still accounted for about 22% of national GDP, about 46% of FDI, and about 60% of exports—and generated in excess of 30 million jobs.

中国经济成功的关键是发展了有竞争力的制造业。中国如何前进的？三十年前，中国还是一个贫穷的农业经济体，现已成为世界上最大的制造中心之一。经济特区发挥了重要作用，是一个试验台，试验经济改革，吸引外商直接投资，促进发展工业集群，吸引新技术，使用新的管理做法。虽然他们的重要性减弱了，近期世界银行的一份研究估计，2007 年，中小企业仍然占约 22% 的 GDP，约 46% 的外商直接投资，约 60% 的出口，产生了超过 3 千万个工作岗位。

African countries want to learn from such success, and China is ready to help.

非洲国家想要学习这些成功经验，中国愿意相助。

The Chinese government is supporting the establishment of industrial zones in several countries in Africa, with the hope that the success of China's special economic zones can be replicated. This is a welcome initiative to expand Chinese investment in Africa beyond the minerals, energy, and infrastructure sectors into activities that offer greater opportunities for creating jobs and transferring know-how.

中国政府正在支持建立工业区，在几个非洲国家建立并且希望中国经济特区的成功能被复制。这是个受欢迎的计划，以扩展中国的投资，使非洲不再仅限于矿物、能源和基础设施的发展，而是扩展到能提供更大机遇的活动，以创造就业机会，转移专有知识。

The World Bank Group is exploring with the Chinese government and with several African governments, ways in which we can work together to ensure win-win-win outcomes.

世界银行集团正在探索与中国政府和几个非洲政府的合作，以确保三赢的结果。

We believe there are a number of things that the Bank can bring to the table:

我们认为有几个方面世界银行可以提供帮助：

First, we can help develop the necessary legal, regulatory, and institutional framework for the zones to offer a world-class business environment, attractive not only to Chinese firms, but also to other foreign investors, and equally importantly, to domestic firms as well.

一，我们能够帮助发展所需的法律、监管和机构框架，使特区能够提供世界一流的商业环境，吸引中国公司，也吸引其他外国投资者和同样重要的国内公司。

Second, we can support measures to ensure linkages to the local economy by creating a level playing field for both foreign and local firms and through interventions to provide opportunities for local supply chain, skills, and technology enhancement.

二，我们能够支持措施，确保联系当地经济，方法是建立公平竞技场，国外和当地公司公平竞争，通过干预以提供机遇，让当地供应链获益，技能和技术得到提高。

Third, we can support complementary infrastructure, as well as the establishment of efficient trade facilitation and logistics procedures and infrastructure.

三，我们能够支持互补的基础设施，建立有效的贸易便利化、物流程序和基础设施。

Fourth, we can help governments to integrate the zone development plans into broader master plans at city or regional level in order to promote more efficient and integrated mixed-use of land and to avoid the risk of the zones becoming enclaves.

四，我们能够帮助政府整合特区发展规划，形成更广泛的主体计划，在城市和地区水平整合，以促进更有效的、整合的混合用地，从而避免特区成为飞地的风险。

Fifth, through the IFC and MIGA, we can offer financing and insurance to the zone development companies and can support them in undertaking feasibility studies and in developing phased development plans of international standards.

五，通过国际金融公司和多边投资担保机构，我们能够提供融资和保险给特区开发公司，支持他们进行可行性研究，发展分阶段开发方案，达到国际标准。

Finally, and most relevant to this program, we can help to facilitate mutual learning and sharing of knowledge.

最后，最有关于本项目的是：我们能够促进相互学习，分享知识。

One aspect will be to work with relevant Chinese partners to ensure that African policymakers and practitioners get access not only to the strong expertise in zone construction that is offered by the Chinese zone development companies, but also to other aspects of China's successful SEZ experience, including such areas as development, management, promotion, and marketing of zones. Another aspect will be to share—both with our African and Chinese partners—lessons from SEZ experience in other countries.

一个方面将是与相关的中国合作伙伴合作，确保非洲政策制定者和实践者获得有力的专长，建立特区。中国的特区开发公司可以相助，还能获得其他方面中国成功的特区发展经验，其中包括发展、管理、宣传和营销。另外一方面也要分享，无论是我们的非洲还是中国伙伴都一样，这就是中小企业在其他国家的经验。

Let me now turn briefly to infrastructure. Africa lags on infrastructure development, with major deficits in transport, roads, water, telecoms, and energy.

我现在来简要说说基础设施。非洲落后的基础设施发展，其主要不足在于交通、道路、水、电信和能源。

China's experience can be instructive for African countries. It also suffered from infrastructure deficits at the beginning of its development process but succeeded in putting in place world-class infrastructure—covering both urban and rural areas. Africa may also draw from China's attention to rural infrastructure as a way to improving productivity and overcoming poverty.

中国的经验有指导意义，非洲国家可以获益。中国当初也是基础设施不足，刚开始发展时是那样，但是现在成功地发展起世界级的基础设施：覆盖城市和乡村。非洲可以学习中国关注农村基础设施的做法，以提高生产力，克服贫困。

Let me return to an earlier theme—the changing global economic and development landscape—and to look at this from the perspective of sharing knowledge.

我回到上一个主题：变化中的全球经济和发展状况，从分享知识的角度谈谈。

Development is no longer a North-South transfer. It is South-South, even South-North, with lessons for all with open minds.

发展不再是从北至南的转移，而是南至南，甚至南至北，经验是只要开放都能学到。

It is Africa learning from China on SEZs and infrastructure; it is China learning from Africa about effective community-driven development approaches; it is the United States learning from China about high-speed railways; and so on.

非洲从中国学习中小企业和基础设施的经验；中国学习非洲有效的社区驱动的发展；美国学习中国如何建设高速铁路；等等。

Nor is development any longer about simplistic panaceas, theory untested by realities, or one-size-fits-all structures. Rather, development is about a humble pragmatism, learning from experience, and applying sound principles while adapting to local needs.

发展不再是关于简单的万能药，不是理论不经实践检验，不是通用的结构。而是关于谦卑的实用主义、学习经验、运用合理的原则、适应当地需要。

This logic was recognized by Deng Xiaoping when, in 1985, he told Ghana's President Jerry Rawlings: "Please don't try to copy our model. If there is any experience on our part, it is to formulate policies in light of one's own national conditions." This was wise advice. There is indeed a lot that African countries can learn from China's experience. The key, however, is to adapt that experience to Africa's own needs, circumstances and conditions. This is precisely the type of understanding and adaptation that the World Bank Group aims to support though this and other China-Africa experience-sharing programs.

这一逻辑的认识邓小平就有，1985年，他告诉加纳总统杰瑞·罗林斯："请不要复制我们的模式。如果有什么经验——对我们而言，那就是制定政策时要考虑自己的国情。"这是明智的建议。确实有许多事情非洲国家能够从中国的经验中学习。但是，关键是调整经验，适应非洲需要、情况和条件。正是这种理解和调整才是世界银行集团旨在支持的，通过这个以及其他中非经验分享项目来支持。

In closing, I want to again thank our Chinese partners: the Ministry of Finance, the Ministry of Commerce, and the Leading Group on Poverty Alleviation. It is exciting to see representatives from so many African countries here in China to share experiences. We look forward to learning from all of you.

I wish you a successful program. Thank you.

最后，我要再次感谢我们的中国伙伴：财政部、商务部和扶贫工作领导小组。令人激动的是看到代表们来自许多非洲国家，到中国来分享经验。我期待听到大家的发言。

我祝项目成功。谢谢。

汉译英

1. 温家宝总理的讲话

使用提要

1. 所有练习单元的讲话稿均以两种形式提供。第一种采用常见的讲话稿形式，便于练习限时视译。第二种采用对照、对比形式，便于练习、琢磨三词一译的技巧。
2. 限时视译部分是讲话稿全文，可以根据需要选用。但是在技巧琢磨部分里，只有前半部分的讲话配有参考译入语以保证每个单元的练习长度大体相同。
3. 为了示范如何在视译的讨论阶段达到两个方案的要求，本单元和第二单元的参考译入语都有两个版本。其他单元只有一个版本。
4. 限时视译的速度在前两个单元可以从每秒 4 个汉字开始，然后每过 2–3 个单元就增加一个汉字，争取在第 6–7 个单元时达到每秒 6 个汉字的速度。
5. 在使用或者参照译入语时必须注意：

5.1. 参考译入语只是诸多可能版本之一，不是最佳版本。有些不一定合适的处理是有意保留，而且没有刻意保持连贯一致，即同个表达法在同一讲话里的处理可能各不相同。这些做法都是为了从同传培训一开始就建立作为实战参照的质量标准。如果教材的译入语是经过修饰后的完善版本，这不仅是概念上的误导，而且会导致培训生无法达到教材里的准确度而丧失练习的信心。

5.2. 由于上述原因，一定不可用笔译的准确标准来衡量同传的译入语版本，因为听同传的感觉和阅读文字完全不一样。

5.3. 本教材有意没有提供视译中具体采取的是三词一译所需 9 大技巧中的哪一个，这是为了避免把练习的重点放在讲解技巧的概念上。

英译汉三词一译10大技巧

1. 先存后译
2. 反话正说
3. 预测先说
4. 弃卒保车
5. 减字近半
6. 增加时态
7. 实词开句
8. 增补主语
9. 译所指也

限时视译

未来中国的走向

（温家宝总理2011年在英国皇家学会的演讲）

尊敬的纳斯会长，

各位会员、各位使节，

女士们、先生们：

今天，我应邀访问久负盛名的英国皇家学会，深感荣幸。刚才，英国皇家学会授予我“查理二世国王奖”。这不仅是我个人的荣誉，也是对中国科技进步的肯定，同时也是中英两国科技界友谊与合作的象征。对此，我向你们表示衷心的感谢！

英国皇家学会，是英国最高科学学术机构，也是世界上历史最悠久的科学学会。牛顿、达尔文、爱因斯坦、霍金等科学巨匠，为人类科技事业发展作出过划时代的贡献。在座的各位会员，同样以自己的杰出成就造福社会。我向你们表示崇高的敬意！

担任中国总理以来，这是我第四次访问贵国。这一次和上一次时隔两年，感觉大不相同。2009 年初，贵国遭受一场罕见的大雪，同时也经历着国际金融危机的煎熬。我从达沃斯到伦敦一路走来，感受到一种忧郁不安的气氛。我当时说，“信心比货币和黄金更宝贵”。如今仲夏的伦敦，人们又恢复了往日的从容和自信。我对贵国应对危机所作的努力和可喜进展，表示由衷的钦佩！

我要告诉朋友们的是，经过这场国际金融危机的洗礼，中国前进的步伐更加稳健了。在这里，我想说一件事。

2008 年 5 月 12 日，中国西南部发生毁灭性的特大地震。当时，我站在震中汶川的废墟上，对前来采访的中外记者说，“过三年再来，一个新的汶川会拔地而起”。三年过去了，我们一边应对国际金融危机的冲击，一边举全国之力进行灾后重建。上个月，我第十次来到震区，欣喜地看到：灾区最漂亮的是住房，最坚固的是学校，最现代的是医院，最满意的是居民。我邀请在座各位朋友，有机会到中国汶川走一走、看一看。如果你们身临其境，一定会为这里发生的奇迹感到震撼，也会从中真实地感受到中国的生机和活力。

对中国改革开放以来的发展变化，世界上有各种各样的解读；对未来中国的走向，人们也非常关注。我愿意借今天这个机会，谈谈我的看法。

上世纪80年代初，中国改革开放的总设计师邓小平，曾提出我国现代化进程分“三步走”的战略构想。第一步，基本解决温饱问题；第二步，全面建设小康社会；第三步，到本世纪中叶，基本实现现代化，达到世界中等发达国家水平。2010年到2020年，是中国全面建设小康社会的关键阶段。“三步走”战略的核心和本质，都是坚持以人为本，增进全体中国人的福祉。沿着这条社会主义现代化道路前进，中国必将会有一个更加光明的未来。

未来的中国，将是一个经济发达、人民富裕的国家。集中精力发展经济，不断改善人民生活，始终是中国政府的第一要务。我们将坚持科学发展，着力转变经济发展方式，走绿色、低碳、可持续的发展道路。我们将扩大国内需求特别是消费需求，进一步释放城乡居民消费潜力，使消费成为拉动经济增长的根本动力。我们将更加注重改善民生，努力扩大就业，优先发展教育、卫生等公共事业，深化收入分配制度改革，增加城乡居民收入，加快建立覆盖城乡居民的社会保障体系，让各族人民共享发展成果。

中国经济的振兴和可持续发展，根本靠科技。中国政府已经制定并组织实施了国家中长期科技发展规划。我们持续增加科技投入，近五年，中央财政共投入近1000亿美元，年均增长22.7%。从今年开始实施的“十二五”规划，我们力争把研究开发投入占国内生产总值的比重从现在的1.75%提高到2.2%。同时，我们将加快培育和发展战略性新兴产业。现阶段重点培育和发展节能环保、新一代信息技术、生物、高端设备制造、新能源、新材料、新能源汽车等产业。所有这些，都将促进当前发展并为长期发展提供有力支撑。

从世界范围看，克服国际金融危机，保证经济的稳定、平衡和可持续发展，根本也要靠科技。当今世界正处于新科技革命的前夜，新技术革命和产业革命初现端倪，诸多领域正酝酿着激动人心的重大突破。这场新科技革命，必将进一步深化我们对宇宙自然和人类自身的认识，必将开辟生产力发展的新空间，创造新的社会需求，必将深刻影响人类的生产方式、生活方式和思维方式，从而从根本上改变21世纪人类社会发展进程。科技无国界。让我们共同迎接这一伟大时代的到来！

未来的中国，将是一个充分实现民主法治、公平正义的国家。在人类历史上，在反对封建专制斗争中形成的民主、法治、自由、平等、人权等观念，是人类精神的一次大解放。只是不同社会、不同国家，实现的途径和形式有所不同。人民民主是社会主义的生命，没有民主就没有社会主义。真正的民主离不开自由。真正的自由离不开经济权利和政治权利的保障。坦率地说，目前中国社会还存在着贪污腐败、分配不公以及损害人民群众权益的种种弊端。解决这些问题的根本途径，是坚定不移地推进政治体制改革，建设社会主义民主法治国家。

我们要尊重和保障人权，依法保障全体社会成员平等参与、平等发展的权利。我们要健全对政府权力的制约和监督机制，保证人民赋予的权力真正为人民谋福利。中国曾经是封建主义影响很深的国家，新中国成立后曾经历十年“文革”的浩劫，在开放的环境下又出现一些新的情况和问题。发扬民主，健全法制，加强对权力的有效监督，仍然是一项长期而艰巨的任务。我们要创造条件让人民监督和批评政府，使政府不敢懈怠、避免产生腐败。人民的责任感和民主精神，将带动社会的进步。人民参与社会管理和公共事务越多，推动社会进步的能量就越大。

近些年来，我们在深化经济体制改革的同时，积极稳妥地推进政治体制改革。在推进政府决策科学化、民主化，加强人民对政府的监督等方面，也有许多进步。例如，实行政务公开，政府预算公开，推行电子政务、听证制度和专家咨询制度等。我已连续三年在作《政府工作报告》之前，在网上同网民交流。今年春，我在新华网在线交流时，收到网民来贴 40 多万条，手机信息 11 万多条，页面访问量近 3 亿人次。同这些普通民众的交流，是心对心的交流，可以直接体察人民的喜怒哀乐和对政府的诉求，有利于改进政府工作。

未来的中国，将是一个更加开放包容、文明和谐的国家。一个国家、一个民族，只有开放包容，才能发展进步。唯有开放，先进和有用的东西才能进得来；唯有包容，吸收借鉴优秀文化，才能使自己充实和强大起来。

我们不仅要在经济领域、科技领域继续扩大对外开放，而且在文化建设、社会管理等领域也要大胆博采众长。中国在推进现代化过程中遇到的诸多问题，如能源问题、环境问题、贫富差距问题、司法公正问题和廉政问题等，许多发达国家都曾经遇到过。对各国的成功经验，我们要认真借鉴；对别人走过的弯路，我们不应重复；对世界面临的难题，我们要同国际社会一道来破解。

我们要创造更加良好的政治环境和更加自由的学术氛围，让人民追求真理、崇尚理性、尊重科学，探索自然的奥秘、社会的法则和人生的真谛。做学问、搞科研，尤其需要倡导“独立之精神，自由之思想”。正因为有了充分的学术自由，像牛顿这样在人类历史上具有伟大影响的科学家，才能够思潮奔腾、才华迸发，敢于思考前人从未思考过的问题，敢于踏进前人从未涉足的领域。不久前，我同中国科学家交流时提出，要大力营造敢于创造、敢冒风险、敢于批判和宽容失败的环境，鼓励自由探索，提倡学术争鸣。

我们历来主张尊重世界文明的多样性，倡导不同文明之间的对话、交流与合作。我国已故著名社会学家费孝通先生，上世纪30年代曾就读于伦敦政治经济学院并获得博士学位，一生饱经沧桑。他在晚年提出："各美其美，美人之美，美美与共，世界大同。"费老先生的这一人生感悟，生动反映了当代中国人开放包容的胸怀。

未来的中国，将是一个坚持和平发展、勇于担当的国家。走和平发展道路，是中国政府和人民根据时代潮流和自身利益作出的战略抉择，是中国积极参与经济全球化、最终实现现代化的必由之路。中国的和平发展，对世界不是威胁，而是机遇。中国已经成为世界经济增长的重要引擎，近五年对世界经济增长的贡献率在20%以上。自2001年中国加入世界贸易组织以来，年均进口近7500亿美元商品，为相关国家和地区创造了1400多万个就业岗位。未来5年，中国进口规模累计有望超过8万亿美元，将给世界各国带来更多商机。

21世纪应是合作的世纪，而不是冲突和争霸的世纪。中国是世界和平的坚定维护者。我们一贯主张和平解决国际争端，反对使用武力。中国将同国际社会一道，共担责任、共迎挑战，继续推动国际体系朝着更加公平、公正、包容的方向发展。

女士们、先生们：

建设有中国特色的社会主义，是13亿中国人民的庄严选择。中国30多年的变化，得益于改革开放；中国未来的发展，仍然要靠改革开放。改革开放，要贯穿中国现代化建设的始终。倒退没有出路，停滞也没有出路。只有坚定信心、继续前进，中国才能建设成为富强、民主、文明、和谐的社会主义现代化国家，中国人民才能更加普遍和以更高水准过上有尊严的幸福生活。尽管前进的道路上还会有这样那样的艰难险阻，但这一历史进程不可逆转！

女士们、先生们：

英国是世界上最早实现工业化的发达国家，在高科技、高等教育、金融服务、医疗卫生、低碳经济等领域，都具有中国所需要的技术和管理经验。中国广阔的市场、丰富的人力资源和巨大的发展潜力，可以为英国经济发展提供有力的支持。中国政府积极推进大型企业、研究型大学和科研机构同英国的合作，鼓励双方高端人才的交流和合作研究。

英国伟大思想家培根说过，"智者创造机会，而不是等待机会"。富有思想和智慧的中英两国人民，一定能创造更多的机会，推动两国合作迈上新的台阶！我对中英关系的明天充满信心，更充满期待！

谢谢大家！

技巧琢磨

尊敬的纳斯会长，各位会员、各位使节，
女士们、先生们：

今天，我应邀访问久负盛名的英国皇家学会，深感荣幸。刚才，英国皇家学会授予我“查理二世国王奖”。这不仅是我个人的荣誉，也是对中国科技进步的肯定，同时也是中英两国科技界友谊与合作的象征。对此，我向你们表示衷心的感谢！

President of the Royal Society,
Members,
Ambassadors,
Ladies and Gentlemen,

Today, I'm visiting the prestigious Royal Society of the UK. This is a great privilege. Your Society has awarded me the King Charles II medal. This is not just an honour for myself, but one for China's progress in science and technology, and one for China UK friendship and cooperation in science and technology. I thank you for this.

Sir Paul Nurse,
Members,
Ambassadors,
Ladies and Gentlemen,

Here I am, at the Royal Society at your invitation. I feel deeply honoured. The Society awarded me the King Charles Second medal. This is not just an honour to me, but also to the science and technology of China, for Sino-UK friendship and cooperation in science and technology. I would like to say thank you for that.

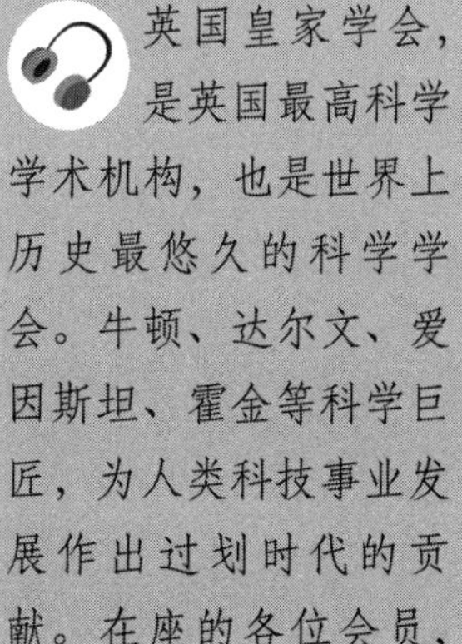

英国皇家学会，是英国最高科学学术机构，也是世界上历史最悠久的科学学会。牛顿、达尔文、爱因斯坦、霍金等科学巨匠，为人类科技事业发展作出过划时代的贡献。在座的各位会员，

The Royal Society is the UK's highest scientific institution and the world's oldest scientific society. Newton, Darwin, Einstein and Hopkins are giants of science. In the development of science, they have each made historic contributions. Your members present today have also contributed to the benefits of the society. I salute you.

The Royal Society is the highest academic institution for science in the UK. It has the longest history among science associations. Newton, Darwin,

同样以自己的杰出成就造福社会。我向你们表示崇高的敬意！	Einstein and Hopkins are giants who have, in science and technology, made historic contributions. All of you have also contributed your achievement. To you, I'd like to express my highest degree of respect.
担任中国总理以来，这是我第四次访问贵国。这一次和上一次时隔两年，感觉大不相同。2009年初，贵国遭受一场罕见的大雪，同时也经历着国际金融危机的煎熬。我从达沃斯到伦敦一路走来，感受到一种忧郁不安的气氛。我当时说，"信心比货币和黄金更宝贵"。如今仲夏的伦敦，人们又恢复了往日的从容和自信。我对贵国应对危机所作的努力和可喜进展，表示由衷的钦佩！	❶ Since I became Premier of China, this is my fourth visit to the UK. Between this time, two years have passed, and it feels different this time. At the beginning of 2009, your country had an unusually heavy snow. You suffered from the financial crisis. I came from Davos and could sense the unease. Back then I said, 'confidence is worth more than gold'. In the mid-summer of London, people have regained their calm and confidence. You have faced down the crisis. I take my hat off to you. ❷ Since I became the Chinese Premier, I've visited your country four times. This time, if compared with the last, there is a distinct difference. Early in 2009, your country suffered a rare snow at the same timeas the international financial crisis. From Davos to London, I felt a sense of worry. I said confidence was worth more than money. This summer in London, people have once again their confidence back. Your country is dealing with the crisis resolutely and has achieved progress. I salute you.
我要告诉朋友们的是，经过这场国际金融危机的洗礼，中国前进的步伐更加稳健了。在这里，我想说一件事。	❶ I'd like to tell you, friends, that after this financial crisis, China's development has become more steady. I'd like to mention one event. ❷ I'd like to tell my friends present that after the financial crisis, China is becoming steadier in pace. Here is what I want to share with you.
2008年5月12日，中国西南部发生毁灭性的特大地震。当时，我站在震中	❶ On May 12th 2008, in China's South West, there was a devastating earthquake. I stood in the ruins and said to Chinese and foreign journalists: 'In three years come back, a new Wenchuan will arise.' Three years have passed, we tackled international financial crisis whilst

汶川的废墟上，对前来采访的中外记者说，“过三年再来，一个新的汶川会拔地而起”。三年过去了，我们一边应对国际金融危机的冲击，一边举全国之力进行灾后重建。上个月，我第十次来到震区，欣喜地看到：灾区最漂亮的是住房，最坚固的是学校，最现代的是医院，最满意的是居民。我邀请在座各位朋友，有机会到中国汶川走一走、看一看。如果你们身临其境，一定会为这里发生的奇迹感到震撼，也会从中真实地感受到中国的生机和活力。

rebuilding the disaster region. Last month was my 10th visit to the region. I was delighted to see that the most beautiful things were the houses, the most solid were the schools, the most modern were the hospitals, the most satisfied were the people. I invite you all to come to Wenchuan. If you were there, you would see the miracle and be amazed, and feel the vitality of China.

❷ May 2008, in the South West of China, there was a very destructive earthquake. I stood on the ruins of Wen Chuan and said to journalists ‘return in three years and you'll see a new Wen Chuan’. Three years have gone by. We're dealing with the financial crisis and using our national strength to rebuild the disaster region. Last month, I visited the region for the tenth time. I was delighted that the best looking buildings were housing, the strongest buildings were schools, the most modern were hospitals, and the happiest were the locals. I would like you to visit the region and have a look. Once you're there, you'll be struck by what you see and will have a true sense of China's dynamism.

对中国改革开放以来的发展变化，世界上有各种各样的解读；对未来中国的走向，人们也非常关注。我愿意借今天这个机会，谈谈我的看法。

❶ The reform in China has brought about changes. There are different interpretations. As for our future direction, people are watching. I'd like to take this opportunity to talk about my view.

❷ The reform in China and the changes have led to different interpretations. The future of China is being watched. I'd like to take this opportunity to talk about what I think.

上世纪80年代初，中国改革开放的总设计师邓小平，曾提出我国现代化进程分“三步走”的战略构想。第一步，基本解决温饱问题；第二步，全面建设小康社会；第三步，到本世纪中叶，基本实现现代化，达到世界中等发达国家水平。2010年到2020年，是中国全面建设小康社会的关键阶段。“三步走”战略的核心和本质，都是坚持以人为本，增进全体中国人的福祉。沿着这条社会主义现代化道路前进，中国必将会有一个更加光明的未来。

❶ During the early 1980s, the reform architect, Mr Deng Xiaoping, said that China's modernisation needed to take three steps. The first step was to feed and clothe the nation, the second step was to build a Xiaokang society and the third step was, by the middle of the current century, to achieve modernization comparable to a middle income country. From 2010 to 2020, China's development of a Xiaokang Society is at a crucial stage. The Three Step strategy is fundamentally about being people-centred, about enhancing welfare for the Chinese people. Continuing with socialist modernisation, China will have an even brighter future.

❷ In the 1980s, the reform architect in chief, Deng Xiaoping said China's modernization would take three steps. Step one was to feed and clothe the nation. Step two was to have a moderately prosperous society. Step three was to achieve basic modernization becoming a middle income country. 2010 to 2020 is step two. The third step is fundamentally about the people, about enhancing the well being of the nation. This is a socialist modernisation path. China will have a brighter future.

未来的中国，将是一个经济发达、人民富裕的国家。集中精力发展经济，不断改善人民生活，始终是中国政府的第一要务。我们将坚持科学发展，着力转变经济发展方式，走绿色、低碳、可持续的发展道路。我

❶ The China of the future will be a developed country with a prosperous population. Focusing on the economy and improving livelihoods have always been the government's top priority. We shall uphold scientific development, shift our development model and pursue green, low-carbon and sustainable development. We will expand domestic demand, unlock spending potentials so that consumption will pull the economy. We will focus even more on improving livelihoods, boosting employment, and on education, healthcare and public services. The income distribution system needs to be further reformed. Urban and

们将扩大国内需求特别是消费需求，进一步释放城乡居民消费潜力，使消费成为拉动经济增长的根本动力。我们将更加注重改善民生，努力扩大就业，优先发展教育、卫生等公共业，深化收入分配制度改革，增加城乡居民收入，加快建立覆盖城乡居民的社会保障体系，让各族人民共享发展成果。	rural income needs to be increased. We will accelerate the coverage of urban and rural social security systems. No ethnic groups will be left out. ❷ Looking ahead, China will be a developed country with prosperity for its people. We'll focus on our economy and standard of living. That'll be our government's top priority. we'll continue with scientific development. We'll drive the transition of growth mode, becoming green, low carbon and sustainable. We'll expand domestic demand, particularly consumer demand, further releasing urban consumption potentials. Consumption will become a fundamental driver of economy. We'll focus more on improved standards of living, on employment, education, health. Income distribution will be further reformed and income increased. We'll accelerate the urban social security system so that the entire nation can share the benefit of development.

2.习近平副主席的讲话

使用提要

1. 本单元的讲话稿仍然是以两种形式提供。第一单元的使用提要里已经说明了使用方法。
2. 本单元和第一单元一样，为了示范如何在视译的讨论阶段达到两个方案的要求，参考译入语都有两个版本。其他单元只有一个版本。
3. 视译时每次练习的长短可以继续按照每秒 4 个汉字计算。
4. 在使用或者参照译入语时必须注意：

   4.1. 参考译入语只是诸多可能版本之一、二，不是最佳版本。有些不一定合适的处理是有意保留，而且没有刻意保持连贯，即同个表达法在一个讲话里的处理都可能各不相同。这些做法都是为了从同传培训一开始就建立作为实战参照的质量标准。如果教材的译入语是经过修饰后的完善版本，这不仅是概念上的误导，而且会导致培训生无法达到教材里的准确度而丧失练习的信心。

   4.2. 由于上述原因，一定不可用笔译的准确标准来衡量同传的译入语版本，因为听同传的感觉和阅读文字完全不一样。

   4.3. 本教材有意没有提供视译中具体采取的是三词一译所需 9 大技巧中的哪一个，这是为了避免把练习的重点放在讲解技巧的概念上。

英译汉三词一译10大技巧

1. 先存后译	2. 反话正说	3. 预测先说	4. 弃卒保车
5. 减字近半	6. 增加时态	7. 实词开句	8. 增补主语
9. 译所指也			

限时视译

着眼长远，携手开创中美合作新局面

（习近平副主席在中美经贸合作论坛开幕式上的演讲）

尊敬的布赖森部长，
尊敬的布朗州长、维拉莱戈萨市长，
女士们，先生们，朋友们：

今天，我很高兴在尼克松总统访华和中美《上海公报》发表40周年之际，来到美丽的洛杉矶，出席中美经贸合作论坛开幕式。洛杉矶是美国对华经贸交往的重要门户，洛杉矶关税区每年吞吐着40%的中美贸易总量。中美经贸合作论坛在这里举行，为两国工商界加强交流、深化合作提供了良好平台。我谨对论坛的开幕表示热烈祝贺！向所有为推动中美经贸关系发展作出贡献的朋友们，表示诚挚的问候和良好的祝愿！

40年来，特别是中美建交33年来，中美两国已从昔日几乎彼此隔绝走到今天相互交往日益密切、利益交汇日益加深。不仅两国政府层面建立起不同级别、不同领域的60多个双边对话机制，两国普通民众往来也日益密切。现在，中美两国每年人员往来超过300万人次，平均每天有近1万人往返于太平洋两岸。中美关系已发展成为当今世界最重要、最富活力和最具潜力的双边关系之一。回顾中美经贸关系的发展历程，我对以下3点感受极为深刻。

第一，经贸合作已成为中美两国关系的最大亮点。现在，互利互惠的中美经贸关系正呈现合作领域持续拓展、合作规模日益扩大、合作层次不断提高的发展态势，双边贸易额已从建交当年不足25亿美元发展到2011年的4466亿美元，增长近180倍，按目前增长速度，今年有望突破5000亿美元。两国早已互为第二大贸易伙伴，中国已连续10年成为美国增长最快的出口市场之一，既是美国农产品第一大出口市场，也是美国汽车、飞机等机电产品的重要海外市场。2011年，美国向中国出口农产品达到233亿美元，平均每个农场向中国出口农产品超过1万美元，每个农民向中国出口农产品接近4000美元。

两国双向协议投资总规模已接近1700亿美元。目前在华美国投资项目6万多个，2010年在华实现销售收入2232亿美元。中国美国商会去年的一项调查显示，2010年，85%的在华美资企业实现收入增长，41%的在华美资企业利润率超过全

球平均利润率。中国企业赴美投资积极性也不断高涨，目前已在美设立直接投资企业1600多家，覆盖制造、批发零售、商务服务、金融、科研技术服务和地质勘探等行业。可喜的是，这样的投资势头方兴未艾。

第二，互利共赢是中美经贸合作的最大特点。有一种观点认为，美国在两国经贸合作中吃了亏，而中国占了便宜。事实并非如此。40年来特别是建交33年来，中国从发展中美经贸关系中固然收益良多，美国也同样获利丰厚。所以中美双方都是赢家，是实实在在的互利双赢。

首先，美国从中国进口的大量质优价廉的产品，提高了美国民众实际消费能力和生活水平，为美国经济保持增长提供了助力。据美中贸易全国委员会公布的研究结果，中美经贸合作促进了美国经济增长，使美国消费品价格相对较低，这相当于美国每个家庭每年可支配收入增加1000美元。

其次，日益密切的中美经贸关系为美国创造了大量就业机会。据不完全统计，2001年至2010年，美国对华出口共为美国增加了300多万个就业岗位。中国在美投资企业也为促进美国就业作出了贡献。比如，中国海运集团在洛杉矶投资兴建的中海运西港池码头连同配套服务行业，共为美国创造就业机会近1万个。中国万向集团在美投资的近30个项目，为美国创造就业机会近5000个。中国海尔集团自1999年在美国南卡罗来纳州建立中国海尔工业园以来，为坎登市创造了上千个就业岗位，该市每10个家庭中就有一个家庭有海尔的员工。更值得一提的是，2009年美国有一家著名跨国公司经营遇到严重困难，但这家公司在华合资企业产品销售额却占有中国市场最高份额，成为这家公司全球最大收入来源。正是在华合资企业的赢利给了这家公司宝贵的现金流和底气，使它得以重整旗鼓、重归股市，最终挽回了该公司及其上下游企业在美国境内数以万计的就业岗位。

第三，结构互补是中美经贸合作的最大优点。中国拥有丰富的熟练劳动力和后发市场潜力，已发展成为当今世界主要商品制造基地；美国拥有最先进的高端制造业和现代服务业，又是世界最大的消费市场。中美经济结构的互补，既产生了内在的合作需求，也形成了巨大的合作利益。中国始终从战略高度和长远角度看待和处理中美经贸合作和摩擦，注重为中美经贸关系顺利发展创造条件、解决问题。两国建立了多个对话合作机制，就双方共同关心的全局性、战略性、长期性问题及时、深入交换意见，为两国凝聚共识、化解分歧、推进合作发挥了重要作用，也为促进世界经济强劲、可持续、平衡增长以及加强全球经济治理作出了积极贡献。

女士们、先生们！

2011年，中国国家主席胡锦涛同奥巴马总统一道确定了两国建设相互尊重、互利共赢的合作伙伴关系的大方向，充分体现了新形势下中美关系的特点与要求。在新的历史起点上推动互利共赢的中美经贸关系持续健康稳定发展，是两国政府的共同责任，也是两国企业的共同期待。为此，我提出以下四点建议。

第一，把握市场机遇，促进贸易平衡发展。中国政府在2011年至2015年的国民经济和社会发展第十二个五年规划期间，将加快转变经济发展方式，推进经济结构调整，实行扩大内需战略，鼓励更多消费、更多进口、更多向海外投资、更多创新创造；美国政府正在实施出口倍增计划，积极引进海外投资。两国宏观经济政策的相向而行为深化经贸合作提供了新的重要机遇。2012年是中国实施“十二五”规划承上启下的重要一年。中国经济将按照稳中求进的总基调，继续保持平稳较快发展，而决不会出现所谓“硬着陆”。预计到2015年中国社会消费品零售总额将达到32万亿元人民币，约合5万亿美元，国内市场规模将位居世界前列，进口规模累计有望达到8万亿美元，对外投资将超过5000亿美元，这将给世界各国带来巨大商机。希望美国把握机遇，扩大具有竞争优势的民用高技术产品对华出口。

我看到的一个统计资料反映，美国对高技术产品的严格管制导致很多有优势的美国公司丧失了在中国的潜在市场机会：2001年至2011年，中国进口高技术产品从560亿美元增至4630亿美元，年均增幅23.5%。同一时期自美国进口的高技术产品，则由2001年占中国高技术产品进口总额的16.7%降到2011年的6.3%。如果美国2011年对华高技术产品出口能够保持2001年的比重，则美国对华出口额可增加近500亿美元。由此可见，放宽对华出口管制对美国有很大好处。扭转中美贸易不平衡，最有效的办法不是限制中国对美出口，而是要扩大美国对华出口。

第二，营造良好环境，提高双向投资水平。2001年中国加入世界贸易组织以来，全面履行入世承诺，在清理修订法律法规、大幅降低外资准入门槛、全面开放对外贸易经营权、反对各种形式的保护主义方面做了大量工作。特别是中国企业同美国企业一样，凭借自身艰苦努力，依靠不断创新和公平竞争，使自己的产品在国际市场上赢得了更多买家。今后，我们还将继续拓展对外开放广度和深度，鼓励一切在华企业，包括在华外资企业，在中国国内市场上公平竞争、积极创新，在赢得市场的同时推动技术进步和社会发展。鼓励创新离不开对知识产权的保护。当前，中国正在着力营造更加公开透明的法律政策环境，继续从司法和行政两个方面加强知识产权保护，包括建立副总理级的知识产权保护协调机制，为本国企业和在华外资企业提供更加安全的经营环境。我们也希望美方继续为中国企业赴美投资创造公平、便利的环境，客观理性看待中国企业的投资行为，避免政治因素干扰经济合作，保证投资安全审查的公开、公正、透明，加紧推动双边投资协定谈判进程，增强中国企业对美投资的信心。

第三，拓展合作领域，培育新的经贸增长点。继续推进产业转型升级，深化经济结构调整，是中美塑造各自发展新模式的共同战略取向。希望两国企业敏锐抓住两国产业结构调整的契机，加快推动在清洁能源、信息技术、电动汽车、新材料、医药和医疗器械、再制造等新兴领域开展合作，为深化经贸合作注入新的动力。我们要鼓励两国企业加强在高铁、公路、港口、桥梁、智能电网、体育和医疗中心、宜居社区等领域的项目建设、融资，以及技术交流等方面合作。希望在座的中美两国企业家更加积极地参与其中，不断探索新的合作方式和途径，努力把新的合作机遇变成更多实实在在的合作成果。

第四，共同应对挑战，加强全球治理合作。中方愿同美方保持和加强在应对国际金融危机、多哈回合谈判、国际货币基金组织改革等全球性经贸问题上的沟通和协调，发挥负责任、建设性大国作用，共同应对各种地区性、全球性挑战，推动落实二十国集团领导人戛纳峰会取得的积极成果，共同为加强全球治理体系改革、维护和促进世界经济稳定和持续发展作出贡献。中美两国也要继续加强在亚太区域合作中的沟通和协调，构建中美在亚太地区的良性互动、互利共赢格局。

女士们、先生们！

中国过去30多年的快速发展靠的是改革开放。30多年来，中国虽然取得了举世瞩目的发展成就，但仍然是世界上最大的发展中国家。在本世纪上半叶，中国要相继实现到2020年建成惠及十几亿人口的更高水平的小康社会、到2050年建成富强民主文明和谐的社会主义现代化国家这两大奋斗目标，必须继续坚定不移地依靠改革开放。同时，也要求保持稳定的国内环境与和平的周边环境、国际环境。我们真诚希望包括美国在内的国际社会理解中国人民渴望彻底摆脱贫困、实现富民强国的心情，相信中国人民走和平发展道路的诚意和决心，尊重中国人民对国家主权、安全、领土完整和社会稳定的珍视，以各种方式支持中国走和平发展道路。一个繁荣稳定的中国，不会对任何国家构成威胁，而只会成为维护世界和平、促进全球发展的积极力量。

让我们携起手来，共同努力，推动中美经贸关系长期健康稳定发展，共同开创中美经贸合作的美好明天！

最后，衷心预祝本次论坛取得圆满成功！

谢谢大家。

技巧琢磨

尊敬的布赖森部长，
尊敬的布朗州长、维拉莱戈萨市长，
女士们，先生们，朋友们：

今天，我很高兴在尼克松总统访华和中美《上海公报》发表40周年之际，来到美丽的洛杉矶，出席中美经贸合作论坛开幕式。洛杉矶是美国对华经贸交往的重要门户，洛杉矶关税区每年吞吐着40%的中美贸易总量。中美经贸合作论坛在这里举行，为两国工商界加强交流、深化合作提供了良好平台。我谨对论坛的开幕表示热烈祝贺！向所有为推动中美经贸关系发展作出贡献的朋友们，表示诚挚的问候和良好的祝愿！

Respected Secretary Bryson,
Governor Brown, Mayor Villaraigosa,
Ladies and Gentlemen, Dear Friends,

I am delighted to be here. President Nixon visited China and the Sino-US Shanghai Communiqué was issued 40 years ago. I am here, in the beautiful city of Los Angeles, to attend the opening session of the China-US Economic and Trade Cooperation Forum. Los Angeles is an important gateway in Sino-US trade. In Los Angeles Customs District, each year, 40% of the Sino-US total trade passes through here. The forum serves the business communities of our two countries well. It enables deeper cooperation and is an excellent platform. I congratulate you on the opening of the forum. To those of you that have been promoting Sino-US trade ties, I'd like to extend my greetings and best wishes.

Secretary,
Governor,
Mayor,
Ladies and Gentlemen, Friends,

I'm very pleased that we're here to mark the 40th anniversary of President Nixon's visit to China and the Sino-US Shanghai Communiqué and to attend China-US Economic and Trade Cooperation Forum. Los Angeles is a US-China gateway in trade. In Los Angeles, you handle 40% of the bilateral trade total. The forum here serves the businesses of both countries. It strengthens exchange and cooperation. It's an excellent platform. On the opening of the forum, I'd like to say congratulations and to those that have been promoting bilateral trade, I'd like to say thank you!

40年来，特别是中美建交33年来，中美两国已从昔日几乎彼此隔绝走到今天相互交往日益密切、利益交汇日益加深。不仅两国政府层面建立起不同级别、不同领域的60多个双边对话机制，两国普通民众往来也日益密切。现在，中美两国每年人员往来超过300万人次，平均每天有近1万人往返于太平洋两岸。中美关系已发展成为当今世界最重要、最富活力和最具潜力的双边关系之一。回顾中美经贸关系的发展历程，我对以下3点感受极为深刻。

❶ Over the past 40 years, in particular the past 33 years of diplomatic relations, things have changed. China and the US were isolated from each other, but now, we enjoy closer relations with our interests increasingly converging. The two governments have multiple level and multi-sector relations with more than 60 dialogue mechanisms. People from the two countries are visiting much more frequently. Between us, more than 3 million people visit annually. Every day, around 10,000 people travel across the Pacific. Sino-US relations have become the world's most important, dynamic and promising bilateral tie. Looking back, I'm very struck by the following 3 aspects:

❷ For 40 years, particularly since the diplomatic relations established 33 years ago, our two countries have moved much closer. There is increasing engagement, not just at the government level where there are now multi-level and multi-sector dialogues numbering more than 60. Ordinary people have much closer relations too. Between our countries, there are more than 3 million visits a year. On average, there are nearly ten thousand people travelling across the Pacific Ocean each day. Our relationship has become one of the most important, dynamic and promising bilateral relationships. A review of the Sino-US trade relationship has made me feel very strongly about these three things:

第一，经贸合作已成为中美两国关系的最大亮点。现在，互利互惠的中美经贸关系正呈现合作领域持续拓展、合作规模日益扩大、合作层次不断提高的发展态势，双边贸易额已从建交当年

❶ First, trade and economic cooperation has become the biggest highlight. The mutually beneficial Sino-US ties are expanding in scale and complexity. Bilateral trade used to be less than 2.5 billion US dollars in early years. In 2011, it reached 446.6 billion, a growth of 180 fold. At the current rate, it's expected to exceed 500 billion US dollars. We have long become the 2nd largest trading partner of each other. For 10 years running, China has been the fastest growing export market for the US. It's the number one

不足25亿美元发展到2011年的4466亿美元，增长近180倍，按目前增长速度，今年有望突破5000亿美元。两国早已互为第二大贸易伙伴，中国已连续10年成为美国增长最快的出口市场之一，既是美国农产品第一大出口市场，也是美国汽车、飞机等机电产品的重要海外市场。2011年，美国向中国出口农产品达到233亿美元，平均每个农场向中国出口农产品超过1万美元，每个农民向中国出口农产品接近4000美元。

export market for American agricultural products. US automobiles, aircrafts and machinery as well as electrical products are selling in large volumes to China. In 2011, the US exported to China agricultural products worth 23.3 billion US dollars. On average, each farm in America exported over 10,000 dollars worth of products to China, and each American farmer, nearly 4,000 dollars.

❷ One, trade has become the brightest highlight. Mutually beneficial trade is expanding across sectors and increasing its scale. Cooperation is moving up the value chain. Bilateral trade used to be less than 2.5 billion US dollars. In 2011, it was 446.6 billion, an increase of nearly 18 times. At the current rate, this year is likely to be more than 500 billion. We have long become second largest trading partner of each other. For ten consecutive years, China is the fastest growing export market of the US. For US agricultural products, we're the largest export market. For US automobile, aircraft, machinery and electrical products, we're your major overseas market. In 2011, you exported to us agri-products worth 23.3 billion. That's equivalent to each farm exporting more than ten thousand dollars or each farmer, nearly 4,000 dollars.

两国双向协议投资总规模已接近1700亿美元。目前在华美国投资项目6万多个，2010年在华实现销售收入2232亿美元。中国美国商会去年的一项调查显示，2010年，85%的在华美资企业实现收入增长，41%

❶ Two-way contracted investment is now approaching 170 billion dollars. In China, US-invested projects now stand at over 60,000. In 2010, their sales reached 223.2 billion dollars. The US Chamber of Commerce in China did a survey last year showing that in 2010, 85% of the US-invested companies saw their revenue grow, and 41% of them saw their profit margin higher than the global average. The Chinese companies are coming to invest in the US more proactively, having invested directly in over 1,600 projects, covering manufacturing, wholesale and retail,

的在华美资企业利润率超过全球平均利润率。中国企业赴美投资积极性也不断高涨，目前已在美设立直接投资企业1600多家，覆盖制造、批发零售、商务服务、金融、科研技术服务和地质勘探等行业。可喜的是，这样的投资势头方兴未艾。

business services, finance, R&D service, geological exploration and so on. I am delighted to see that such investment continues to boom.

❷ Two-way investment is approaching 170 billion. In China, US companies have invested more than 60,000 projects. In 2010, their sales were 223.2 billion. US Chamber of Commerce in China did a survey, showing that in 2010, 85% of their companies increased income, 41% of them saw their profitability exceeding the global average. Chinese businesses are increasingly looking to the US. Direct investment involves 1,600 companies, ranging from manufacturing, wholesale and retailing, business services, finance, research and technology services as well as geographical exploitation. The thing is, this investment is continuing.

第二，互利共赢是中美经贸合作的最大特点。有一种观点认为，美国在两国经贸合作中吃了亏，而中国占了便宜。事实并非如此。40年来特别是建交33年来，中国从发展中美经贸关系中固然收益良多，美国也同样获利丰厚。所以中美双方都是赢家，是实实在在的互利双赢。

❶ Second, mutual benefit has been the most prominent feature of Sino-US cooperation. There is a view that in this cooperation, the US suffers while China wins. It's not true. Over the past 40, especially the past 33 years, developing Sino-US trade has brought benefits to China, so has it to the US. We are both winners, and this is a truly win-win situation.

❷ Two, mutual benefit between us is the biggest highlight. Some people believe that the US has lost out to China. The reality is for the past 40 years, particularly the 33 years of diplomatic relationship, China has gained a great deal, but so has the US. Both have been winners. It's been truly mutually beneficial.

3. 李克强副总理的讲话

使用提要

1. 本单元的讲话稿仍然以两种形式提供：限时视译和技巧琢磨。但是目前为止应该已经掌握了两个版本的原则，所以参考译入语只提供一个版本。
2. 限时视译每次材料的长短，应该开始按照每秒 5 个汉字要求，争取在 2-3 个单元之后能够开始增加到每秒 6 个汉字。
3. 在使用或者参照译入语时必须注意：

   3.1. 参考译入语只是诸多可能版本之一，不是最佳版本。有些不一定合适的处理是有意保留，而且没有刻意保持连贯，即同个表达法在一个讲话里的处理都可能各不相同。这些做法都是为了从同传培训一开始就建立作为实战参照的质量标准。如果教材的译入语是经过修饰后的完善版本，这不仅是概念上的误导，而且会导致培训生无法达到教材里的准确度而丧失练习的信心。

   3.2. 由于上述原因，一定不可用笔译的准确标准来衡量同传的译入语版本，因为听同传的感觉和阅读文字完全不一样。

   3.3. 本教材有意没有提供视译中具体采取的是三词一译所需 9 大技巧中的哪一个，这是为了避免把练习的重点放在讲解技巧的概念上。

英译汉三词一译10大技巧

1. 先存后译	2. 反话正说	3. 预测先说	4. 弃卒保车
5. 减字近半	6. 增加时态	7. 实词开句	8. 增补主语
9. 译所指也			

限时视译

在中国发展高层论坛上的致辞

（国务院副总理李克强）

各位来宾，女士们，先生们，朋友们，

很高兴参加本年度中国发展高层论坛，令与会每一位来宾都感到惊喜的是，昨天夜里中国的北京下了去年入冬以来第一场有真正意义的或者叫做有规模的雪，这是一个好兆头，它给粮食生产和城市环境改善都带来了好气象，人们会有好心情，好心情下会有好建议。中国发展高层论坛这几年来一直围绕着世界与中国经济发展，特别是应对金融危机展开深入的研讨，提出了很多很好的建议。本次论坛的主题是中国与世界宏观经济和结构调整，这个主题本身具有很强的针对性、现实性，也有长远意义。在此，我代表中国政府对论坛的召开表示热烈的祝贺，对远道而来的嘉宾表示热烈的欢迎。

当前，世界经济复苏虽然出现了一些变化，有一些好兆头，但是前景仍不明朗，国际金融危机、欧洲主权债务危机还在发展，全球流动性明显增加，经济下滑、通货膨胀压力并存，国际大宗商品市场动荡不已，人们对前景忧虑挥之不去。与此同时，支撑全球经济逐步恢复增长的因素依然存在，科技创新与产业升级正在进行，储蓄与消费、出口与进口、实体经济与虚体经济等结构性调整越来越受到重视，人们期待通过调整和创新拓展积极因素，更有效地应对复杂局面，推动世界经济强劲可持续，平衡增长。

中国经济和世界经济已高度融合，相互影响日益加深，当前中国经济继续保持了较快增长，总体态势平稳，长期向好的基本面没有改变，但中国依然是世界上最大的发展中国家，发展中国家不平衡、不协调的问题依然突出。

前几天，十一届全国人大第五次会议批准了政府工作报告，对经济社会发展做出了全面部署，我们将按照“十二五”发展主题主线的要求和今年的工作安排，把握好稳中求进的总基调，加强和改善宏观调控，提高政策的针对性、灵活性和前瞻性，以保持经济平稳较快发展和物价总水平基本稳定。并努力在转变发展方式、深化改革开放、保障改善民生上取得新的突破。对于经济结构进行战略性调整，是我国加快转变经济发展方式的主攻方向，也是实现今年经济社会发展的关键目标。

推进结构调整，有利于激发经济增长的活力和动力，增强发展的可持续性，提高抗风险能力，有利于增强有效供给，抑制不合理需求，促进共同平衡，也有利于推动经济转型和模式创新，提高发展的质量和效益，促进经济和社会协调发展。

当前，我们将在诸多方面特别是以下几个重点方面做出进一步的努力：一是立足扩大内需，扩大内需是中国经济社会发展的战略基点，特别是在今年国际市场仍然不景气，扩大内需对中国来说具有更重要的现实意义。中国扩大内需城镇化是最大的潜力，去年中国城镇人口比重已经超过 50%，但还远低于发达国家的水平，也低于世界平均水平。

我们将统筹城乡发展，在严格保护耕地、保障粮食安全、不断改善农村生产生活条件的情况下积极稳妥地推进城镇化，推动工业化、城镇化和农业现代化协调发展，实现“三化”并举，这样可以释放巨大的消费潜力，带动投资扩大和相关产业发展，拉动经济持续增长。扩大内需还需要把服务业放在更加突出的位置，与发达国家和同等收入水平发展中国家相比，中国服务业比重明显偏低，要在大力发展先进制造业、高新技术产业的同时，加快发展生产和生活性服务业，这样不仅可以大量地容纳就业，而且能够提升工业发展水平，是壮大实体经济的有效途径。

扩大内需还要和改善民生更好地结合起来，我们正在进行的保障房建设、新一轮医改、集中连片扶贫攻坚，这不仅是重大的民生工程，也是重大的发展工程，同时又是调解收入分配的重大举措，有利于保障人民群众基本生活。我们要围绕保障人民基本需求来实施好这些重大工程，并注重在发展经济与提高居民收入同步的过程当中，提高居民的消费能力，增强居民的消费信心，促进消费和投资良性互动，使改善民生成为发展之基，使全国人们共享发展成果。

二是强化创新驱动。创新是经济社会发展的最大活力，推进经济结构调整要坚持以企业为主体，以市场为导向，加强政府引导，增强各方面资金投资，全面的推进技术创新、管理创新和产品创新，提高经济的自主增长能力和创新驱动，从而来实现结构和产业升级。今年中国的研发费用的支出预计可达到 1 万亿元人民币，这将有力地支持发明创造和技术革新。

创新需要人才，发展需要高素质的劳动者。经过多年努力，中国已培育了数千万各类科研人员和工程师，拥有数以亿计勤劳和熟练的产业工人，每年还有几百万大学毕业生进入工作一线，我们将努力把人口众多的特点转化为人力资源、人力资源丰富的优势，并全面推进科技创新，加大知识产权保护力度，鼓励创新创造，促进经济增长由主要依靠物质资源消耗向主要靠科技进步、劳动者素质提高、管理创新转变，为保持经济的长期平稳较快发展奠定坚实基础。

三是依靠改革开放。中国的经济发展到了转变经济发展方式的关键阶段，刻不容缓。转变方式的根本在于创新体制机制，改革开放是实现经济转型和推动现代化建设的根本动力。目前，中国的改革已进入攻坚期，我们将深化财税、金融、价格、企业、收入分配制度等方面的改革，努力在重点领域和关键环节有所突破，更好地发挥市场在资源配置中的基础性作用，坚决破除制约经济社会发展的体制机制障碍，增强发展的内生动力。中国的扩大内需、推动创新、实现转型是在扩大开放的条件下进行的。我们不仅要扩大内需，也要稳定和拓展出口。

在促进进出口平衡的过程中，创新引进外资和对外投资的方式，为各类企业公平竞争、共同发展提供良好环境。今天到会的有中外许多企业家，大家都十分关心中国开放型经济的发展，我在这里也可以告诉各位，预计中国今年对外贸易额和境外直接投资额还有可能保持两位数的增长，进口总额将超过 1.9 万亿美金，这样一个大的数字为国外企业在中国市场参与平等竞争提供巨大的商机。更重要的是，在“十二五”期间，据我们测算，按照平稳的增长势头，中国的进出口总额有可能达到 10 万亿美金以上，这无疑是酝酿着巨大的商机和潜力。

女士们，先生们，当前中国经济的持续增长和结构调整，未来中国经济的长期平稳较快发展，有利于增进中国人民的福祉，也有利于促进国际合作发展，中国发展高层论坛既是一个碰撞思想、凝聚共识的平台，也是一个加强交流、促进合作的平台，希望在座的各位在研讨中相互启迪，在合作上取得丰硕成果。

最后，祝 2012 中国发展高层论坛圆满成功，祝各位嘉宾身体健康，工作顺利，生活愉快。谢谢大家！

技巧琢磨

各位来宾，女士们，先生们，朋友们，

很高兴参加本年度中国发展高层论坛，令与会每一位来宾都感到惊喜的是，昨天夜里中国的北京下了去年入冬以来第一场有真正意义的或者叫做有规模的雪，这是一个好兆头，它给粮食生产和城市环境改善都带来了好气象，人们会有好心情，好心情下会有好建议。中国发展高层论坛这几年来一直围绕着世界与中国经济发展，特别是应对金融危机展开深入的研讨，提出了很多很好的建议。本次论坛的主题是中国与世界：宏观经济和结构调整，这个主题本身具有很强的针对性、现实性，也有长远意义。在此，我代表中国政府对论坛的召开表示热烈的祝贺，对远道而来的嘉宾表示热烈的欢迎。

Guests, ladies and gentlemen, friends,

I am delighted to attend the China development forum.Guestswere perhaps pleasantly surprised last night that we had the first proper snow or substantial snow. This is a good omen.In terms of food production and urban environment, it's a good thing. It makes people feel good. Good mood produces good ideas. The forum has been focusing on the world and China's economic development. In particular, we've been talking about how to tackle the financial crisis. There have beenmany excellent suggestions.This year, the theme is China and the World: Macro economy and Economic Restructuring.It is highly relevant, pragmatic and bears long-term importance. On behalf of the Chinese government, I congratulate on the opening of this forum and extend my welcome to all the guests.

当前，世界经济复苏虽然出现了一些变化，有一些好兆头，但是前景仍不明朗，国际金融危机、欧洲主权债务危机还在发展，全球流动性明显增加，经济下滑、通货膨胀压力并存，国际大宗商品市场动荡不已，人们对前景忧虑挥之不去。与此同时，支撑全球经济逐步恢复增长的因素依然存在，

The world economic recovery has shown some good signs, but the future is uncertain. The financial crisis and European sovereign debt crisis are on-going. Global liquidity is increasing significantly. Downturn and inflation pressure co-exist. The global commodity market is volatile. Worries about the future aren't disappearing. However, economic recovery has the factors it needs to restore

科技创新与产业升级正在进行，储蓄与消费、出口与进口、实体经济与虚体经济等结构性调整越来越受到重视，人们期待通过调整和创新拓展积极因素，更有效地应对复杂局面，推动世界经济强劲可持续，平衡增长。

growth. Technology innovation and industrial upgrades are continuing. Savings and consumption, export and import, real economy and virtual economy are being restructured in increasing earnest. The expectation is that re-structuring and innovation will help us deal more effectively with complex situations and drive the world economy towards sustainable and balanced growth.

中国经济和世界经济已高度融合，相互影响日益加深，当前中国经济继续保持了较快增长，总体态势平稳，长期向好的基本面没有改变，但中国依然是世界上最大的发展中国家，发展中国家不平衡、不协调的问题依然突出。

Chinese economy and global economy are highly integrated, impacting on each other. China has maintained a relatively fast growth.Overall, it's stable and positive in its fundamentals. But, China is still thelargest developing nation. As such, imbalance and lack of coordination are still problems.

前几天，十一届全国人大第五次会议批准了政府工作报告，对经济社会发展做出了全面部署，我们将按照“十二五”发展主题主线的要求和今年的工作安排，把握好稳中求进的总基调，加强和改善宏观调控，提高政策的针对性、灵活性和前瞻性，以保持经济平稳较快发展和物价总水平基本稳定。并努力在转变发展方式、深化改革开放、保障改善民生上取得新的突破。对于经济结构进行战略性调整，是我国加快转变经济发展方式的主攻方向，也是实现今年经济社会发展的关键目标。

A few days ago, the 11th NPC held its 5th conference and approved the Government Work Report. In terms of economic and social development, there is a comprehensive plan.We will follow the 12th FiveYear Plan and the plan for this year. We will pursue stable progress, improvemacro-control and ensure our policies are targeted, flexible and forward-looking, so as to maintain stable and relatively fast economic growth andstable prices. We will shift the development mode, deepen reform and improve livelihoods. Economic restructuring is ofa strategic nature. It'll enable us to accelerate the transition. It is also a key goal for this year.

推进结构调整，有利于激发经济增长的活力和动力，增强发展的可持续性，提高抗风险能力，有利于增强有效供给，抑制不合理需求，促进共同平衡，也有利于推动经济转型和模式创新，提高发展的质量和效益，促进经济和社会协调发展。

Driving forward restructuring will stimulategrowth, improve sustainability and resilience. It'll help strengthen effective supply, constrain irrational demand, and achieve balance. It'll facilitateour transition and innovation, improve the quality and efficiency of development, and advance economic and social development in harmony.

当前，我们将在诸多方面特别是以下几个重点方面做出进一步的努力：一是立足扩大内需，扩大内需是中国经济社会发展的战略基点，特别是在今年国际市场仍然不景气，扩大内需对中国来说具有更重要的现实意义。中国扩大内需城镇化是最大的潜力，去年中国城镇人口比重已经超过 50%，但还远低于发达国家的水平，也低于世界平均水平。

Of the many things, we will focus our efforts on the following. First, we need to expand domestic demand. That is a strategic basis. Given that the global market is not doing well, expanding domestic demand has become even more important. Urbanization has the greatest potential. Last year, China's urban population was more than 50% of the total. But, that's still lower than that of the developed countries and the world average.

4. 杨洁篪外交部长的讲话

使用提要

1. 本单元的讲话稿仍然以两种形式提供。第一种采用常见的讲话稿形式，便于练习限时视译。第二种采用对照、对比形式，便于练习、琢磨三词一译的技巧。
2. 限时视译的速度仍然可以是每秒 5 个汉字。
3. 在使用或者参照译入语时必须注意：

   3.1. 参考译入语只是诸多可能版本之一，不是最佳版本。

   3.2. 参考译入语完全按照实战的标准提供，没有经过修饰。不可用笔译的标准衡量，因为听同传的感觉和阅读文字完全不一样。

   3.3. 为了体现实战里的情况，参考译入语没有刻意保持连贯。同个表达法在一个讲话里的处理都可能各不相同。

   3.4. 本教材有意没有提供视译中具体采取的是三词一译所需 9 大技巧中的哪一个，这是为了避免把练习的重点放在讲解技巧的概念上。

英译汉三词一译10大技巧

1. 先存后译	2. 反话正说	3. 预测先说	4. 弃卒保车
5. 减字近半	6. 增加时态	7. 实词开句	8. 增补主语
9. 译所指也			

限时视译

在“全球反恐论坛”成立仪式上的讲话

（外交部长杨洁篪）

尊敬的克林顿国务卿女士，达乌特奥卢外长先生，
尊敬的潘基文秘书长先生，
各位同事，女士们，先生们：

今天是全球反恐事业的重要日子，由30个国家和组织参加的“全球反恐论坛”在这里正式成立。论坛以提高相关国家反恐能力建设、推动国际反恐合作为己任，为各国在反恐领域加强交流和合作提供了一个重要平台，体现了国际社会为应对恐怖主义新挑战而共同努力的坚定决心。论坛的成立必将对全球反恐合作进程产生重要而积极的影响。

近十年来，反恐成为国际社会的重要议程。各国政府充分认识到恐怖主义对国际安全、稳定与发展的危害，下大力气反恐，加大投入，提高能力，完善政策，加强合作。经过努力，恐怖势力的活动能力和空间受到削弱和挤压，全球反恐斗争形势在不断朝好的方向发展。但同时，我们在反恐方面仍然面临许多新挑战和新问题，特别是国际金融危机深层次影响尚未根本消除，一些国家和地区动荡加剧，制约了相关国家的反恐能力和意愿，让暴力极端思想有机可乘。国际恐怖势力不断变换策略和手法，大肆利用网络传播恐怖极端思想，恐怖主义的本土化和个体化问题日益突出。恐怖活动不仅在贫困动荡的地区肆虐，也已将触角伸入原本富足平和的国家。我们必须认识到，国际反恐形势依然严峻，各国与恐怖主义的斗争将是长期的、艰巨的。

各位同事，女士们，先生们，

当前形势下，如何赢得反恐斗争的胜利，使人类拥有一个和平、安宁、繁荣的21世纪，仍是我们必须认真思考和应对的问题。中方认为，国际社会应从以下几方面加大努力：

第一，促进世界经济复苏，推动各国共同发展。“没有发展，万事空谈”。解决好目前突出的发展问题，特别是发展中国家发展不足的问题，有利于遏制恐怖极端思想的蔓延。

第二，维护国际和地区稳定，和平解决地区争端。冲突和动荡是恐怖主义滋生的温床。各国应努力实现国际关系民主化，坚持通过对话和协商，以和平方式解决国际和地区争端，实现经济发展和人民安居乐业，杜绝恐怖主义的滋生。

第三，深化国际反恐合作，实现共同安全。各国应本着互信互利、平等协作的原则，进一步加强在反恐领域的合作与对话，特别要提高发展中国家的反恐能力。继续支持联合国在国际反恐斗争中发挥核心作用，充分发挥其他国际反恐合作机制的作用，推动《联合国全球反恐战略》的平衡实施。

恐怖主义是世界各国共同面临的问题。中国作为恐怖主义的受害者和国际反恐大家庭中的一员，一贯坚定致力于防恐、打恐和治恐的工作，努力维护国家安全、地区和平与稳定。在反恐工作中，中国政府始终坚持标本兼治的原则，促进经济发展与社会稳定的和谐统一，努力消除恐怖主义滋生的土壤。同时，不断推进反恐立法、机制建设和能力保障。中国政府积极推动和参与国际和地区反恐合作，维护地区和世界的和平与稳定，为国际反恐斗争做出了积极贡献。

各位同事，女士们，先生们，

当今世界正处于大发展大变革大调整之中，维护和平、促进发展，是包括中国在内的世界各国人民的共同愿望。要解决恐怖主义这一影响世界和平与发展的重大问题，需要各国和衷共济，真诚合作。今天成立的全球反恐论坛是我们在合作应对恐怖主义道路上迈出的新一步。我们希望论坛能通过扎实有效的工作，为提高各国反恐能力发挥积极作用，为国际反恐合作注入新动力。中国愿与世界各国并肩努力，以坚定的决心、共同的智慧和强大的力量去推动人类社会的发展与繁荣，促进不同族群、不同文明、不同国家间的和谐包容，最终实现世界的持久和平与安全。

谢谢大家！

技巧琢磨

尊敬的克林顿国务卿女士，
达乌特奥卢外长先生，
尊敬的潘基文秘书长先生，
各位同事，女士们，先生们：

今天是全球反恐事业的重要日子，由30个国家和组织参加的“全球反恐论坛”在这里正式成立。论坛以提高相关国家反恐能力建设、推动国际反恐合作为己任，为各国在反恐领域加强交流和合作提供了一个重要平台，体现了国际社会为应对恐怖主义新挑战而共同努力的坚定决心。论坛的成立必将对全球反恐合作进程产生重要而积极的影响。

Secretary of State Clinton, Foreign Minister Davutoglu,
Secretary General Ban Ki Moon,
Colleagues, ladies and gentlemen,

Today global counterterrorism is having an important day. Thirty countries and organizations have participated in the Global Counterterrorism Forum. The forum aims at improving counterterrorism capability and promoting international cooperation. It provides countries with a counterterrorism communication and cooperation platform. This reflects that the international community is facing new terrorism challenges and we're working together to tackle them. The forum will contribute to global counterterrorism cooperation.

近十年来，反恐成为国际社会的重要议程。各国政府充分认识到恐怖主义对国际安全、稳定与发展的危害，下大力气反恐，加大投入，提高能力，完善政策，加强合作。经过努力，恐怖势力的活动能力和空间受到削弱和挤压，全球反恐斗争形势在不断朝好的方向发展。但同时，我们在反恐方面仍然面临许多新挑战和新问题，特别是国际金融危机深层次影响尚未根本消除，一些国家和地区动荡加剧，制约了相关国

In the last decade, counterterrorism has become a major international agenda. Governments recognize that terrorism threatens international security, stability and development. They need to improve investment, capability, policy and cooperation. With their efforts, terrorist capabilities have been weakened. Global counterterrorism is progressing in the right direction. But we still face many new challenges and issues, especially when the financial crisis is not yet over. Some countries and regions are becoming more unstable, constraining their antiterrorism capabilities. Extremism sets in. International terrorism

家的反恐能力和意愿，让暴力极端思想有机可乘。国际恐怖势力不断变换策略和手法，大肆利用网络传播恐怖极端思想，恐怖主义的本土化和个体化问题日益突出。恐怖活动不仅在贫困动荡的地区肆虐，也已将触角伸入原本富足平和的国家。我们必须认识到，国际反恐形势依然严峻，各国与恐怖主义的斗争将是长期的、艰巨的。

continues to change tactics, using the internet to spread extremist ideas. Localization and individualisation are pressing problems. Terrorist activities are not only troubling the poor regions but also reaching the rich and peaceful countries. We must realize that international counterterrorism is still a tough task that requires long-term efforts.

各位同事，女士们，先生们，当前形势下，如何赢得反恐斗争的胜利，使人类拥有一个和平、安宁、繁荣的21世纪，仍是我们必须认真思考和应对的问题。中方认为，国际社会应从以下几方面加大努力：

Colleagues, ladies and gentlemen, Given the situation, how to win the fight against terrorism and maintain peace and prosperity in the 21st century is something we must think about seriously. China believes that the international community should work on the following:

第一，促进世界经济复苏，推动各国共同发展。"没有发展，万事空谈"。解决好目前突出的发展问题，特别是发展中国家发展不足的问题，有利于遏制恐怖极端思想的蔓延。

First, we need to boost economic recovery so that all countries can develop together. Without development nothing is real. We need to resolve the issue of development, especially in developing countries. This will help to contain terrorist ideology.

第二，维护国际和地区稳定，和平解决地区争端。冲突和动荡是恐怖主义滋生的温床。各国应努力实现国际关系民主化，坚持通过对话和协商，以和平方式解决国际和地区争端，实现经济发展和人民安居乐业，杜绝恐怖主义的滋生。

Second, we need to maintain international and regional stability, peacefully resolving disputes. Conflicts benefit terrorism, breed terrorism. Countries should strive for democratic international relations, using dialogues to resolve disputes peacefully both internationally and regionally, to achieve economic development and prosperity for their people, and to eliminate terrorism.

第三，深化国际反恐合作，实现共同安全。各国应本着互信互利、平等协作的原则，进一步加强在反恐领域的合作与对话，特别要提高发展中国家的反恐能力。继续支持联合国在国际反恐斗争中发挥核心作用，充分发挥其他国际反恐合作机制的作用，推动《联合国全球反恐战略》的平衡实施。

Third, we need to enhance international cooperation for common security. Countries should trust and help each other, enhance antiterrorism cooperation. We particularly need to help the developing countries improve capabilities. We should continue to support the UN to play its core role and make use of other antiterrorism cooperation mechanisms, so as to drive forward the UN global antiterrorism strategy.

恐怖主义是世界各国共同面临的问题。中国作为恐怖主义的受害者和国际反恐大家庭中的一员，一贯坚定致力于防恐、打恐和治恐的工作，努力维护国家安全、地区和平与稳定。在反恐工作中，中国政府始终坚持标本兼治的原则，促进经济发展与社会稳定的和谐统一，努力消除恐怖主义滋生的土壤。同时，不断推进反恐立法、机制建设和能力保障。中国政府积极推动和参与国际和地区反恐合作，维护地区和世界的和平与稳定，为国际反恐斗争做出了积极贡献。

Terrorism is an issue for the whole world. China is a victim of terrorism as well as a member of the international antiterrorism family. We are committed to the prevention and the fight against terrorism. We work to maintain national security and regional stability. The Chinese government has consistently been dealing with both the symptoms and the causes together, promoting economic development and social stability, in order to remove terrorist hotbeds. We continue to develop antiterrorism legislation, mechanism and capability. The Chinese government actively promote and participate in international cooperation to maintain regional and world peace and stability. We have made positive contributions.

各位同事，女士们，先生们，当今世界正处于大发展大变革大调整之中，维护和平、促进发展，是包括中国在内的世界各国人民的共同愿望。要解决恐怖主义这一影响世界和平与发展的重

Colleagues, ladies and gentlemen, The world is experiencing major development and changes. Maintaining peace and development is crucial to China and the rest of the world. We need to resolve the issue of terrorism because it affects world peace and development. We need to help each

大问题，需要各国和衷共济，真诚合作。今天成立的全球反恐论坛是我们在合作应对恐怖主义道路上迈出的新一步。我们希望论坛能通过扎实有效的工作，为提高各国反恐能力发挥积极作用，为国际反恐合作注入新动力。中国愿与世界各国并肩努力，以坚定的决心、共同的智慧和强大的力量去推动人类社会的发展与繁荣，促进不同族群、不同文明、不同国家间的和谐包容，最终实现世界的持久和平与安全。

谢谢大家！

other and work together. The counterterrorism forum is just such cooperation and a new step. We hope to work effectively for the improvement of counterterrorism capability, and provide new dynamism. China is willing to work with other countries. Our resolve is to share wisdom and forces to promote development and prosperity for mankind irrespective of ethnicity, civilisation or country. We want to see harmony and inclusion as well as sustained peace and security.

Thank you!

5. 陈竺卫生部长的讲话

使用提要

1. 本单元的讲话稿仍然以两种形式提供。第一种采用常见的讲话稿形式，便于练习限时视译。第二种采用对照、对比形式，便于练习、琢磨三词一译的技巧。
2. 限时视译的速度仍然可以是每秒 5 个汉字。
3. 在使用或者参照译入语时必须注意：

   3.1. 参考译入语只是诸多可能版本之一，不是最佳版本。

   3.2. 参考译入语完全按照实战的标准提供，没有经过修饰。不可用笔译的标准衡量，因为听同传的感觉和阅读文字完全不一样。

   3.3. 为了体现实战里的情况，参考译入语没有刻意保持连贯。同个表达法在一个讲话里的处理都可能各不相同。

英译汉三词一译10大技巧

1. 先存后译	2. 反话正说	3. 预测先说	4. 弃卒保车
5. 减字近半	6. 增加时态	7. 实词开句	8. 增补主语
9. 译所指也			

限时视译

慢性非传染性疾病防控刻不容缓

（卫生部长陈竺在世界卫生大会上的一般性辩论发言）

尊敬的主席先生、尊敬的总干事女士，各位部长、各位同事：

首先请允许我对主席先生的当选表示祝贺。我相信在您的领导下，本届大会一定能够取得圆满成功。

我愿借此机会对在日本地震和海啸、美国飓风灾害中失去亲人、遭受不幸的家庭表示同情和慰问。这些事件说明在遭遇自然灾害时，人类是如此脆弱，因此，我们需要在人与自然、发展与环境实现和谐。当前，全球化使各国相互联系、相互依存，利益交融达到前所未有的程度，携手合作、同舟共济符合各国共同利益。在此，我祝贺成员国政府间工作组历时四年就《共享流感病毒以及获得疫苗和其他利益的大流行流感防范框架》达成共识。广大发展中国家将不仅只提供流感病毒，并且在《框架》的安排下，合理、合法、公平地分享流感疫苗和抗病毒药物的利益。这充分体现了各国的团结与合作，必将为今后国际社会共同应对威胁人类自身安全的公共卫生挑战树立一个典范。

女士们，先生们，

根据中国最新的人口普查数据，中国 60 岁及以上人口占 13.26%，人口老龄化进程加快。中国已成为世界上首个“未富先老”的发展中大国。中国有 2 亿高血压患者，每年新发 280 万癌症患者，糖尿病患病率已达到 9%。慢性非传染性疾病占中国人群死因构成升至 85%，每年约 370 万人因慢性非传染性疾病过早死亡。慢性非传染性疾病已经给社会经济发展造成了巨大的威胁。防控慢性非传染性疾病，任重道远。

中国政府高度重视慢性非传染性疾病防控工作，参照世界卫生组织的“全球战略行动计划”，坚持预防为主，降低发病率；坚持早发现，减少经济负担；坚持以人为本，提高生活质量；坚持政府主导，全社会共同参与。中国当前进行的医药卫生体制改革正在实现基本医疗卫生服务全民覆盖，包括为全民建立健康档案，为 35 岁以上人群提供高血压、糖尿病健康管理服务，为 65 岁以上老年人提供健康检查服务等。中国政府已在经济社会发展规划中将人均期望寿命提高 1 岁列为核心指标。我们深知，要实现这一目标，实现慢性非传染性疾病的有效防控是关键，为此，我们还将以创建健康城市为抓手，积极开展健康促进、控烟、提高社会服务综合管理能力，并进一步加强以全科医师为重点的基层医疗卫生队伍建设，提高综合服务能力。卫生改革正在为人们带来看得见、摸得着的实惠。

主席先生，各位同事，

慢性非传染性疾病防控是一项刻不容缓的工作。如果控制不好，未来 20-30 年，全球将会出现慢性非传染性疾病的“井喷”。必须重视导致慢性非传染性疾病的健康社会决定因素。国际社会必须增强使命感和紧迫感，必须坚定地实施慢性非传染性疾病全球战略行动计划。我愿提出如下建议：

第一，各国将慢性非传染性疾病防控纳入到衡量本国社会经济发展状况的核心指标，国际社会进一步推动将慢性非传染性疾病防控指标纳入千年发展目标。慢性非传染性疾病是“社会传染病”，各国政府要像重视 GDP 一样重视慢性非传染性疾病预防控制工作，将其纳入当地经济社会发展总体规划，建立部门间协调机制，加强社会动员，共同参与。国际社会要积极筹措资金，保障经费投入。

第二，进一步加强卫生体系建设。强有力的卫生体系不仅是应对传染病以及突发公共卫生事件的基础，更是防控慢性非传染性疾病的关键。各国政府应将卫生体系建设作为重点工作内容。发达国家和国际组织应将加强卫生体系建设作为对外援助的一个重要领域，增加援助力度，帮助发展中国家建设卫生体系。

第三，充分发挥世界卫生组织在全球卫生发展日程中的领导作用，支持陈冯富珍总干事领导秘书处的改革进程。希望世界卫生组织在今年 9 月联合国关于慢性非传染性疾病峰会的筹备中发挥领导作用，在全球建立统一明确的慢性非传染性疾病防控目标与评价指标，制订清晰的行动路线，协调整合国际资源，建立广泛的国际合作和伙伴关系。

主席先生、各位同事，

在此，我也要对总干事陈冯富珍女士表示祝贺，感谢您带领世界卫生组织秘书处，为全球卫生改革和发展发挥的卓越领导和协调作用。

谢谢大家。

技巧琢磨

尊敬的主席先生、尊敬的总干事女士，各位部长、各位同事：

首先请允许我对主席先生的当选表示祝贺。我相信在您的领导下，本届大会一定能够取得圆满成功。

Distinguished Chairman, Director General, Ministers and colleagues,

First, I'd like to say congratulations to the chairman. Under your leadership, the conference will be a great success.

我愿借此机会对在日本地震和海啸、美国飓风灾害中失去亲人、遭受不幸的家庭表示同情和慰问。这些事件说明在遭遇自然灾害时，人类是如此脆弱，因此，我们需要在人与自然、发展与环境实现和谐。当前，全球化使各国相互联系、相互依存，利益交融达到前所未有的程度，携手合作、同舟共济符合各国共同利益。在此，我祝贺成员国政府间工作组历时四年就《共享流感病毒以及获得疫苗和其他利益的大流行流感防范框架》达成共识。广大发展中国家将不仅只提供流感病毒，并且在《框架》的安排下，合理、合法、公平地分享流感疫苗和抗病毒药物的利益。这充分体现了各国的团结与合作，必将为今后国际社会共同应对威胁人类自身安全的公共卫生挑战树立一个典范。

I'd like to take this opportunity to say to those who have suffered in the Japanese earthquake and tsunami and the American Hurricane, those who have lost loved ones, that my thoughts are with them. It shows that in front of natural disasters, human beings are very fragile. Therefore we need to see man and nature, development and environment in harmony. Globalization has meant countries are interconnected, inter-dependant and our interests are linked closer than ever before. Cooperation meets our common interests. I congratulate the inter-governmental working group. In the last four years, they worked on, Sharing of influenza viruses and access to vaccines and other benefits pandemic influenza preparedness framework. A consensus was reached. Developing countries will not only provide influenza viruses, but also, under the framework, legally and fairly share vaccines and anti-virus drugs. This demonstrates international unity. It'll help the international community in its joint effort on life threatening problems in public health.

女士们，先生们，

根据中国最新的人口普查数据，中国60岁及以上人口占13.26%，人口老龄化进程加快。中国已成为世界上首个“未富先老”的发展中大国。中国有2亿高血压患者，每年新发280万癌症患者，糖尿病患病率已达到9%。慢性非传染性疾病占中国人群死因构成升至85%，每年约370万人因慢性非传染性疾病过早死亡。慢性非传染性疾病已经给社会经济发展造成了巨大的威胁。防控慢性非传染性疾病，任重道远。

Ladies and gentlemen,

The latest census of China indicates that the number of Chinese above sixty accounts for 13.26%. Aging is accelerating. China has become the first country that is getting old before getting rich. China has 200 million high blood pressure patients. Every year, there are 2.8 million new cancer cases. Diabetes is found in 9% of the population. Chronic NCDs related death has increased to 85%. Every year, 3.7 million die. NCDs have become a major threat. The prevention and control will be a long-term effort.

中国政府高度重视慢性非传染性疾病防控工作，参照世界卫生组织的“全球战略行动计划”，坚持预防为主，降低发病率；坚持早发现，减少经济负担；坚持以人为本，提高生活质量；坚持政府主导，全社会共同参与。中国当前进行的医药卫生体制改革正在实现基本医疗卫生服务全民覆盖，包括为全民建立健康档案，为35岁以上人群提供高血压、糖尿病健康管理服务，为65岁以上老年人提供健康检查服务等。中国政府已在“十二五”经济社会发展规划中将人均期望寿命提高1岁列为核心指标。我们深知，要实现这一目标，实现慢性非传染性疾病的有效防控

The Chinese government attaches great importance to chronic NCDs. Based on the WHO's global strategic action plan, we focus on prevention to reduce morbidity. We aim at early detection to reduce costs. We focus on improving people's quality of life. The government leads with full public participation. The health care reform is aiming at primary care for all. That includes nationwide health records. For those above 35, high blood pressure and diabetes health management will be provided. For those above 65, there will be health check-ups. The Chinese government has written into its 12th five-year-plan that the life expectancy is to be raised by one year. It's a core indicator. We know well that in order to achieve the target, chronic NCDs control is the key. We will develop healthy cities, promote health, contain smoking and

是关键，为此，我们还将以创建健康城市为抓手，积极开展健康促进、控烟、提高社会服务综合管理能力，并进一步加强以全科医师为重点的基层医疗卫生队伍建设，提高综合服务能力。卫生改革正在为人们带来看得见、摸得着的实惠。

improve management of social services. GPs will be the focus of grassroots level health care delivery teams. There needs to be better capabilities. Healthcare reform is bringing visible benefits to our people.

主席先生，各位同事，

慢性非传染性疾病防控是一项刻不容缓的工作。如果控制不好，未来20-30年，全球将会出现慢性非传染性疾病的“井喷”。必须重视导致慢性非传染性疾病的健康社会决定因素。国际社会必须增强使命感和紧迫感，必须坚定地实施慢性非传染性疾病全球战略行动计划。我愿提出如下建议：

Chairman, colleagues,

Chronic NCD prevention and control are an urgent task. Unless we do it well, in the next two to three decades, there will be chronic NCD ‘blast’. We must pay attention to what causes those diseases in a healthy society. The international community must have a stronger sense of mission and urgency and must implement the NCD global strategic action plan. I’d like to propose the following:

6. 国土资源部长徐绍史的讲话

使用提要

1. 本单元的讲话稿有意选择了政府部长在国内发表的讲话，其中的考虑是国内的译员经常需要为政府领导人和官员的对外讲话提供同传服务。在这种场合，领导人或者官员经常大段、大段的引用国内讲话时的内容或者用语，这种讲话往往没有正式发表的文字稿。所以，必须采用对内讲话的材料练习才能掌握。
2. 本单元的材料仍然以两种形式提供。第一种采用常见的讲话稿形式，便于练习限时视译。第二种采用对照、对比形式，便于练习、琢磨三词一译的技巧。
3. 限时视译的速度需要根据进展争取提高到每秒 6 个汉字，这是实战同传必须达到的速度。
4. 在使用或者参照译入语时必须注意：

   4.1. 参考译入语只是诸多可能版本之一，不是最佳版本。

   4.2. 参考译入语完全按照实战的标准提供，没有经过修饰。不可用笔译的标准衡量，因为听同传的感觉和阅读文字完全不一样。

   4.3. 为了体现实战里的情况，参考译入语没有刻意保持连贯。同个表达法在一个讲话里的处理都可能各不相同。

英译汉三词一译10大技巧

1. 先存后译	2. 反话正说	3. 预测先说	4. 弃卒保车
5. 减字近半	6. 增加时态	7. 实词开句	8. 增补主语
9. 译所指也			

限时视译

在国土资源调查评价成果展开幕式上的致辞

（国土资源部长徐绍史）

尊敬的司马义·铁力瓦尔地副委员长，尊敬的罗富和副主席，
各位领导、各位来宾、同志们：

上午好！

在纪念中国共产党九十华诞之际，由国土资源部、发展改革委、财政部共同举办的“基础·先行——国土资源调查评价成果展”，今天在国家博物馆隆重开幕了。这次展览的主要目的，是向全社会全面系统地回顾总结国土资源调查评价工作的最新成果，介绍宣传我国的资源国情，更好地服务于经济社会发展。首先，我代表展览各主办单位向出席今天开幕式的各位领导、各位来宾和新闻界的朋友们表示热烈的欢迎！向参加国土资源调查的全体同志致以诚挚的慰问和崇高的敬意！也借此机会，向长期以来关心、支持国土资源事业发展的司马义·铁力瓦尔地副委员长、罗富和副主席，以及发展改革委、财政部等有关部门和社会各界表示衷心的感谢！

国土资源是经济社会发展的重要物质基础，国土资源调查评价是支撑经济社会发展的先行性、基础性工作。1998 年以来，国土资源部会同发展改革委、财政部，按照党中央、国务院的决策部署，组织开展了历时 12 年的国土资源调查评价工作。先后实施了国土资源大调查、青藏高原地质矿产调查、新疆“358”地质矿产调查、油气资源战略调查、危机矿山接替资源勘查、海洋资源调查和第二次全国土地调查、全国耕地后备资源和农地分等定级调查等一系列重大调查专项，取得了一大批具有全局意义的开创性成果，为国家重大战略决策、经济社会发展、国土资源管理提供了坚实的支撑和保障，为加快我国的现代化建设和构建和谐社会作出了积极贡献。回首 12 载风雨历程，我们感慨而自豪，这是国土资源调查评价工作波澜壮阔的 12 年，也是艰苦奋进的 12 年，更是硕果累累的 12 年。

12 年来，我们完成了 5000 多个调查项目，发现了 900 余处矿产地，形成了 10 大后备资源勘查基地，显著提升了国内资源的保障能力。12 年来，我们开展了大量的基础地质调查，地质工作程度大幅提高，有力满足了南水北调、青藏铁

路、西气东输等重大基础设施建设和经济社会发展对基础地质资料的需求。12年来，我们初步查明了全国地质灾害现状，建立了重点地区预警预报系统，提高了防灾减灾能力，特别是面对近年来我国发生的南方严重雨雪冰冻灾害、北方和西南地区严重干旱、“5·12”汶川地震、“4·14”玉树地震，以及甘肃舟曲特大山洪泥石流等一系列自然灾害，我们充分运用地质调查评价成果，第一时间提供灾区影像图，第一时间开展应急调查，为国家及时了解灾情、指挥救灾以及灾后重建发挥了不可替代的作用，有效地保障了民生。12年来，我们查清了全国耕地后备资源状况，摸清了全国土地资源家底；海洋资源环境调查和基础测绘调查也取得了长足发展，为服务国家经济社会发展提供了有力支撑。

12年来国土资源调查评价取得的成果，是全国国土资源调查评价和地质勘查行业广大干部职工、科技工作者风餐露宿、跋山涉水、挑战极限，付出大量心血、汗水和智慧的结晶；也是国土资源人和地勘行业干部职工、科技工作者“胸怀祖国、服务大局、顽强拼搏、锐意改革、团结协作、甘于奉献”时代精神的生动写照。我相信，这种精神必将成为推进国土资源事业改革发展的不竭动力和宝贵财富，必将永载史册。

同志们，“十二五”是我国全面建设小康社会的关键时期，也是深化改革开放、加快转变经济发展方式的攻坚时期，工业化、城镇化、农业现代化三化同步快速推进，实现经济社会的全面、协调、可持续发展，这对提高国土资源保障能力、全面加强和改进国土资源管理工作提出了新的更高要求。我们将继续深入贯彻落实科学发展观，按照中央以科学发展为主题、以加快转变经济发展方式为主线的部署要求，加快已有调查评价成果的深度开发和利用，着力提高转化应用成效和社会化服务水平；我们将紧紧围绕经济社会发展大局，坚持统筹规划、合理布局，积极探索新机制、新举措，采用新思路、新方法，团结和依靠各方力量，进一步做好国土资源调查评价工作，为缓解我国资源约束、服务经济社会发展，作出新的更大贡献！

预祝国土资源调查评价成果展取得圆满成功！谢谢大家。

技巧琢磨

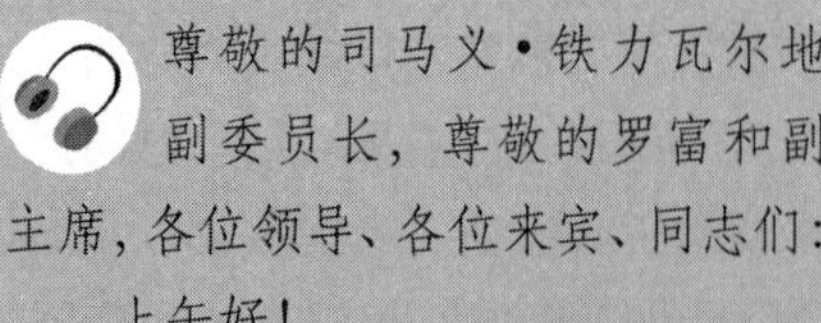

尊敬的司马义·铁力瓦尔地副委员长，尊敬的罗富和副主席，各位领导、各位来宾、同志们：

上午好！

在纪念中国共产党九十华诞之际，由国土资源部、发展改革委、财政部共同举办的“基础·先行——国土资源调查评价成果展”，今天在国家博物馆隆重开幕了。这次展览的主要目的，是向全社会全面系统地回顾总结国土资源调查评价工作的最新成果，介绍宣传我国的资源国情，更好地服务于经济社会发展。首先，我代表展览各主办单位向出席今天开幕式的各位领导、各位来宾和新闻界的朋友们表示热烈的欢迎！向参加国土资源调查的全体同志致以诚挚的慰问和崇高的敬意！也借此机会，向长期以来关心、支持国土资源事业发展的司马义·铁力瓦尔地副委员长、罗富和副主席，以及发展改革委、财政部等有关部门和社会各界表示衷心的感谢！

Distinguished Vice Chairman Simayi Tieliwaerdi, Vice Chairman Luo Fuhe, Dear guests,

Good morning!

The Communist Party of China is celebrating its 90th birthday. The Ministry of Land and Resources, National Development and Reform Commission and Ministry of Finance have jointly organized the exhibition of land and resources assessment, and we're celebrating its opening at the National Museum. The exhibition aims at reviewing the survey and assessment results of our land resources, providing information on China's resources, and better serving economic and social development. First, on behalf of the organizers, I'd like to say officials, guests and friends from the media, welcome to you all! To everyone who took part in the assessment, I appreciate what you've done and I salute you! Also, to those who have been supporting our work, to Vice Chairman Simayi Tieliwaerdi and Vice Chairman Luo Fuhe, the Development and Reform Commission and Ministry of Finance and other departments and people involved, thank you!

国土资源是经济社会发展的重要物质基础，国土资源调查评价是支撑经济社会发展的先行性、基础性工作。1998年以来，国土资源部会同发展改革委、财政部，按照党中央、国务院的决策部署，组织开展了历时12年的国土资源调查评价工作。先后实施了国土资源大调查、青藏高原地质矿产调查、新疆“358”地质矿产调查、油气资源战略调查、危机矿山接替资源勘查、海洋资源调查和第二次全国土地调查、全国耕地后备资源和农地分等定级调查等一系列重大调查专项，取得了一大批具有全局意义的开创性成果，为国家重大战略决策、经济社会发展、国土资源管理提供了坚实的支撑和保障，为加快我国的现代化建设和构建和谐社会作出了积极贡献。回首12载风雨历程，我们感慨而自豪，这是国土资源调查评价工作波澜壮阔的12年，也是艰苦奋进的12年，更是硕果累累的12年。

National land and resources are the basis of development. The assessment supports such development as its precursor. Since 1998, MLR has been working with NDRC and MoF to implement the Party and State Council's decisions. We've worked for twelve years on our land and resources assessment, including an overview on geology and minerals of the Tibetan plateau, Xinjiang 358 geology and mineral project, oil and gas strategy, mine substitutes, marine resources and the second national land survey, arable land reserves and agricultural land rating. We have achieved a substantial amount of ground-breaking results, contributing to our national strategy, economic and social development and resource management. It helps to accelerate our modernization and the development of a harmonious society. Looking back on the 12 years, we're very proud. The assessment over the past 12 years has been eventful, hard work and rewarding.

12年来，我们完成了5000多个调查项目，发现了900余处矿产地，形成了10大后备资源勘查基地，显著提升了国内资源的保障能力。12年来，我们开展了大量的基础地质调查，地质工作程度大幅提高，有力满足了南水北调、青藏铁路、西气东输等重大基础设

We completed some five thousand projects, discovering some nine hundred mineral sites, identifying ten reserve survey bases, significantly improving our domestic resource security. We conducted a large scale geology survey. Geological work was scaled up, meeting the needs of trans-regional water supply, the Tibetan railway and trans-regional

施建设和经济社会发展对基础地质资料的需求。12年来，我们初步查明了全国地质灾害现状，建立了重点地区预警预报系统，提高了防灾减灾能力，特别是面对近年来我国发生的南方严重雨雪冰冻灾害、北方和西南地区严重干旱、“5·12”汶川地震、“4·14”玉树地震，以及甘肃舟曲特大山洪泥石流等一系列自然灾害，我们充分运用地质调查评价成果，第一时间提供灾区影像图，第一时间开展应急调查，为国家及时了解灾情、指挥救灾以及灾后重建发挥了不可替代的作用，有效地保障了民生。12年来，我们查清了全国耕地后备资源状况，摸清了全国土地资源家底；海洋资源环境调查和基础测绘调查也取得了长足发展，为服务国家经济社会发展提供了有力支撑。

gas supply infrastructure projects as well as economic development in terms of geological data. We now have geological disaster updates and have set up key pre-alert systems. We've improved prevention and reduction capabilities. In recent years, China suffered serious rain and snow disasters in the south. In the north and south west, there was drought. The Wenchuan earthquake, Yushu earthquake and Gansu mudslides among others. We made good use of the assessment results to provide images of disaster areas and at the first opportunity, conducted emergency surveys. It helped with understanding the disaster, managing relief and reconstruction. We've saved lives. We now have a clear picture of our farming land reserves and total land resources. The marine resources survey and basic mapping survey also achieved remarkable results, contributing to China's economic and social development.

7. 傅莹副部长担任大使时的离任讲话

使用提要

1. 本单元的材料仍然以两种形式提供。第一种采用常见的讲话稿形式，便于练习限时视译。第二种采用对照、对比形式，便于练习、琢磨三词一译的技巧。
2. 限时视译的速度应该努力达到每秒 6 个汉字，这是实战同传必须达到的速度。
3. 在使用或者参照译入语时必须注意：
   3.1. 参考译入语只是诸多可能版本之一，不是最佳版本。
   3.2. 参考译入语完全按照实战的标准提供，没有经过修饰。不可用笔译的标准衡量，因为听同传的感觉和阅读文字完全不一样。
   3.3. 为了体现实战里的情况，参考译入语没有刻意保持连贯。同个表达法在一个讲话里的处理都可能各不相同。

英译汉三词一译10大技巧

1. 先存后译	2. 反话正说	3. 预测先说	4. 弃卒保车
5. 减字近半	6. 增加时态	7. 实词开句	8. 增补主语
9. 译所指也			

限时视译

在离任招待会上的讲话

傅　莹

感谢各位出席今晚的招待会。此时我百感交集。20 世纪 20 年代，时任中国驻英国的公使是顾维钧，是我非常敬仰的一位外交家。当有人问他中国人最残酷的一句话是什么时，他说：天下没有不散的筵席。离任就像是席末杯中的那最后一口酒，甘醇中已经有了些许的苦涩。

作为外交官，又是蒙古族人，我是个天生的游牧者，似乎一生都在不断地履新和离别之间徘徊。在布加勒斯特、金边、雅加达、马尼拉和堪培拉，都有过美好的岁月，而每次告别都依依不舍。现在即将离开伦敦和英国，心里更充满了难舍的眷恋。我会怀念在这里结交的许多好朋友，正是在他们的支持和帮助下，我才得以更好地了解英国和英国人民。

三年来，我走过英国许多的城镇和街巷，著名中国作家王蒙曾写道：抵达伦敦如同抵达一幅早已熟悉的油画。我深有同感。英国的生活丰富多彩，无论是在如同隔世的剧场里欣赏名剧，还是足球场上狂热的喝彩，抑或是赛马场里激奋的人群，都令人印象深刻，使我感受到英国人对生活的认真和考究。

不少人问我，最留恋英国的是什么？与许多中国人一样，我从小就接触到英国文学，有幸在这里追寻名著作者的足迹，简·奥斯汀临窗撰写《傲慢与偏见》的小圆桌在我的脑海里留下深深的印记；博朗蒂姐妹汲取灵感的荒原引发我无限的遐想；威廉·华兹华斯静谧的湖畔故居让我流连忘返。这都使我触摸到英国的文化精华，也是将中国众多游客源源不断吸引来的文化魅力。

在我任内的三年，两国关系稳步发展。胡锦涛主席和温家宝总理分别来到英国，布朗首相也访问过北京。两国的领导人和部长之间还经常性会晤或打电话，次数之多，几乎数不清了。两国地方之间的交流也日趋频繁。三年来，中国在英投资增长了六倍，留学生和游客人数也在以双位数增长。听说，去年中国游客在邦德街的购物金额增长了一倍半多。英国保持了欧盟对华最大投资国和第三大贸易伙伴的地位。去年夏天在北京休假期间，我想挑选一张床垫，最终相中的那款竟然是一个英国 19 世纪的品牌。

“英国设计”这几个字在中国是相当有分量的。英国不仅仅是世界金融中心，我访问过英国中东部和中西部地区，对该地区企业世界领先的创意设计能力印象深刻。这与中国强大的制造能力形成了很强的互补，双方应该加强合作，开发巨大的合作潜力。

中英伙伴关系的民众基础在不断加强。在英中贸协、四十八家集团俱乐部、筷子俱乐部等众多的工商、教育和民间友好团体的推动下，英国民众对中国产生了浓厚的兴趣，也创造了众多的商机，我们应该继续推动这一良好的势头。

记得不久前出席特色学校校长年会的时候了解到，英国特色学校联盟的目标是给所有想学中文的孩子提供中文课程，充分说明两国关系的民众基础是深厚的。英国民众在2008年地震后对中国的关心和慷慨帮助令我终身难忘。记得当时一个19岁的男孩Issac Lewis从威尔士家乡步行240英里，一路筹款到伦敦来。我对双边关系的前景非常乐观。

但是，今天既然是在朋友们中间，我也想说，过去的三年也是我外交生涯最为波澜起伏的一段经历。每当两国不能达到彼此的要求或出现意见不一致时，英方会倾向于评判和指责中国。每次遇到问题和困难，我都试图从两国的历史智慧中寻求灵感，与英国同事一道，通过坦诚沟通找到化解分歧的思路，维护双边关系稳定发展的大局。

西方需要做出是否接受中国作为平等伙伴的决断，做伙伴就意味着在出现问题的时候，要接触对话，而不是批评说教。英方不能叶公好龙，表面上说欢迎中国崛起，但实际上并不了解中国。如果西方对华接触的目标是改变中国，那西方就永远不会满意，双方在国际合作中也难以同心协力。中国正处在改革的进程中，世界上有哪一个大国能像中国这样把改革作为国家的根本政策方向？这正是因为我们认识到自己有许多需要改进之处。但中国的改革将以自己的方式按自己的步伐进行，改革的目标是服务中国人民的利益，而不是为了满足西方的要求。

只有尽快消除成见，更好地了解中国，双方才能认识到彼此的不同和多元化，才能建立以理解和尊重为基础的稳固的双边关系。中国也需要努力学习如何更好地向世界介绍自己，我给同事们留下的建议是：沟通，沟通，再沟通。这对于中英两国尤为重要，因为两国关系已经超出了双边范畴，越来越需要在全球性问题上更紧密地合作。

即将离开英国的时刻，工作上有了一些句号，做成了一些事情，但是也有不少“逗号”，不少工作还没有完成，还有一些“问号”。但是我对中英关系的坚定承诺没有改变，相信在双方共同努力下，中英关系的明天将更加美好。我希望各位热烈欢迎我的继任刘晓明大使，一如既往地支持他的工作。我也要感谢使馆的同事在过去三年里给我的大力支持，感谢海德饭店为我们今天的酒会提供这样好的场地。

下周一我就要离开伦敦了。临走之前，我会最后一次去公园慢跑，最后一次到牛津街漫步。人还未离开，已经开始想念英国了。希望我们的友谊长存。

技巧琢磨

感谢各位出席今晚的招待会。此时我百感交集。20 世纪 20 年代，时任中国驻英国的公使是顾维钧，是我非常敬仰的一位外交家。当有人问他中国人最残酷的一句话是什么时，他说：天下没有不散的筵席。离任就像是席末杯中的那最后一口酒，甘醇中已经有了些许的苦涩。

Thank you for being here tonight. There is much I want to say. In the 1920s, the then Chinese envoy was Gu Weijun, I hold him as a diplomat in very high regard. Someone asked him what the cruelest Chinese saying was. He replied: All feasts end. Leaving my post is like savoring the last drop of wine. One can already taste a bit of dryness.

作为外交官，又是蒙古族人，我是个天生的游牧者，似乎一生都在不断地履新和离别之间徘徊。在布加勒斯特、金边、雅加达、马尼拉和堪培拉，都有过美好的岁月，而每次告别都依依不舍。现在即将离开伦敦和英国，心里更充满了难舍的眷恋。我会怀念在这里结交的许多好朋友，正是在他们的支持和帮助下，我才得以更好地了解英国和英国人民。

As a diplomat and a Mongolian, I am born a nomad. My whole life has been about arriving at and leaving posts. In Bucharest, Djakarta, Manila and Canberra, there were good times. Yet every departure was hard. Now, I am about to leave London, the UK, it seems even harder. I will miss many friends I've made here. Their support and help have enabled me to better understand the UK and its people.

三年来，我走过英国许多的城镇和街巷，著名中国作家王蒙曾写道：抵达伦敦如同抵达一幅早已熟悉的油画。我深有同感。英国的生活丰富多彩，无论是在如同隔世的剧场里欣赏名剧，还是足球场

It's been 3 years. I've been to many places. A leading Chinese writer, Wang Meng once wrote: arriving in London is like approaching a familiar oil painting. I feel the same. Life here is colourful. Be it at a theatre out of this world, shouting at a football match, or the excitement at a horse

上狂热的喝彩，抑或是赛马场里激奋的人群，都令人印象深刻，使我感受到英国人对生活的认真和考究。

race. You can't forget those. I find people here live lives to the full.

不少人问我，最留恋英国的是什么？与许多中国人一样，我从小就接触到英国文学，有幸在这里追寻名著作者的足迹，简•奥斯汀临窗撰写《傲慢与偏见》的小圆桌在我的脑海里留下深深的印记；博朗蒂姐妹汲取灵感的荒原引发我无限的遐想；威廉•华兹华斯静谧的湖畔故居让我流连忘返。这都使我触摸到英国的文化精华，也是将中国众多游客源源不断吸引来的文化魅力。

Many people ask me: what will I miss the most? Like many Chinese, I read English literature from a young age. I am fortunate to trace the authors' footsteps here. Jane Austin with her *Pride and Prejudice* and the little round table she used is etched into my mind. Bronte sisters were inspired by wilderness, and so have I been. William Wordsworth's lakeside home made me feel as if I never wanted to leave. I've touched the gems of British culture, and many Chinese tourists come here falling for its charm.

在我任内的三年，两国关系稳步发展。胡锦涛主席和温家宝总理分别来到英国，布朗首相也访问过北京。两国的领导人和部长之间还经常性会晤或打电话，次数之多，几乎数不清了。两国地方之间的交流也日趋频繁。三年来，中国在英投资增长了六倍，留学生和游客人数也在以双位数增长。听说，去年中国游客在邦德街的购物金额增长了一倍半多。英国保持了欧盟对华最大投资国和第三大贸易伙伴的地位。去年夏天在北京休假期间，我想挑选一张床垫，最终相中的那款竟然是一个英国 19 世纪的品牌。

My 3 years in London have seen two countries develop their relations steadily. President Hu and Premier Wen both visited London, Prime Minister Brown visited Beijing. Leaders and ministers of both sides often met and spoke on the phone. I've lost count of those. Between the two countries, there has been increased engagement at a local level. Over the past 3 years, Chinese investment grew by 6 times, students and tourists grew at double digits. I am told that last year, Chinese tourists shopping at Bond Street spent 1.5 times more than before. The UK, within the EU, is the largest investor and 3rd largest trading partner of China. I was on summer leave in Beijing and wanted to buy a mattress. In the end, the one I chose was British, a brand from the 19th century.

“英国设计”这几个字在中国是相当有分量的。英国不仅仅是世界金融中心，我访问过英国中东部和中西部地区，对该地区企业世界领先的创意设计能力印象深刻。这与中国强大的制造能力形成了很强的互补，双方应该加强合作，开发巨大的合作潜力。

'Designed in Britain' carries strong weight in China. The UK is not only the financial center. I visited the Midlands, the world-leading design capability impressed me. China has manufacturing strength, we can complement each other. We need to enhance our cooperation and unlock potentials.

中英伙伴关系的民众基础在不断加强。在英中贸协、四十八家集团俱乐部、筷子俱乐部等众多的工商、教育和民间友好团体的推动下，英国民众对中国产生了浓厚的兴趣，也创造了众多的商机，我们应该继续推动这一良好的势头。

People to people engagement between China and the UK is strengthening. CBBC, the 48 Group, the Chopstick Club together with many other business, education and civil groups have been working to that end. British people are very interested in China. This has created many business opportunities. We need to continue this trend.

8. 中国驻印大使张炎的讲话

使用提要

1. 本单元的材料仍然以两种形式提供。第一种采用常见的讲话稿形式，便于练习限时视译。第二种采用对照、对比形式，便于练习、琢磨三词一译的技巧。
2. 限时视译的速度必须达到每秒 6 个汉字，这是实战同传必须达到的速度。
3. 在使用或者参照译入语时必须注意：

 3.1. 参考译入语只是诸多可能版本之一，不是最佳版本。

 3.2. 参考译入语完全按照实战的标准提供，没有经过修饰。不可用笔译的标准衡量，因为听同传的感觉和阅读文字完全不一样。

 3.3. 为了体现实战里的情况，参考译入语没有刻意保持连贯。同个表达法在一个讲话里的处理都可能各不相同。

英译汉三词一译10大技巧

1. 先存后译	2. 反话正说	3. 预测先说	4. 弃卒保车
5. 减字近半	6. 增加时态	7. 实词开句	8. 增补主语
9. 译所指也			

限时视译

在河南旅游推介会上的讲话

（中国驻印度大使张炎）

尊敬的河南省副省长孔玉芳女士，
各位来宾，女士们、先生们：

很高兴出席河南省旅游推介会。首先，欢迎河南省副省长孔玉芳女士访问印度。你的来访不仅加强了中印旅游合作，并且将具有深厚文化底蕴和独特自然风光的多彩河南带到了“不可思议”的印度。我还想对在座的印度朋友们表示感谢，你们的出席表明了印度政府对中印两国文化与旅游交往的重视。

中印作为近邻，拥有2000多年友好交往与相互影响、相互借鉴的历史。佛教文化从印度传入中国，印度也从中国的茶叶、瓷器和丝绸产品中获益。历史上，中国僧人法显、玄奘和伟大的航海家郑和、印度的达摩祖师以及其他许许多多人士为中印两个文明古国的交往做出了自己的贡献。近代，印度著名的思想家及诺贝尔奖得主泰戈尔、中国学者谭云山教授和季羡林博士为促进两国文化交流和友谊做出不懈努力。这些交往极大地促进了两国人民的相互了解和友谊，并且成为两个伟大国家繁荣发展的不竭动力。

女士们，先生们：

河南位于中国中东部地区，是中国古代文明的摇篮，孕育了中国历史上许多伟大的人物，是中国古代发明创造及武术的故乡。中国的8大古都有4个在河南，即郑州、开封、洛阳和安阳。20个朝代的帝王选择在河南建都。深厚的历史文化底蕴给河南留下了举世闻名的名胜古迹和自然景观，吸引着海内外游客。这些古迹包括登封“天地之中”历史建筑群、龙门石窟、安阳殷墟等。以龙门石窟为例，它体现了中印两国文化的相互深远影响，迄今已吸引了很多印度游客来访。坐落在洛阳城中的白马寺是河南与印度悠久历史交往的另一个生动写照。2010年10月，印度总统帕蒂尔访华，亲自为白马寺“印度风格佛殿”揭幕。

由于具有丰富的历史文化遗产和迷人的自然风光，河南成为广受国内外游客欢迎的旅游目的地。现有的旅游界盛会，如“世界旅游城市市长论坛”“洛阳牡丹花展”“三门峡国际黄河旅游节”等，为中国与包括印度在内的各国开展合作提供了有利平台。

女士们，先生们：

近年来，中印关系取得全面发展，旅游合作呈现良好态势。2010 年，到访中国大陆的印度人数超过 57.3 万人次，实现了两国旅游交往的重大突破。今年上半年，印度访华人数为 35.2 万人次，比去年同期增长 11.8%，中国访印人数为 6.4 万人次，比去年同期增长 17.8%。现在，每周有 40 多个直航航班往返中印各大城市。中印已互为旅游市场发展迅速的客源国。

今年是“中印交流年”和“中国文化旅游”年，这必将增进两国人民交往，加强相互理解和合作。然而，与两国庞大的人口数量和充满活力的经济相比，目前两国的旅游合作水平还远不令人满意。中国正为加强两国旅游合作做出巨大努力。此次中国国家旅游局派出由 70 多人组成的庞大代表团参加即将在新德里举办的“2011 亚太旅游协会旅游交易会”。希望双方共同努力，使旅游合作成为中印关系的新亮点。

最后，祝孔玉芳副省长访印取得丰硕成果，祝旅游推介会圆满成功。

谢谢。

技巧琢磨

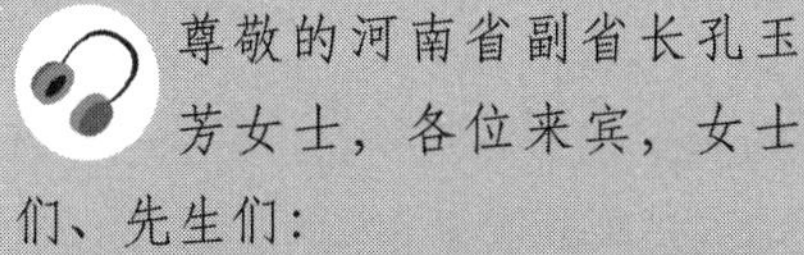

尊敬的河南省副省长孔玉芳女士，各位来宾，女士们、先生们：

很高兴出席河南省旅游推介会。首先，欢迎河南省副省长孔玉芳女士访问印度。你的来访不仅加强了中印旅游合作，并且将具有深厚文化底蕴和独特自然风光的多彩河南带到了“不可思议”的印度。我还想对在座的印度朋友们表示感谢，你们的出席表明了印度政府对中印两国文化与旅游交往的重视。

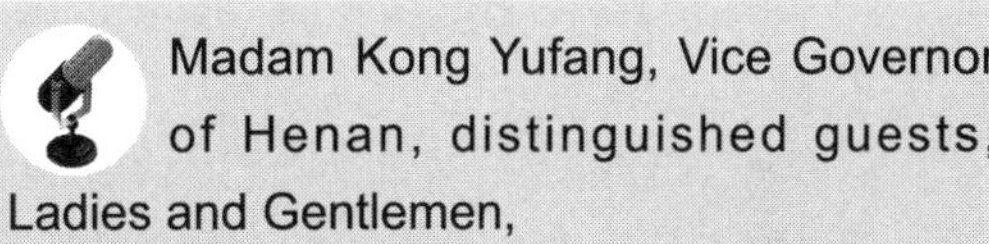

Madam Kong Yufang, Vice Governor of Henan, distinguished guests, Ladies and Gentlemen,

I am delighted to attend the Henan Tourism Promotion event. First, I welcome Madam Kong Yufang to India. Your visit enhances Sino-Indian tourism cooperation. Cultural heritage and sceneries are what Henan is known for, and you've brought them to the incredible India. I also want to thank all the Indian friends. Your presence demonstrates that for the Indian government, bilateral tourism is very importantm.

中印作为近邻，拥有2000多年友好交往与相互影响、相互借鉴的历史。佛教文化从印度传入中国，印度也从中国的茶叶、瓷器和丝绸产品中获益。历史上，中国僧人法显、玄奘和伟大的航海家郑和、印度的达摩祖师以及其他许许多多人士为中印两个文明古国的交往做出了自己的贡献。近代，印度著名的思想家及诺贝尔奖得主泰戈尔、中国学者谭云山教授和季羡林博士为促进两国文化交流和友谊做出不懈努力。这些交往极大地促进了两国人民的相互了解和友谊，并且成为两个伟大国家繁荣发展的不竭动力。

We are neighbours. For 2000 years, we've enjoyed friendly relations. We've influenced and learned from each other. Buddhist culture came to China from India. India benefited from Chinese tea, porcelain and silk products. In history, Chinese monks Fa Xian and Xuan Zang, the navigator Zheng He, and the Damo from India, among many others contributed to the relationship between us. In modern times, the great thinker and Nobel Laureate Tagore, Professor Tan Yunshan and Dr. Ji Xianlin have contributed to the cultural ties and friendship between us. This level of engagement has promoted our two-way understanding and friendship. Our two great nations have prospered as a result.

女士们，先生们：

河南位于中国中东部地区，是中国古代文明的摇篮，孕育了中国历史上许多伟大的人物，是中国古代发明创造及武术的故乡。中国的8大古都有4个在河南，即郑州、开封、洛阳和安阳。20个朝代的帝王选择在河南建都。深厚的历史文化底蕴给河南留下了举世闻名的名胜古迹和自然景观，吸引着海内外游客。这些古迹包括登封“天地之中”历史建筑群、龙门石窟、安阳殷墟等。以龙门石窟为例，它体现了中印两国文化的相互深远影响，迄今

Ladies and Gentlemen,

Henan is in the eastern part of central China, the cradle of ancient Chinese civilization. It gave birth to many great figures. Chinese inventions and martial arts can find origins there. China has 8 ancient capitals, 4 of which are in Henan. They're Zhengzhou, Kaifeng, Luoyang and Anyang. 20 dynasties chose Henan as their capitals. A long history and rich culture heritage have left Henan with world-renowned historic sites and tourist attractions, drawing visitors from home and abroad. Some of them include the Dengfeng cluster, Longmen Grottoes and Anyang Yinxu. The Longmen Grottoes for example, embody the Chinese and Indian cultures from history. It has already attracted many visitors from

已吸引了很多印度游客来访。坐落在洛阳城中的白马寺是河南与印度悠久历史交往的另一个生动写照。2010年10月，印度总统帕蒂尔访华，亲自为白马寺“印度风格佛殿”揭幕。

India. In Luoyang, we have the White Horse Temple where Henan and India's historical links are clearly visible. In Oct 2010, the Indian President Patil visited China. She inaugurated the Indian style Buddhist Hall.

由于具有丰富的历史文化遗产和迷人的自然风光，河南成为广受国内外游客欢迎的旅游目的地。现有的旅游界盛会，如“世界旅游城市市长论坛”“洛阳牡丹花展”“三门峡国际黄河旅游节”等，为中国与包括印度在内的各国开展合作提供了有利平台。

Historical heritage and sceneries make Henan popular among domestic and foreign tourists. Tourism events, such as the International Mayors Forum on Tourism, Luoyang Peony Fair, and International Yellow River Festival in Sanmenxia provide China as well as India and other countries with a platform for cooperation.

女士们，先生们：

近年来，中印关系取得全面发展，旅游合作呈现良好态势。2010年，到访中国大陆的印度人数超过57.3万人次，实现了两国旅游交往的重大突破。今年上半年，印度访华人数为35.2万人次，比去年同期增长11.8%，中国访印人数为6.4万人次，比去年同期增长17.8%。现在，每周有40多个直航航班往返中印各大城市。中印已互为旅游市场发展迅速的客源国。

Ladies and Gentlemen,

In recent years, our bilateral relations are flourishing. Cooperation in tourism is doing well. In 2010, visitors to China mainland from India were over 573,000, a major breakthrough. In the first half of this year, Indian visitors to China were 352,000, an increase of 11.8% year on year. Chinese visitors to India were 64,000, an increase of 17.8% YOY. Every week, more than 40 direct flights shuttle between Chinese and Indian cities. China and India have become each other's market and source of visitors.

今年是“中印交流年”和“中国文化旅游”年，这必将增进两国人民交往，加强相互理解和合作。然而，与两国庞大

This year is China-India Exchange Year and the year of China Cultural Tour. It'll enhance people-to-People links, promote mutual understanding and

的人口数量和充满活力的经济相比，目前两国的旅游合作水平还远不令人满意。中国正为加强两国旅游合作做出巨大努力。此次中国国家旅游局派出由70多人组成的庞大代表团参加即将在新德里举办的“2011亚太旅游协会旅游交易会”。希望双方共同努力，使旅游合作成为中印关系的新亮点。

cooperation. However, between us, we have two large populations and two vibrant economies. Given that, the current level of cooperation is not satisfactory. China wants to strengthen bi-lateral cooperation and is working hard on it. China National Tourism Administration is sending a 70 strong delegation to New Delhi to attend the PATA Travel Mart 2011. I hope with joint efforts, cooperation in tourism will be a new highlight in our bilateral relations.

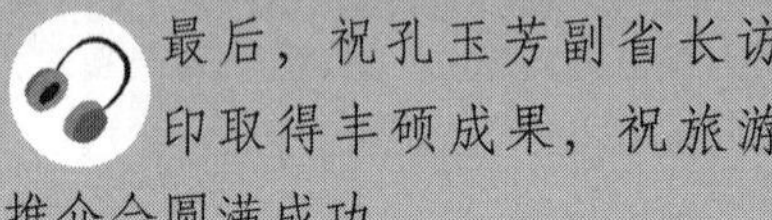

最后，祝孔玉芳副省长访印取得丰硕成果，祝旅游推介会圆满成功。

谢谢。

Finally, I wish Vice Governor a fruitful visit, and this event a great success.

Thank you.

9. 中国代表团在联合国的发言

使用提要

1. 本单元的材料仍然以两种形式提供。第一种采用常见的讲话稿形式，便于练习限时视译。第二种采用对照、对比形式，便于练习、琢磨三词一译的技巧。
2. 限时视译的速度必须达到每秒 6 个汉字，这是实战同传必须达到的速度。
3. 在使用或者参照译入语时必须注意：

   3.1. 参考译入语只是诸多可能版本之一，不是最佳版本。

   3.2. 参考译入语完全按照实战的标准提供，没有经过修饰。不可用笔译的标准衡量，因为听同传的感觉和阅读文字完全不一样。

   3.3. 为了体现实战里的情况，参考译入语没有刻意保持连贯。同个表达法在一个讲话里的处理都可能各不相同。

英译汉三词一译10大技巧

1. 先存后译	2. 反话正说	3. 预测先说	4. 弃卒保车
5. 减字近半	6. 增加时态	7. 实词开句	8. 增补主语
9. 译所指也			

限时视译

在联合国网络犯罪问题专家组首次会议上的发言

（中国外交部条法司李燕端参赞）

主席先生，

互联网技术的快速发展及其应用大大促进了人类社会的发展与进步，但同时各种新型网络犯罪活动也随之滋生，特别是由于互联网的开放性和全球化，网络犯罪的跨国性尤为突出，需要各国合作应对。如何加强国际合作以有效打击网络犯罪，维护网络安全已成为国际社会面临的一个紧迫问题。在此形势下，设立联合国网络犯罪专家组，全面深入研究网络犯罪问题，并探讨国际社会合作打击网络犯罪的新对策具有重要意义，中方对此表示欢迎，并愿在专家组会议上同各方充分交流，共同推动专家组会议取得成功。

主席先生，

中国是世界上互联网用户最多的国家之一，已超过4亿，同时，中国也是全球网络违法和犯罪行为的主要受害国之一，尤其是近年来，中国的网络犯罪数量呈快速上升势头，中国公安机关办理的网络犯罪案件数量从1998年的142起猛增至2008年的3.5万起，10年间增加了近250倍，2010年更是达到4.9万起。同时，网络犯罪更趋复杂，各种犯罪相互渗透，形成分工合作的利益链条，特别是不法分子利用境外网络资源实施犯罪活动比较突出。据统计，中国所调查的网络犯罪案件中，超过90%的诈骗、钓鱼、色情、赌博等违法网站和超过70%的僵尸网络控制端位于国外。

中国高度重视打击网络违法犯罪活动，通过立法、执法、司法、技术等多种措施，全面打击网络犯罪，取得了明显成效。根据中国法律，网络犯罪不仅包括侵害电脑数据和系统保密性、整体性和可用性的犯罪，如非法截取数据、侵入重要计算机信息系统等，也包括利用计算机网络实施的其他违法犯罪行为，如诈骗、赌博、侵犯知识产权等。为不断完善相关法律法规，中国于2009年出台了刑法第七修正案，将非法控制僵尸网络、非法盗窃网络账号、为攻击破坏活动提供木马程序等行为独立入罪，为依法打击有关行为提供了充分法律依据。该修正案出台后，中国已打掉了80余个制作提供黑客工具的网络犯罪团伙。目前，中方正研究制定有关网络攻击破坏、网上侵犯知识产权犯罪的相关司法解释。

中国在国内大力打击网络犯罪的同时，积极探索通过多种渠道开展国际合作。中国大力加强打击网络犯罪国际执法协作，2004年至今中国公安机关共协助40多个国家调查网络犯罪案件700多起；按照同有关国家签订的司法协助条约，及时向请求国提供司法协助；中国计算机网络应急技术处理协调中心（CNCERT）等互联网行业机构主动同外国行业机构建立合作关系，共同处理网络安全事件。例如，2010年2月，CNCERT与美国微软公司等联合打击一个名为Waledac的全球大型僵尸网络，微软公司书面来函表示感谢。

主席先生，

由于网络犯罪范围的不确定性、跨国性、技术对抗性以及各国法律的差异，没有任何一国能够单独应对网络犯罪的威胁。过去十年间，国际上就打击网络犯罪进行了大量的合作，但仍然存在一些不足，有效的合作措施和合作机制尚待完善，能力欠发达的发展中国家仍处于不利地位。因此，国际社会应该从法律、执法、技术等各方面加强和改善现有国际合作，以更有效地打击网络犯罪。中方支持联合国网络犯罪专家组就网络犯罪问题进行全面研究，希望各国通过交流，相互借鉴有益做法，凝聚共识，不断加强打击网络犯罪国际合作，包括对制定新的打击网络犯罪国际公约的可行性进行探讨，中国代表团愿为此做出积极努力。

谢谢主席先生。

技巧琢磨

主席先生， 互联网技术的快速发展及其应用大大促进了人类社会的发展与进步，但同时各种新型网络犯罪活动也随之滋生，特别是由于互联网的开放性和全球化，网络犯罪的跨国性尤为突出，需要各国合作应对。如何加强国际合作以有效打击网络犯罪，维护网络安全已成为国际社会面临的一	Mr Chairman, Internet technology, with its rapid growth and application, has driven development of the mankind. However, internet crimes are part of this growth, and especially since the internet is open and global, cybercrime has become transnational, requiring cross border cooperation. Strengthening international cooperation to fight this crime and protect internet safety, has become a pressing issue. Therefore, the establishment of the UN expert

个紧迫问题。在此形势下，设立联合国网络犯罪专家组，全面深入研究网络犯罪问题，并探讨国际社会合作打击网络犯罪的新对策具有重要意义，中方对此表示欢迎，并愿在专家组会议上同各方充分交流，共同推动专家组会议取得成功。

group on cybercrime to study this matter and discuss how the international community can collectively combat this crime is a major initiative. China welcomes that, and is willing to participate in expert group meetings to engage in dialogue, and jointly ensure the group's success.

主席先生，

中国是世界上互联网用户最多的国家之一，已超过4亿，同时，中国也是全球网络违法和犯罪行为的主要受害国之一，尤其是近年来，中国的网络犯罪数量呈快速上升势头，中国公安机关办理的网络犯罪案件数量从1998年的142起猛增至2008年的3.5万起，10年间增加了近250倍，2010年更是达到4.9万起。同时，网络犯罪更趋复杂，各种犯罪相互渗透，形成分工合作的利益链条，特别是不法分子利用境外网络资源实施犯罪活动比较突出。据统计，中国所调查的网络犯罪案件中，超过90%的诈骗、钓鱼、色情、赌博等违法网站和超过70%的僵尸网络控制端位于国外。

Mr. Chairman, in terms of internet users, China is a major country, with over 400m users. At the same time, in terms of cybercrime, China is a major victim. Especially in recent years, China's cybercrime rate has shot up. The police has been handling increasing number of cases, 142 in 1998, rising to 35,000 in 2008. In 10 years cases have increased by 250 times, and in 2010 reached 49,000. Cybercrimes are complex and interconnected, with cooperation between interest groups, especially when criminals exploit international networks for criminal activities. Statistics show that of China's cybercrimes, over 90% are fraud, phishing, pornography or gambling sites. Over 70% of botnet controllers are abroad.

中国高度重视打击网络违法犯罪活动，通过立法、执法、司法、技术等多种措施，全面打击网络犯罪，取得了明显成效。根据中国法律，网络犯罪

China attaches great importance to cyber crime. By legislature, enforcement, judicial and technology means, we have achieved clear success. According to Chinese law, cybercrime includes not only

不仅包括侵害电脑数据和系统保密性、整体性和可用性的犯罪，如非法截取数据、侵入重要计算机信息系统等，也包括利用计算机网络实施的其他违法犯罪行为，如诈骗、赌博、侵犯知识产权等。为不断完善相关法律法规，中国于2009年出台了刑法第七修正案，将非法控制僵尸网络、非法盗窃网络账号、为攻击破坏活动提供木马程序等行为独立入罪，为依法打击有关行为提供了充分法律依据。该修正案出台后，中国已打掉了80余个制作提供黑客工具的网络犯罪团伙。目前，中方正研究制定有关网络攻击破坏、网上侵犯知识产权犯罪的相关司法解释。

attacking databases and systems such as illegal database entry, or breaking into IT systems, but also using IT for other crimes, like fraud, gambling and IP infringement. To strengthen legislation, in 2009 China passed a criminal law 7th revision, to include illegal botnets, stealing of account data and helping attacks with Trojan horses as specific crimes. It provides a strong legal basis for our initiative. After the law was revised, we eliminated some 80 manufacturers of hacking tools. China is working on fighting cyberattacks and IP crime. We're developing judicial interpretations.

中国在国内大力打击网络犯罪的同时，积极探索通过多种渠道开展国际合作。中国大力加强打击网络犯罪国际执法协作，2004年至今中国公安机关共协助40多个国家调查网络犯罪案件700多起；按照同有关国家签订的司法协助条约，及时向请求国提供司法协助；中国计算机网络应急技术处理协调中心（CNCERT）等互联网行业机构主动同外国行业机构建立合作关系，共同处理网络安全事件。例如，2010年2月，CNCERT与美国微软公司等联合打击一个名为Waledac的全球大型僵尸网络，微软公司书面来函表示感谢。

Domestically, we are fighting cybercrime, and at the same time we are actively exploring international cooperation. We have strengthened collaboration in international enforcement. Since 2004, our police have helped more than 40 countries with over 700 cases. In line with our international agreements, we give countries judicial assistance. CNCERT, among other organisations, has approached industry bodies abroad to deal with cyber security issues. For example in February 2010, CNCERT, together with Microsoft, cracked down on Waledac—an international botnet. Microsoft wrote to thank us.

主席先生，

由于网络犯罪范围的不确定性、跨国性、技术对抗性以及各国法律的差异，没有任何一国能够单独应对网络犯罪的威胁。过去十年间，国际上就打击网络犯罪进行了大量的合作，但仍然存在一些不足，有效的合作措施和合作机制尚待完善，能力欠发达的发展中国家仍处于不利地位。因此，国际社会应该从法律、执法、技术等各方面加强和改善现有国际合作，以更有效地打击网络犯罪。中方支持联合国网络犯罪专家组就网络犯罪问题进行全面研究，希望各国通过交流，相互借鉴有益做法，凝聚共识，不断加强打击网络犯罪国际合作，包括对制定新的打击网络犯罪国际公约的可行性进行探讨，中国代表团愿为此做出积极努力。

谢谢主席先生。

Mr Chairman,

Cybercrime is not fixed. It's transnational and technology confrontational. But laws vary. No country alone can manage this threat. Over the last decade, international fight against cybercrime has seen much joint efforts. but it is not enough. Cooperation measures and mechanisms need to be improved. With limited capabilities, developing countries are at a disadvantage. Therefore, the international community must leverage legislation, enforcement and technology to strengthen international cooperation, to become more effective. China supports the UN cybercrime expert group in its research. We hope that countries will share their best practice, build a consensus and continue to strengthen cooperation, including the development of a new international treaty in discussion. China is willing to work towards this.

Thank you.

10. 王毅韧秘书长的讲话

使用提要

1. 本单元的材料仍然以两种形式提供。第一种采用常见的讲话稿形式，便于练习限时视译。第二种采用对照、对比形式，便于练习、琢磨三词一译的技巧。
2. 限时视译的速度必须达到每秒 6 个汉字，这是实战同传必须达到的速度。
3. 在使用或者参照译入语时必须注意：

   3.1. 参考译入语只是诸多可能版本之一，不是最佳版本。

   3.2. 参考译入语完全按照实战的标准提供，没有经过修饰。不可用笔译的标准衡量，因为听同传的感觉和阅读文字完全不一样。

   3.3. 为了体现实战里的情况，参考译入语没有刻意保持连贯。同个表达法在一个讲话里的处理都可能各不相同。

英译汉三词一译10大技巧

1. 先存后译
2. 反话正说
3. 预测先说
4. 弃卒保车
5. 减字近半
6. 增加时态
7. 实词开句
8. 增补主语
9. 译所指也

限时视译

在国际原子能机构部长级核安全大会上的讲话
（国家原子能机构秘书长王毅韧）

尊敬的主席先生，

日本福岛核事故是由特大地震和次生海啸叠加造成的超设计基准事故，引起国际社会的广泛关注。中国国家核事故应急协调委员会在第一时间启动了国家核应急机制。3 月 17 日，中国政府决定，立即组织对我国核设施进行全面安全检查，加强在运核设施的安全监管，用最先进的标准对所有在建核电站进行安全评估，在核安全规划批准前暂停审批新的核电项目。

中国是日本的近邻，对日本发生特大灾害，特别是严重核事故导致的后果，感同身受，温家宝总理亲自前往灾区看望受灾民众，对日本大地震造成的重大人员伤亡和财产损失表示慰问。根据《核事故或辐射紧急情况援助公约》中的义务，中国政府在第一时间即向日本政府表达了愿意提供辐射监测、医疗救护等援助的愿望。5 月 20 日，中国专家代表团访问日本，就福岛核事故进行了交流，制定了在核安全和核应急领域合作的工作计划。

主席先生，

历史和现实告诉我们，核安全无国界。吸取日本福岛核事故的经验教训，加强核安全领域的国际合作，共同促进核能安全发展，是当前摆在我们面前的一项重要而紧迫的任务。为此，中方提出以下四点主张。

第一、认真总结经验教训。中国有一句成语，“吃一堑，长一智”。美国三哩岛核事故和前苏联切尔诺贝利核事故发生后，都引起世界各国对核安全的极大关注，曾经影响了不少国家的核电发展进程，同时也极大地推动了核电技术的升级和管理水平的提高，使后来建设的核电站安全性能有了明显提升。日本福岛核事故的发生，再一次对人类认知能力提出挑战，也为人类追求核电的更高安全性提供了机遇。福岛核事故对世界核能安全发展具有重要的借鉴和启示作用，我们建议由国际原子能机构牵头，针对核事故发生前后的技术风险、管理体制、决策机制、缓解措施、应急手段、信息发布等进行深刻反思，全面总结经验教训，使其成为各国的共同财富。

第二、进一步完善核安全标准。经过成员国几十年的共同努力，机构在核安全领域制订了一系列的标准、导则和行动计划，这些技术文件对提高核安全水平发挥了积极作用。福岛核事故产生的严重后果警示我们，必须提高忧患意识，重新审视并完善核电的安全标准，特别是要高度重视超设计基准的多重自然灾害或极端自然灾害与次生灾害叠加事故的影响。建议机构优先考虑开展对核电厂选址标准的审查工作，对地震高发地区以及可能受到其他自然灾害影响的核电站厂址提出更高的要求，切实提高对叠加自然灾害的抵御能力。机构还应当采取有效措施，推动机构核安全标准在更广泛的范围内被接受和采用。

第三、加强核安全信息共享和交流。日本福岛核事故表明，及早、全面向国际社会以及受影响或可能受影响的国家通报有关核事故的信息，对减少跨国界的辐射后果，做好公众沟通工作，是十分重要的。各国应通过建立双边或多边的合作机制，加强核安全信息的共享与交流。我们建议对《及早通报核事故公约》进行审查，制定相应的补充条款，根据国际原子能机构的事故（件）分级，对不同程度核事故的通报内容作出具体规定。

第四、充分发挥国际原子能机构的主导作用。促进和平利用核能事业的发展，是国际原子能机构的宗旨之一。面对福岛核事故后的新情况，作为核领域唯一的政府间国际组织，国际原子能机构应利用自身的资源优势和权威地位，在事故评估、标准审查、信息发布、国际公约修订和核安全国际合作中发挥主导作用，重树人们对核安全的信心。建议机构推动建立地区核应急与响应中心，确保发生核事故时，成员国间具备相互支援、资源共享的条件和能力。同时，机构还应充分发挥自身优势，加强公众宣传，普及核能知识，提高公众对核能的认知度。

主席先生，

中国政府高度重视核安全问题，始终坚持安全第一的原则。通过制定和完善核安全法规，实施独立和有效的核安全监管，建立核应急响应体系，确保了中国核设施的安全运行，取得了良好的核安全纪录。中国政府近期组织的、对在运核设施的全面安全检查表明，中国核设施的安全是有保障的。尽管如此，我们还将认真总结、吸取福岛核事故的经验教训，采取针对性措施，进一步提高核设施应对极端自然灾害的能力以及核应急响应能力。中国正在抓紧组织编制核安全专题规划，研究制定确保核安全的综合治理措施，确保核电持续安全发展。

主席先生，

核能的和平利用是20世纪人类最伟大的科学技术成就之一。进入新世纪以来，核能在保障能源供应、控制温室气体排放等方面继续发挥着不可替代的作用。人类文明的进步总是伴随着风险和挑战，福岛核事故阻挡不了全球核电发展的步伐。我相信，只要在科学的基础上认真吸取事故教训，针对薄弱环节采取得力措施，核能一定会为人类社会进步、经济发展作出更大的贡献。

谢谢各位！

技巧琢磨

尊敬的主席先生，

日本福岛核事故是由特大地震和次生海啸叠加造成的超设计基准事故，引起国际社会的广泛关注。中国国家核事故应急协调委员会在第一时间启动了国家核应急机制。3月17日，中国政府决定，立即组织对我国核设施进行全面安全检查，加强在运核设施的安全监管，用最先进的标准对所有在建核电站进行安全评估，在核安全规划批准前暂停审批新的核电项目。

Mr Chairman,

The Fukushima accident was caused by a big earthquake and a secondary tsunami, which went beyond its design benchmarks. It has raised global concerns. China's National Nuclear Emergency Coordination Committee activated the emergency mechanism swiftly. On 17th March, the government decided that the facilities were to be thoroughly examined and transportation facilities be enhanced in its safety regulation. We will apply the most advanced standards to all stations under construction. Nuclear safety planning will be suspended for all new projects.

中国是日本的近邻，对日本发生特大灾害，特别是严重核事故导致的后果，感同身受，温家宝总理亲自前往灾区看望受灾民众，对日本大地震造成的重大人员伤亡和财产损失表示慰问。根据《核事故或辐射紧急情况援助公约》中的义务，中国政府在第一时间即向日本政府表达了愿意提供辐射监测、医疗救护等援助的愿望。5月20日，中国专家代表团访问日本，就福岛核事故进行了交流，制定了在核安全和核应急领域合作的工作计划。

China is Japan's neighbor. Japan suffered the disaster and its consequences. We empathise with them. Premier Wen visited the disaster region and the local people. Japan's earthquake has caused substantial casualties and losses. Premier Wen expressed his condolences. In line with *Convention on Assistance in the Case of a Nuclear Accident or Radiological Emergency*, the Chinese government expressed to the Japanese government its willingness to provide monitoring devices and medical assistance. On 20th May, Chinese experts visited Japan, and Fukushima was their topic. They developed a nuclear safety and emergency cooperation working plan.

主席先生，

历史和现实告诉我们，核安全无国界。吸取日本福岛核事故的经验教训，加强核安全领域的国际合作，共同促进核能安全发展，是当前摆在我们面前的一项重要而紧迫的任务。为此，中方提出以下四点主张。

Mr Chairman,

History and reality tell us that nuclear safety has no national boundaries. We must learn from the Fukushima accident and work more on nuclear safety internationally, to promote nuclear safety. This issue is right in front of us. It's important and pressing. China has 4 proposals in this regard.

第一、认真总结经验教训。中国有一句成语，“吃一堑，长一智”。美国三哩岛核事故和前苏联切尔诺贝利核事故发生后，都引起世界各国对核安全的极大关注，曾经影响了不少国家的核电发展进程，同时也极大地推动了核电技术的升级和管理水平的提高，使后来建设的核电站安全性能有了明显提升。日本福岛核事故的发生，再一次对人类认知能力提出挑战，也为人类追求核电的更高安全性提供了机遇。福岛核事故对世界核能安全发展具有重要的借鉴和启示作用，我们建议由国际原子能机构牵头，针对核事故发生前后的技术风险、管理体制、决策机制、缓解措施、应急手段、信息发布等进行深刻反思，全面总结经验教训，使其成为各国的共同财富。

First, learn lessons. A Chinese proverb says 'a fall in the pit, a gain in the wit'. The Three-Miles Island and Chernobyl disasters raised international concerns on nuclear safety. Both have impacted on nuclear power development in many countries. They have greatly boosted technology upgrading and management improvement. Susbsequent developments are clearly safer. The Fukushima disaster is yet anotherchallenge. It also means that our pursuit for better safety now has a new opportunity. Fukushima has provided an important reference point. We propose that IAE take the lead. Areas such as technologycal risk, management, decision making mechanism, mitigation, emergency response, information release need to be re-examined thoroughly. Lessons need to be learned and shared.

第二、进一步完善核安全标准。经过成员国几十年的共同努力，机构在核安全领域制订了一系列的标准、导则和行动计划，这些技术文件对提高核安全水平发挥了积极作用。福岛核事故产生的严重后果警示我们，必须提高忧患意识，重新审视并完善核电的安全标准，特别是要高度重视超设计基准的多重自然灾害或极端自然灾害与次生灾害叠加事故的影响。建议机构优先考虑开展对核电厂选址标准的审查工作，对地震高发地区以及可能受到其他自然灾害影响的核电站厂址提出更高的要求，切实提高对叠加自然灾害的抵御能力。机构还应当采取有效措施，推动机构核安全标准在更广泛的范围内被接受和采用。

Second, enhance nuclear safety standards. Member countries have, for several decades, been working on this. The IAE has developed standards, guidance and action plans. They've contributed to nuclear safety. But Fukushima is a warning. We must raise awareness, review and enhance safety standards, with a particular focus on design benchmarks based on multiple natural disasters or extreme natural disaster coupled with a secondary desaster. I propose that the Agency give priority to site selection and approval process. Earthquake-prone and natural disaster-affected regions will have to meet more demanding requirements. This will enable the site to cope with multiple desasters. The Agency should take effective measures to promote its safety standards to the wider community.